Preface

I wrote this book because I love one of the characters and we got to live out a dream come true. I remember reading Moneyball back in 2004 and then watching the movie several years later. That was a story of an undervalued group of professional baseball players that turned themselves into one of the most successful franchises in Major League Baseball.

Moneyball started with a simple question, "how did one of the poorest teams in baseball, the Oakland Athletics, win so many games?" The question I attempt to answer in this book is, "How can parents develop a group of kids to reach the biggest stage in the world at 12 years old, the Little League World Series?" This is a story of how a group of kids from a small town earned the right to compete on a global stage in front of over 4 million TV viewers.

Since the late 1980's, people have argued about whether Little League baseball or Select/Travel baseball is the "right" way to develop kids and support their dreams of playing baseball at a high level. Little League is a true community-based sport and teams (at least during the regular season) are selected via a draft. You will have a few really good players and then several kids that are still learning. Select/Travel ball is an opportunity to put a group of more advanced players together and go play against other "hopefully" stacked teams.

In the Little League World Series, it's the culmination of several thousand All-Star teams competing against each other to earn one of the coveted 20 team spots in Williamsport each August. You see teams from California who have historically dominated, with almost twice the number of appearances (50) of any other state in the union. Texas is next with 30 appearances.

Pennsylvania has 25, Florida has 24, and New York and Connecticut are tied at 22.

However, just because you arrive, you now have an entirely new mountain to climb to become a World Champion. California has 8 championships (16% win rate), Connecticut, Hawaii, New Jersey, and Pennsylvania are all tied at 4, New York and Georgia have 3, Texas and Michigan have 2, and then Alabama, Florida, Kentucky, Louisiana, New Mexico, and Washington have 1 each. For the last 75 years...

Yes, this is an incredibly tough mountain to climb. The average is 1 in 11 appearances to win the whole thing. Even with the 456 appearances in total, only 152 have emerged in one of the top 3 spots (33%). I know I threw you in the deep end of the pool with those statistics, so please bear with me.

Buckle up, this entire book, we are going to show you the math. We are going to measure kid's performances, show you their averages, and show you how incredible they are able to perform by 12 years old with a lot of practice and good instruction.

There is a quote that Navy SEAL's use (who borrowed it from the Greek poet Archilochus) to emphasize a core truth about performance: "Under pressure, you don't rise to the occasion, you sink to the level of your training."

In baseball, we talk about averages. They take into account your good days and your bad days. Your excellent days and the days you can't hit the broad side of a barn. The days you hit smoking lines drives right at the shortstop who catches them all, and other days you hit weak grounders that just happen to find holes in the infield. Over extended lengths of time and many games, you can measure player's performance, and you want to bring the kids with the best averages together. You can trust that day in and day out, that player will generally perform to that number (within one or two standard deviations, if you really want to be the Ivy League economics/statistics nerd with me 😊).

On the way to Willamsport, every single one of these kids that plays, has parents cheering them on from the stands, has extended family watching them on TV, and has entire states rooting for them to succeed. These kids play their absolute hearts out all summer to try to earn the opportunity to play in Williamsport. They hold nothing back. It is such an incredibly pure way to play the game. As Brad Pitt famously says, "How can you not be romantic about baseball?" Every single one of these kids loves getting to play this game. So, here is our fairy tale and love story that came true for 12 ordinary kids.

Advance Reader Commentary

As someone who grew up playing baseball in small towns across the South, this book is highly relatable and well-written. Baseball stories are not reserved for the Big Leagues alone, and the best ones often come from places we may not expect. Tim has done a great job capturing what baseball looks like in communities across the country. – Gaines Johnson, President of The World Baseball League and former Strategy Executive for the Olympic Games

Awesome book! - Erik Whinery, Owner of ATX Sandlot and former D1 catcher at Northern Colorado

It was really fun to be taken through each game pitch-by-pitch and to see how the parents were feeling! Such a summer of great memories for all involved! - Jon Peters, Little League Coach and author of "When Life Grabs You by the Baseballs"

Really well-written and a great account of our summer! - Jim Hurst, Julian's grandfather

Acknowledgements

A huge Texas thank-you and hug to all Boerne and San Antonio residents who supported the team with your cheers, your social media posts, and your generous financial donations to fund the trips to Abilene, Waco, and Williamsport. This book is for you!

Thank you to Jon Peters, my Little League Coach in Brenham, TX, who was the first high school baseball player to ever make the cover of Sports Illustrated as "Superkid" in 1989 because you set a national high school record with 53 consecutive victories, 7 no-hitters, and led Brenham to three state championships (1986-88). You inspired an entire generation of kids to know that through God's gifts and hard work, greatness is possible, even if you are from a small town.

Thank you to my Dad for driving my brother and I to practices, games, and volunteering as an umpire. Thank you for always telling us, "You can be anything you want to be; you just have to set your mind to it."

ISBN: 979-8-9950395-01

First edition: February 2026

Printed in the United States of America

Table of Contents

Introduction

It was still over 100 degrees in Waco, TX at 745pm on a very special Tuesday, August 6, 2024. Brandt Deeke comes to the plate with his teammate Kole Cao on second base and 2 outs. He is Louisiana's last hope to keep this game alive. As it seems to happen so often in baseball, Brandt is the #12 hitter in their lineup, and now the outcome on this Little League Regional Championship game rests on his young shoulders. Doc Mogford is pitching for Texas West; this kid throws hard and he's accurate. He can touch 70 mph and the plate is only 46 feet away. This is a David v. Goliath moment as both teams' families and the other fans wait with bated breath to see how this turns out.

Brandt watches a wild pitch go over the catcher Caden Guffey's head for ball one that allows his teammate Kole Cao to advance to 3rd. He swings at strike one and then hits a ground ball to Boerne's Kole Newson at 3rd base that takes a hard bounce but he is in front of it, it hits the heel of his glove, slides into his stomach, he grabs it and throws to Julian at first to get the last out and that does it!!! After 5 ½ innings and a come-from-behind to take the lead, Boerne has done it! They've beaten Louisiana 6-3 in the top of the 6th inning, and the boys from Boerne, TX are going to Williamsport!!!!

The stadium erupts, the kids rush to the mound to surround Doc, throwing their gloves in the air, screaming and cheering, because what has been a 14-game winning streak to this point, in three different cities across Texas, for the past two months, the dream has now come true! The kids have punched their ticket to the Little League World Series!

But this story didn't start on this hot Tuesday afternoon in Waco...This journey started on another hot Texas Wednesday night in Ingram (west of San Antonio about an hour) two months earlier. So let's start at the beginning! My name is Tim Christ and my son Kaleb, is the 11-year-old on the Boerne team.

This is the Justin Newson "I have a dream" section. Justin is the General Manager of the 2024 Boerne 12U All-Star Team. He grew up in Comfort, a small town about 17 miles west of Boerne. It's much smaller than Boerne (22,000 residents) at just under 2,000 residents. He played Little League growing up and the Boerne teams would always kick the snot out of Comfort during the District tournament. Justin recalls a good group of athletes in Comfort, but it wasn't enough to deal with the depth and skill of the Boerne kids.

Now that we live in Boerne and see the level of training, hours spent developing, and competition, we understand why. The number of college baseball recruits that come out of Boerne it is impressive. However, it seems like the Boerne Little League doesn't live up to the level of talent that exists locally.

When you think about the excellent baseball talent that comes out of Boerne, it includes two boys that played on the Boerne High State Championship team, Bradley Suttle (2005 grad) and Russell Moldenhauer (2006 grad). Suttle was drafted by the Los Angeles Angels but chose instead to go play at The University of Texas. He played there two years and then was drafted in the 4th round by the New York Yankees. Moldenhauer holds Boerne High career records in home runs (29), doubles (24), singles (105), runs (139), and RBI's (133). He batted .510 as a senior with a .657 on-base percentage (OBP). He also holds the record for the most home runs in a College World Series with four in 2009, while playing for the University of Texas. He was drafted by the Washington Nationals in 2010. Seth Johnston (2001), also went to University of Texas and was part of the 2005 College World Series Championship team.

In the last decade you think about names like:

(all sourced from www.perfectgame.org/college/collegecommitments)

2014 grads (committed to): Brady Sullivan (McLennan CC)

2015 grads: Eric Aldaco (Stephen F. Austin)

2016 grads: Cade Bullinger (UTSA), Connor Queen (Texas Tech), Brock Grabarkewitz (Temple College)

2017 grads: Garrison Armstrong (Nebraska), Jonah Bailey (Bossier Parish CC), Bryson Smith (Texas A&M-Corpus Christi), Zachary Zuniga (Vanguard), Alec Kubik (Incarnate Word), Zane Badmaev (Tarleton State)

2018 grads: Jordan Thompson (Incarnate Word), Julio Riggs (Paris Junior College)

2019 grads: Michael Gresham (Blinn College), Douglas Hodo (Texas, drafted by Baltimore in the 6th round), Guiliano Hernandez (Clarendon College)

2020 grads: Luke Boyers (TCU)

2021 grads: Trey Rucker (San Jacinto CC), Brandon Watson (Huston-Tillotson College)

2022 grads: Cole Phillips (Arkansas, drafted by Atlanta in the 2nd round), Rashawn Galloway (Texas State), Andrew Poole (Alvin CC), Myree Zolliecoffer (Mid-America Christian), Sean Moore (Texas A&M-Corpus Christi)

2023 grads: Tyler Garritano (Texas State), Camden Johnson (Wichita State), Riley Pechacek (University of Houston), Rowdy

Miller (Tyler Junior College), Wyatt Chandler (Missouri University), Robert Vela (St. Edward's), Jacob Zendejas (St. Edward's)

2024 grads: Evan Kuhl (Trinity University), Owen Edwards (Dallas), Jordan Ballin (UTSA)

2025 grads: Dylan Perez (Baylor), Hudson McNew (Trinity University), Brooks Perez (Duke), Jackson Melanson (Missouri University), Aidan Smith (Wartburg College), Preston Longhurst (US Merchant Marine Academy), Pearce Kelly (Clarendon College), Jacob Schwope (Sul Ross State), Sawyer Smith (Texas A&M-Kingsville)

2026 grads: Jackson Grimes (UTSA), Garland Whitehead (UTSA), Parker Davis (Odessa College), Angelo Grizzaffi (McLennan CC), Brody Bendele (Ranger College)

Boerne historically had only made it to the Little League State Tournament one time, and that year, they didn't win a single game. Boerne LL seems to consistently lose to the San Antonio Little League teams during District or Section play. Justin kept seeing kids leave Little League for select and never come back. Julian, Ben, and Gage were the only ones that have played Little League consistently the entire time. Kole, Cooper, Jett, and Gray all played 6+ seasons of Little League together. Aiden played a couple years. Dylan played baseball in California and has only been in Texas a few years. Doc played Little League when he lived in Corpus Christi, but hadn't played Boerne Little League. Kaleb played a season of Helotes Little League and played with Catholic Youth Organization for several years.

This is a really tough mountain to climb. Only 28 teams from Texas have reached Williamsport, and only two Texas teams have actually won the World Championship, Houston National LL in 1950 and Westbury American LL in 1966. Since 1950, the Texas teams to get there include:

1950: National, Houston
1951: North Austin
1954: Western, Galveston
1960: NE Optimist, Fort Worth
1961: El Campo
1962: Valley Verde, Del Rio
1963: National, North Houston
1965: Northern, Waco
1966: Westbury American, Houston
1988: Northwest 45, Spring
1995: Northwest 45, Spring
2000: Bellaire
2002: Westside, Fort Worth
2003: Lamar-National, Richmond

2004: Lamar-National, Richmond
2007: Western, Lubbock
2009: McAllister Park, San Antonio
2010: Pearland White
2012: McAllister Park, San Antonio
2013: Universal, Corpus Christi
2014: Pearland East
2015: Pearland West
2016: McAllister Park, San Antonio
2017: Lufkin
2018: Post Oak, Houston
2021: Wylie, Abilene
2022: Pearland
2023: Needville

Justin consistently talked about it with the small group of parents over the years, kind of jokingly, but then it really started to gain traction when Chris Carey became Boerne Little League President in 2023. Chris is from Abilene and he knew the Wylie Little League program well, so he understood what a successful and competitive Little League program can look like. As shown above, Wylie LL reached the Little League World Series in Williamsport in 2021 before being eliminated by Michigan. They are the only team from Wylie to ever get that far. That Wylie team had Ella Bruning, a female pitcher as part of their roster. She was the 20th girl to participate in the LLWS. Pairing up Chris and Justin was a match made in heaven.

Guided by similar parenting values and a shared respect for the game, the goal was to create an All-Star experience that balanced player development, teamwork, and the joy of competing together. They wanted to make it all about the kids. Take the parents out of it. Choose the best kids, without the politics. You may miss a kid or two but if you are approaching it with the mindset of choosing the "best players" for All-Stars, it will set the bar high and show that you have a "morally" right league. It was difficult for us, because we had a to say "no" to a few talented kids for this Boerne team, but in the end, we decided that it was these 12 kids that would give us the best opportunity to go as far as possible.

While some parents with prior Little League experience were understandably cautious, the process was handled in accordance with Little League and Boerne Little League guidelines. Coaches were nominated, player selections were completed, and coaches were then voted on following the selection of the players. Justin Newson (Kole's dad) was selected as General Manager, with Bert Munoz (Aiden's dad) and Jonathan Collins (Gray's dad) approved as coaches. Each committed to leading the team the right way and representing Boerne Little League with integrity, sportsmanship, and respect for the game.

For those of you who are unfamiliar with the Little League World Series, let's provide a brief synopsis, so that way we are all on the same page...yes, pun intended... 😊 Today there are more than two million kids around the world playing Little League, in one of the more than 80 countries around the world and/or the clubs around the country, along with about one million adult volunteers. Little League believes in the power of Youth Baseball and Softball to teach life lessons that build stronger individuals and communities. One of their statements reads:

"To build character, courage, and loyalty by using baseball to teach life lessons, foster teamwork, and create a fun, inclusive environment for personal growth, emphasizing sportsmanship and citizenship over winning."

You will see those themes weaved throughout this book, as baseball will teach you some very hard lessons, but it also rewards you for a lot of hard practice. You will see how the kids conducted themselves, simply being excited to meet new people and play with each other. We are very proud of our Boerne team that they always acted with excellent sportsmanship and were great ambassadors for the city of Boerne.

For these kids, baseball is all about having fun. It's the moments in games when they do something great to help their team. It's the high-fives they get from their players, the opponents, the coaches, and the umpires. It's the energy they put into the game, the energy of the fans, and it's the heart they put into it as they play as hard as they can. It's the laughs when crazy things happen or when they are joking in the dugout. Little League is pure, unadulterated fun with kids just having an absolute blast! There is no simpler joy that brings a bigger smile to their parents' face, than that. The fact that we won a bunch of games is the icing on the cake.

Kids can start in Little League at the age of 4 and join a Tee Ball team (yes, where they hit the ball off a tee as opposed to having it thrown to them by a Coach or the other team's pitcher). Once a kid has played at least one regular season and are 5-6 years old, they can graduate to a coach/machine pitch team (also called Minor League Division). Once the kids are 7-12, they can play any of the Minor League Divisions they want (player pitch, coach pitch, or machine pitch). Players age 9-12 are eligible to play on a "Major League Division."

Driveline Baseball has a podcast episode specifically devoted to "What is the Point of Little League," and that the primary goal is development and engagement. There are different levels of Major League to accommodate where each individual player is at. Some kids are just getting introduced to the game, while some having been playing for 3-4 years, and so it's helpful to keep it safe and fun for all to divide up the kids appropriately by age/skill level.

Kids will play with their respective teams all spring, then will come together and hold an All-Stars tryout day, and then the 12 best kids will be selected for the local All-Star Team. In our case, our 12 kids were equally divided among multiple teams for the Spring 2024 regular Little League season, all the boys tried out during the All-Star tryout day, and then we came together to form the 2024 Boerne All-Stars Team and went to compete in the local Little League District Tournament.

The other thing that people don't think about until they are in it, is that this "is" your entire summer. If you lose in District, then you can backfill whatever other activities you might want to do for those next two months until the kids go back to school. However, if you make it to state and/or regional, you are basically giving up all of June and July for baseball. No family vacation, unless you squeeze it in sometime between the tournaments. For those of us that plan our vacations six months to two years in advance, this creates a real scheduling nightmare. Ask Betty about the Dominican Republic vacation that she gave up so that Kaleb could play in all these games, and she'll tell you that it was so worth it! Welcome to living the "Baseball Life!" Now, let's introduce you to the team!

Boerne's 12 All-Stars

On a hot Wednesday night in the middle of June, this journey begins for these 12 special kids. Here we are, in Ingram, TX, and we have no idea what's going to happen. Are we confident that our kids are good players? Absolutely. Have we also been in a number of games where we started walking kids, where we didn't hit well, and where we ultimately lost the game? Absolutely yes.

Knowing this situation is "win, or don't advance," is completely different than a typical weekend select tournament. In those tournaments, you are just there for the reps. Many times there is something that we worked on over the last couple weeks in practice, or 1-on-1 with Kaleb, that we want to specifically ensure that we do in the game this weekend. This is where we "test" various tweaks we are making to his pitching delivery, batting, or other. If we go three games and out this weekend, no big deal, because we are playing in at least three more games the following weekend.

Boerne is a premier San Antonio suburb of German heritage with really good schools. It attracts an affluent population who commuted into San Antonio to work (pre-COVID), and now a number of folks work from home. Boerne, as the first town just before you get deep into the Hill Country, also attracts a large number of retirees, both military and non-military, because of the temperate climate and "country living."

Each of these games are incredibly stressful. There is no time limit, so you either play 6 complete innings or run-rule the other team, whichever comes first. For two hours-ish, all of us parents and others in the audience are coiled tighter than springs and we are holding our breath for every pitch, because we know that a single bad game sends the team to the loser's bracket, and a second loss knocks you out of the tournament completely. We are rooting like crazy for our team and we are scared to death all at the same time!

This point will become really important at the US Championship game two months later, but all of these early tournaments are double elimination, meaning that every team has to get beaten twice in order to be out of the tournament.

Let's first define what an "ideal outcome" is, and then we can see how close to that we can actually get. In golf, if you could hit a hole-in-one on each of the 18 holes, that would be absolutely perfect. You would score 18 for 18 holes. Now, the odds of that are next to impossible, but that is the ideal outcome.

In this format, the ideal outcome would be to score 15+ runs in 3 innings, and only have to throw 9 pitches. That would be 3 outs for 3 innings, meaning that each kid hit a pop up, line drive out, fly out or ground out, but ALWAYS get out on that single pitch to each of them. That would save your pitcher as they would only commit 9 pitches to the entire game. If you can achieve this, you run rule each team at the end of the 3rd inning and you go on to the next game. That same pitcher could then pitch every single game because they only throw 9 pitches per game. Now, the odds of doing that are pretty slim, but that is the ideal state. The other interesting piece that comes into play here is the sportsmanship piece. In many games, if you have a substantial lead, you'll substitute in one of our less consistent pitchers to "get some reps" but you still have confidence that you will win the game. However, in this format, with it being double elimination, and you are trying to minimize pitching, the rules highly incentivize teams to "try" to crush their opponents as quickly as you can.

For Kaleb, our pre-game routine was just like we have been doing for years. When we talked about it, we discussed what was likely going to happen tonight and what we would like to do. We were simply reinforcing the confidence that he has in his own abilities and saying, just go out there and do what you do. You are a great hitter, so figure out the situation before you step in the box, get your plan together, and then once you are in the box, you know exactly what you are wanting to do.

This was completely new experience for him though, and we had to make sure that we helped him set the right expectations. On his 11U select team, he is one of the top players. He is the leadoff or 2nd batter. He is the kid that is the starting pitcher on Sunday in order to shut down the opponent and help us to earn a second game on Sunday. However, for Little League All-Stars, he's most likely going to be riding the bench on defense, and he's only going to get to bat. These kids are a year older, taller, and stronger than he is. It's incredibly important for him to take advantage of those opportunities that he does get to execute the best he can in each of those instances in order to help the team win. On defense, he can be the cheerleader and keep the energy in the dugout high.

Kaleb's not the only one. He is going to be joined by Gage, Ben, and Dylan. The three of them are going to be doing some defensive rotations, but for the most part, these four kids will be the ones sitting on defense the majority of these games. That is a very difficult pill for the parents to swallow. You know your kid can execute, but they are being sat because the coaches believe the other kids provide a higher likelihood of a good outcome and this format requires you to carry 12 kids. However, only nine boys can be on the field at one time, and who plays is ultimately the coaches' decision. So, for us, we had to ensure we have incredible patience, approach everything with a grateful heart, and counsel our kids to understand how they can best succeed in their role and best help the team.

There are several key differences between Little League and Select/Travel ball. Little League is typically one game per day, and 1-2 games played per week. In Boerne, we played during the week in the evenings, and all the games were at our local Northrup Park. Select/Travel ball is typically comprised of 2 practices during the week and then playing tournaments on the weekends. Saturday is typically pool play, so you play two games to "get seeded" in the brackets. Sunday is single elimination bracket play, and if you play all the way to the championship game you likely play 3-5 games just on Sunday. So, over the course of that weekend you will play at least 3 games and up to 7.

The time commitment is significantly different, because you commit to LL one evening per week and perhaps one other evening for practice. For Select/Travel, you commit two evenings per week to practice and your entire weekend (potentially all day both days) to the tournament. Some of the Select/Travel ball organizations include Perfect Game, FiveTool, and National Championship Sports (NCS), to name a few. Select/Travel also gets its name because games may be local in San Antonio, in New Braunfels (1 hour), Austin (2 hours), Houston (3.5 hours), or Dallas (4.5 hours) from home. One of the key pieces that makes an "emotional" difference for some is that Little League is a not-for-profit entity while the select/travel ball organizations are for-profit. Boerne LL runs about $200 for the spring for 14 games and select/travel can run $1,000-3,000 for the spring of 35+ games. Boerne LL has 800-1,000 kids play every season. It takes a volunteer board of 25 directors, coordinating with 300-400 volunteer coaches and other volunteer members to run it. Little League truly is a "community event," as there are hundreds of local citizens involved in its successful execution every fall and spring. Once you understand that, you can start to understand how many people actively support the All-Star teams, because they truly are representing a large "community" of folks who are dedicated to them having a lot of fun in the game of baseball.

When you as parents are sitting there in the stands, your mind races! Is my son fully prepared today? Is there anything I could have done more, or differently? Part of this journey involves building routines and habits, and helping your kids to learn how to focus and lock in on what is about to happen for the next two hours. We know the game time, so then we work backwards from there. A first-thing in the morning game at 8am, means we are arriving at the field around 6-630a to hit in the cages and warm up. If the drive time is an hour to the field, then we are adding an hour plus another 15 minutes to get breakfast tacos en route, which means we are getting up and leaving the house by 5am. For example, Kaleb will typically eat 2-3 breakfast tacos before a game, and then another 1-2 tacos between games.

Maintaining a high level of energy requires a lot of fuel, and some kids don't perform as well as they could during games because they don't simply have the energy reserves in order to put 100% focus into playing hard for 2 hours, or, if they are playing 3-4 games in day, to eat enough to sustain themselves for that 6-8 hours' worth of intense athletic activity.

Kids will burn 500-750 calories in a single game, not including the 1,500 or so they use every day for just basic functions, so for 3-4 games means you need to plan for them to eat 3,000-4,000 calories that day. When you listen to Patrick Jones Baseball podcast where he interviewed Brandon Guyer, a former MLB player turned certified nutritionist, and other sources, many college programs have now realized that the one key piece of the athletic puzzle they have not yet embraced is the nutrition aspect. These kids need .5-1+ gram of protein per pound of body weight, so our kids that weigh between 92 and 150 lbs. need 46-150 grams of protein every day in their diet. When you think about 4 eggs containing 24 grams, an 8 oz steak containing 45 grams, a protein shake containing 24 grams, and an 8 oz chicken breast containing 55 grams, you start to figure out that it takes very consistent and intentional focus to make sure they consume the appropriate amount of protein per day.

Kids should not be "tired" after the game. If they are worn out and can't go throw a football or go play tag with their teammates after the game, then that is a sign that they do not have the energy supplies they need. I won't say mal-nourished, because that's probably not the right word, and that brings up all sorts of negative legal connotations, but they need to have an internal "motor" that, #1 is conditioned well-enough to run all day, and #2, the food (gas for the motor) to power them all day long, and #3, is hydrated (the oil) to keep things running smoothly.

Nick Saban, famous football coach for Alabama says that the only difference between good players and great players is that great players don't get tired. When good players get tired, lose focus for an instant, are a step too slow, or other, that's when great players beat them and that can become the difference in who wins and loses.

Let's introduce you to the Boerne roster!

Name	2024 Height	2024 Weight
Julian Hurst	5'11"	140
Ben Burkhart	5'8"	125
Doc Mogford	5'8"	130
Kole Newson	5'7"	135
Caden Guffey	5'6"	145
Gage Steubing	5'6"	125
Gray Collins	5'5"	115
Jett Matthews	5'5"	100
Cooper Hastings	5'4"	145
Aiden Munoz	5'3"	125
Dylan Burke	5'1"	105
Kaleb Christ	4'11"	92

As you can see, we've got 9 kids that are 5'4" or taller, we've got 8 that weigh more than 125 lbs., and we've got 7 kids that can all pitch between 66-74 mph, and they are accurate. We've got another 5 kids that are very accurate on the mound that throw 60-66 mph. We were blessed with how many of our kids had already grown and were able to throw 65+ mph and hit home runs with the USA bats. We were also blessed with a group of kids whose parents had been very intentional about their athletic development, and more specifically their baseball prowess, for 7+ years to this point.

Let's talk about bats and pitch counts. There are four types of bats that kids use: wood, BBCOR, USSSA, and USA bats. Many kids will play in wood bat tournaments that provide a very unique experience, as the wood bats don't go nearly as far as the metal bats, but definitely reward the kids that can connect solidly with the barrel. BBCOR bats are what 14U thru college players use.

USSSA bats are bats that are used in Select from 6U-13U. These bats go the furthest, compared to the other bats, and so they are a lot of fun for younger kids to hit the ball further and start hitting home runs at ages 6 and up. Some 12U kids can hit USSSA bats at 70+ mph exit velocity and some will hit them more than 350 feet!!

USA bats are designed to not go as far as the USSSA bats and so these are used in Little League. The ball doesn't come off as "hot" when it is hit, which is really important because the pitcher is only 46 feet away. One of our 12U kids hitting a USSSA bat could hit a ball back at the pitcher over 70 mph and could injure him badly. Not that they can't get hurt with a USA bat, but it reduces the odds. We have hit both bats in our own "scientific experiments" on a number of baseball fields, and what we generally find is that USSSA bats go about 30-40 feet further than USA bats.

When you think about a kid hitting a ball 170' versus 200', that is the difference between a fly ball to the outfield and a home run in Little League. Bats get further complicated because they can be either end-loaded or balanced. End-loaded are typically better for those kids who have grown and are stronger, while the balanced bats are better for the kids that haven't grown as much yet. Kaleb has been swinging balanced bats his entire career.

The pitch count is extraordinarily important topic that we'll address now. If they throw 35 pitches or less, they have to have 1 calendar day of rest. If they pitch up to 50 pitches, 2 days' rest. 65 pitches require 3 days' rest, and 85 pitches require 4 days' rest. 85 pitches in a day is the maximum allowed by LL rules.

James Andrews, the renowned orthopedic surgeon that has performed hundreds of Tommy John surgeries, is the go-to surgeon for high-profile professional athletes including Roger

Clemens, Albert Pujols, Charles Barkley, Troy Aikman, Jack Nicklaus, and others, wrote the book Any Given Monday: Sports Injuries and How to Prevent Them... It is a must-read. He was the doctor consulted by Little League when they decided on these rest days and pitch limits. Make sure you memorize that because there will be a test on it later. 😊

Also, catchers who catch 4 innings or more in a game are not eligible to pitch on that calendar day either. Many of your "top athletes" will be those kids that can do it all, pitch, catch, play shortstop, etc. Unfortunately, you will see some coaches in select put too much strain on certain players, they will catch 3-4 innings in game one, then pitch game 2, then catch game three, all in one day. That is simply too much overuse on that particular athlete, so parents have to be highly intentional and communicative with the coach about what the boundaries are.

When you have a great athlete, some coaches' default approach is to use them as much as he can in order to win the game, but as parents, and with a vision for the long-term, you have to temper that and ensure the long-term health of your athlete. There is a lot of strategy behind, who is on the mound, who can catch them, and then who do you put in the field to back them up?

The way that you build a very good All-Star team, which we define as one that can compete and hopefully win in Regionals to make it to Williamsport, is to try to ensure that you have 12 kids that can do all of the three fundamentals, they are solid in the field, they are accurate pitchers, they all bat over .400, and you have at least 3-4 kids that are also good catchers. With the Little League continuous batting rule, all 12 kids bat in the same order the entire game and on defense you'll have three kids sitting at any one point in time.

However, as you'll see when we get into these games, you need to have kids at the bottom of the lineup that are good hitters, because at some point it will matter. It is very helpful to have 4-7 really good pitchers, depending on how you end up playing in the games, because a single loss means that you are playing back-to-back days and in several extra games, and so you'll need the additional good arms in order to go the distance. In some Little Leagues, the way the All-Star rules work is that the players get to vote on the team members first, then the local Board of Directors will vote on some kids (many times that has to be unanimous), and then the Head Coach gets 3 spots that he can choose the final players.

If you are part of a system where you see the Coach's kid on the team, where he was clearly not one of the "best" 12 players in the league, then you know how he got there. It's really unfortunate because, as you'll see, this takes 12 "really good baseball players" all executing their very best in each at-bat to make it all the way to Williamsport. The Coach is trying to be nice to his son, but he is creating a situation where his son is now the weak link on the team and that may end up sabotaging the efforts of the 11 other kids on the roster.

Another key point for Leagues around the world to understand is that if you want to put a team together and go compete, you are putting a big target on your back. Every single league around you, especially the ones that you ultimately beat, are looking for any rules infractions to force you to forfeit so that they can take that spot. It's incredibly important for the team manager, league President, and Region Administrator to work very closely together to document that you are doing everything in accordance with Little League rules. This is such a small world, that if you try to bring a really good player in to your group, those other families will be quick to report you. We know folks whose "full-time jobs" during All-Star selection/District play are to research the backgrounds of all the coaches and players to see if there is any evidence of impropriety. Welcome to the frustrating nuances of parental politics and youth sports.

Another thing that has happened in the past is that the rules used to state if you carried less than 12 players on your roster, everyone had to play a minimum of 6 outs and have two at-bats. However, if you carried 14, you could let your best defensive 9 players play 100% of the time, and you would only have those additional 5 get an at-bat. So, some coaches would make the choice to carry 14 players, and then 5 kids would sit the bench the entire series, except for their at-bats. Little League International does all they can to provide a set of rules to ensure a fair playing field, but as you can see above, some people will always try to figure out a way to get an edge, instead of simply relying on the talent and skill of their best 12 players. Yuck...ok, let's get back to more positive topics!

As you sit there in the stands, before each swing, you do an introspective analysis and this is what we teach the boys to do between each pitch. First, what is the situation? How many on base, how many outs, what is the score, and how good is this pitcher? Can he hit his spots or is he kind of wild? What is the perfect execution for this batter on this pitch? If there is a runner on 3rd with less than two outs, then the kid at the plate needs to be aggressive, barrel up any pitch that is close to a strike, and hit either a line drive or a hard grounder to score the run. If there is no one on base, then they are being a little more conservative with the strike zone and waiting for a really good pitch to hit, or if the pitcher isn't very good and they can draw four balls to get walked, then that is ideal. They have not even given the other team a chance to get them out.

For the kids playing defense, they need to know, how many outs, left-hand batter or right-hand batter to determine appropriate defensive position, where are the runners, and most importantly, if the ball is hit to me, what am I supposed to do with it? If it's a ground ball to me, what do I do? If it's a line drive right at me and I catch it, what do I do? If it's a pop fly to me and I catch it, what do I do? This entire game is about doing the "optimal" thing at that moment in time, minimizing mental and physical errors, and capitalizing on the other teams' mistakes.

There are two ways to read this book. First, if you are a baseball purist, and you want to live in the pitch-by-pitch detail, all those details are in the Appendix, after you read this introduction chapter you can turn to pages 167-282, go live the games with us, and then turn to page 85 to continue when we arrive in Williamsport. If you are not a baseball purist (there might be three or four of you out there 😊), then you are welcome to read the "Reader's Digest" version in the following pages for the first 14 games, and then you can live the pitch-by-pitch at Williamsport, because, well, it's my book. I sincerely hope that we can make you laugh out loud, cheer, get a knot in your stomach, and maybe even shed a tear as we go through this book, and our experience together!

Game 1 Boerne @ Ingram, Wednesday, June 19, 2024

There are five teams in this District tournament, Fredericksburg (the famous wine town that is becoming the Napa Valley of Texas), Ingram, Kerrville, Medina Valley, and Boerne. Every Little League game starts off with the Little League Pledge:

I trust in God, I love my country, and will respect its laws. I will play fair, and strive to win, but win or lose, I will always do my best."

Our first game is against the Ingram All-Stars team. Ingram is located on the banks of the Guadalupe River in the Texas Hill Country, and is known as "Rock Town," because of a 2/3 replica of Stonehenge (like the one in the United Kingdom). Ingram is home to a number of very popular summer camps for kids. We take a brief pause of remembrance for the tragedy that occurred at Camp Mystic and the local area, with over 135 people losing their lives in the pre-dawn hours of July 4, 2025.

The Guadalupe has a long history of flash flooding going back over 100 years. Little did we know it at the time, in the summer of 2024, but these would be some of the last Little League All-Star games played on these fields, before they were destroyed in the flooding. The community has rallied with donations to rebuild the fields, and our prayers continue to be with them as they move forward from this terrible tragedy. We want to say a special thank you to the Houston Astros owner, Jim Crane, who has graciously donated $2.5 million to assist in the rebuilding efforts. Thanks to his and others generosity, these fields will be built back even better than they were before.

Ingram beat Kerrville 13-3 in the Opening Game of this District Tournament two days earlier, on Monday, June 17th. Game 1 v. Ingram highlights include:

- Julian leads the game off with a single and records a sacrifice fly
- Cooper gets his first single and records his first 5 strikeouts pitching
- Kole moves a runner over and takes his first hit-by-pitch
- Caden hits his first double and his first home run
- Gray scores his first home run and records 3 strikeouts pitching
- Doc draws his first 6-pitch at-bat
- Aiden draws his first walk and hits a single
- Ben rips his first double
- Dylan gets his first single
- Gage draws his first walk and hits a single
- Jett scores his first home run
- Kaleb earns his first single and draws a walk
- Our pitchers earn their first no-hitter game
- First game ends in a run rule!

Little League rules say that if one team is up by 10 runs after 4 innings or up by 15 runs after 3 innings, the game ends. Boerne's first All-Star game concludes in grand fashion, and now the parents can let out their breath...Whew, we won the first one, thank God. The parents are literally shaking we are so nervous for our kids.

Boerne wins game 1 with a score of 15-0, including 15 runs on 14 hits, and 4 homeruns, and that means we get to come back two days later, on Friday night for game 2! Cooper's 71% strike percentage pitching was key for his 34 pitches, and he'll be ready in case he's needed again in the next few days. Gray pitched very well too, throwing 64% strikes. Neither pitcher allowed a hit, and we walked one batter, striking out 8.

Gio Garza threw 54% strike percentage for his 54 pitches and Eli Rodriguez threw 70% for his 23 pitches. Ingram only got to bat 10 players, and their remaining three players didn't get an opportunity at the plate. This game sends Ingram to the loser's bracket.

Kole is the first of our players to take a hit-by-pitch. This is incredibly important in the context of baseball, and shows the level to which kids are team players. The "right" thing to do if the pitcher accidentally throws the pitch at you, is to turn your left shoulder (if you are a right-handed batter) toward the plate, turn your face away from the pitcher, and "take" the hit. Let the ball hit your side, shoulder, back, or helmet. That is the selfless thing to do, and can be incredibly important for your team. It's an automatic runner on base. We have seen way too often a kid diving out of the way of a pitch, then stands back up and either gets out going to first or strikes out. That is an incredibly costly mistake when you should have simply taken the hit-by-pitch for the team.

Fredericksburg lost to Medina Valley 10-0 and then Fredericksburg beat Kerrville 17-4, so Ingram and Fredericksburg face off in the semi-final game. Ingram beats Fredericksburg in a nailbiter 9-8. That earns Ingram the right to play in the final elimination bracket game.

Game 2 Medina Valley @ Boerne, Friday, June 21st

Since we played Wednesday night, as soon as we won the game, we had to pack up the kids, get back to our vehicles, and drive about an hour home to Boerne from the field. The kids were starving, so dinner consisted of Whataburger drive-through to eat on the way home since we were going to get back home around 1030p, and knowing that we had to be back here on Friday night.

One of Kaleb's preferences that we have developed over the last 3 years or so, is to always arrive at the ballpark 2 hours in advance of our game. That allows him to get into the batting cage, hit a couple buckets of balls (80-100 balls), throw a football to warm up (it was good enough for Nolan Ryan and Phil Mickelson), and then get into regular throwing with the rest of the kids as they generally arrive about an hour early.

Game 2 kicks off at 8pm two days later, the baseball version of Friday Night Lights, and we are playing Medina Valley, a group of kids we know very well, and that Kaleb has played with multiple times in various travel ball tournaments over the last few years. Medina Valley is a farming community just west of San Antonio and has been named the "Apple Capital of Texas." Like many communities in Texas, this town has grown up around Medina Lake and is known for its small-town charm, local friendliness, and warm personality.

Even though we feel confident in our team our heart is back again in our throat as soon as the first pitch is thrown. Game 2 v. Medina Valley highlights:

- Caden records his first 12 strikeouts as pitcher, pitches a complete game, and scores his second homerun
- Kole records his first single
- Dylan hits his first home run
- Gage's hustle gets him on 1st base from what would have been a fly out
- Ben draws his first walk
- Julian rips a double
- Cooper rips a double
- Gray rips a single and double
- Doc rips his first home run of the tournament
- Aiden draws a walk
- Ben advances the runners on his at-bat
- Kaleb gets on base and scores
- Our 2nd no-hitter
- Medina Valley has bases loaded and we walk the batter, so we "walk" in a run for the 1st run against Boerne
- Ends in run rule in 4th inning

We finish the game Boerne 11, Medina Valley 1 (10 runs after four innings is a run rule).

The parent's breath a collective sigh of relief. Even though Boerne maintained great control over the game, that little slip in the fourth inning was enough to put your heart back in your throat and keep you on edge until that last run scored. If you feel you are missing out, you are welcome to turn to page 173 and follow the play-by-play!

Boerne's pitching doesn't allow Medina Valley any hits, one error and three walks, resulting in one run. Caden throws 58% strike percentage with a total pitch count of 77 and an incredible 12 strike-outs. Boerne collects 10 hits, three walks, and only two strikeouts.

Walker Kohlleppel pitched 54%, Drew McDougal pitched 55%, and Jase Marquez pitched 44% for a total of 105 pitches. Boerne got 25 at-bats this game, so we were able to just make it into our lineup for a third time. Medina Valley got to the plate 16 times.

This game sent Medina Valley to the loser's bracket, which means they had to play Ingram. Medina Valley then beats Ingram 9-1 in the elimination bracket final game. They earn the right to re-match Boerne in the championship game Sunday evening!

Medina Valley played fantastic against both Ingram and Fredericksburg, batting .537 as a team and accumulating 19 runs on 29 hits, 10 walks, only 8 strike-outs, and four kids took a hit-by-pitch.

Game 3 Boerne @ Medina Valley, Sunday, June 23rd

The goal with each of these District tournaments is to complete them in 5-6 days, which builds in a small buffer for weather delays/rain-outs, so the first two games kicked off on Monday, June 17th and this championship game is scheduled for Sunday, June 23rd at 7:00pm unless a second game is needed, which is scheduled for the following evening on Monday at 8pm.

This is where it gets really interesting from a baseball pitching strategy perspective. Medina Valley is now playing in their 4th game in 6 days, as they played in the opening round (Boerne had a bye), they beat Fredericksburg, but then lost to Boerne in Round 2, which sent them to the loser's bracket, and then they had to win that game to earn the right to re-match Boerne in this Championship game. Medina Valley played us Friday night and lost, had to play the next day Saturday against Ingram, which they won, and now they are playing again on Sunday night.

Each game, each team is going to throw probably 65-100 pitches. Based on every we have learned about youth pitcher health, including Eric Cressey's podcasts, Patrick Jones' podcasts, and other sources, kids under 15 should be throwing no more than 100 pitches per week in games, and as we mentioned earlier, LL restricts it to 85 pitches per day. That means that Medina Valley has completely exhausted the arms of at least 3 of their kids unless they split things up, but if their top kid threw in Game 1, then he has recovered enough to pitch in this do-or-die game as he has had 5 days' rest. The team has thrown a total of 276 pitches in the three prior games, with Hunter Alston throwing 94, Walker Kohlleppel throwing 48, Drew McDougal throwing 45,

Jase Marquez throwing 29, and TJ Fulks, Harris Hitzfielder, and Hollis Bartlett throwing 20 each.

Many Little League teams have one or two "ace" pitchers, a 12-year-old that throws 70+ mph, can throw strikes consistently (we define consistent as throwing 60% strike percentage or better), and has 1-2 off-speed pitches, a curveball and/or a change-up. That combination makes them really dangerous (like, Maverick and Goose dangerous, so in a good way 😊). Then they have 2-3 more kids that "can pitch" but do not possess all three of those qualities together. They won't throw as hard, they will not be as consistent, and they might not have a good secondary pitch.

Every so often you'll find a kid, like Luis Yepez from Venezuela, Antonio Guerrero from Mexico, or Lin Chin-Tse from Taiwan that throws 78-82 mph, and that puts a lot of pressure on a team, because few kids at 12 years old are prepared to step into the box and actually battle against that pitcher. More importantly than having one great pitcher though, would be to have 4-7 really good pitchers, with strike percentages consistently above 60%. However, as Donald Rumsfeld famously quoted, "you go to war with the army you have, not the army you want or wish to have at a later time."

To give you an insider's viewpoint and provide some additional context, our Spring season Little League team went 8-6 against our opponents. We had 10 players on the team, and one of the rules for the Spring season is that you aren't supposed to "stack" the teams. Our 12 All-Star kids got separated onto four different teams, so there were roughly three "really good" players per team. For the 14-game season, Kole Newson batted .618, Kaleb Christ batted .595, and Aiden Munoz batted .526. We had one other kid bat .320, one bat .258, four kids bat between .100 and

.200, and three kids bat under .100. This is absolutely to be expected. Little League gets kids at all different skill levels and all the kids are wanting to improve.

Kole pitched 23 innings, Aiden pitched 14, and Kaleb pitched 9, for a total of 46 innings pitched, or 68% of all the 72 innings pitched during the spring season. Kaleb's strike percentage was 68%, Kole's strike percentage was 66%, and Aiden's strike percentage was 53%. When you look at these three kids, they walked 22 kids out of 74 total walks, so 30% of the total walks for the team. For strikeouts, these three kids struck out 55 of the 122 strikeouts, or 45% of the total.

Strike percentage is a key metric for youth pitchers, defined as how many strikes you throw divided by the number of total pitches. Nolan Ryan's lifetime strike percentage was 65%. You can argue that in the MLB pitchers are going to throw "competitive balls" a lot to try to induce swings and misses or swings and soft contact.

With kids, that is not the right focus. You want kids to throw strikes. If they are accurate enough to throw on the corners, then that's great. When you talk to high school coaches, they want kids that can throw strikes. Walks are what kills a team.

We set a goal of Kaleb throwing 70% strikes per game in Select. In Little League, we set a goal to throw 100% strikes. We have yet to achieve that, but we've gotten really close! Many coaches will change pitchers once a kid walks 3-4 batters to try to keep control of the game and still figure out a way to win. With Kaleb, we have set a higher standard than that, we set a goal to only walk 1 batter (or preferably less) for the entire game. We don't ever pitch around any kid, because if they beat us by barreling up the baseball and hit a home run, then we'll tip our cap to them.

However, we are going to make them beat us, we are not going to give them a free base. If you look at our Williamsport team and you see that even Kaleb, our 11-year-old batted .595 and threw 68% strike percentage during the regular season, you start to understand how good, and deep, our pitching and hitting lineup really was.

But let's get back to this championship game. Medina Valley is the home team, so Boerne bats first. Game 3 highlights include:

- Julian drives in a run and records 7 strike-outs pitching
- Gray is the first to get on base, scores our first run, and then rips a double
- Kole hits a single that drives in a run and moves a runner over
- Caden rips another homerun to score two
- Doc creates a 7-pitch at-bat and takes the hit-by-pitch to get on base and records 4 strike-outs pitching
- Cooper drives in Gray with a double and then hits a single to drive in two more runs
- Jett gets a single and a double
- Aiden smashes a triple and a double
- Dylan hits three singles
- Gage hits a single and moves the runner over
- Ben creates a 6-pitch at-bat and gets on base
- Kaleb gets a single
- Our 3rd no-hitter

A few plays showed great baseball IQ. Kaleb is the runner on third, no outs, all we need to do is put the bat on the ball to score the run, and Julian executes his job to perfection with his grounder. The very first pitch is close enough that he is swinging hard and trying to barrel up the baseball. The fact that he reached 1st instead of being thrown out is simply a bonus, but when we talk about capitalizing on the little mistakes, this is an excellent example. Medina Valley should have gotten at least one out on that play, but now we've scored a run and have another base runner. Gray comes in to bat and hits a double to Hollis in center field, scores Ben, and Julian gets to third. Again, great baseball IQ executed in the moment. Cooper as well swings at the first pitch and hits a single to Hollis again, scoring Julian and Gray! Caden comes to the plate, watches ball one, and then rips a home run over the left field wall for a two-run bomb! The top four guys in the lineup executing to precision exactly what you want MLB players to do! This is incredibly fun to watch play out in front of us! Well done boys!!

We go back to baseball IQ. At the plate, it's simple. We want to let balls go by and swing at strikes. These Little League umpires are really good, and they are not calling anything outside the plate. The strike zone is armpits to knees, but if it's off the plate, it's a ball. That lets the really good hitters be selective about what pitches they will swing at, because they have that certainty. We have some umpires in other tournaments where anything between the two white lines (6" off the plate on both sides) is a strike, and sometimes curveballs that end up in the other batter's box get called as strikes too. However, for this District to LLWS tournament, the umpires are awesome and consistent!

Anytime we swing at a ball, we made a mistake and we give a "free strike" to the pitcher. When we know that their pitchers are going to have to throw 65-100 pitches in a game, and they are always going to start off with their best pitcher available, our goal is to let him rack up his pitch count as quickly as possible. If we can force him to throw 30 pitches in the first inning, and another 30 pitches in the second inning, his arm is wearing down coming back in for a third inning, or the coach may even decide that he needs to protect that arm for a future game. Doc created a 7-pitch at bat. Technically, a quality at-bat (QAB) is 6 pitches or more. Anytime a batter can force a pitcher to throw him that many pitches means that you are probably seeing every pitch he has available, you are wearing him down physically, and you are also frustrating him which makes him more prone to error.

Julian's focus shifts a bit once Boerne has a 14-0 lead. The only thing that kills us at this point are to walk kids, so now our goal is to throw 100% strikes, if they can hit it, that's fine, but let's allow our defense to work. It's unlikely they would get 10+ runs before they rack up three outs, so we'll just play the odds.

Boerne has done it!! They've won District and will be advancing to the Section Tournament! 17-0 final score, Boerne allowed no hits, walked three batters and had 11 strike-outs. Boerne had 19 hits, drew 2 walks, and only had 4 strikeouts. When you look at the game in the rearview mirror, or just from the statistics, you'd say, wow, what a boring game.

Trust me, with this game being the deciding factor between going to Section or having to play a second elimination game, this game was a rollercoaster of emotion the entire two hours! Medina threw 105 pitches in that game to our 33 total batters, with Harris throwing 62% strike percentage on his 85 pitches and Hollis throwing 55% for his 20 pitches. Julian threw 61% strikes for his 46 pitches and Doc threw 53% for his 30 pitches (76 total pitches vs. their 105 pitches), and we faced a total of 16 batters.

The fans erupt, the kids get to pose with the District Champion banner and the scoreboard in the background, and it means that Boerne gets to return to Ingram the following weekend for the Section Tournament! That picture appears in the Boerne Star, the local newspaper, the next day on June 29th and the boys have their first taste of fame!

Quick Re-cap: 3 games and 3 wins, Ingram 15-0, and two games against Medina Valley, winning 11-1, and 17-0. We allowed one run in 3 games, while scoring 43 runs. Oh, and by the way, we threw three no-hitter games. Our pitching roster for those games was Cooper, Gray, Caden, Julian, and Doc. We had eight home runs, with Caden getting three of them, and one each for Julian, Gray, Dylan, Doc, and Jett. Since Medina Valley had already lost one time to Boerne, this was their second loss, and so they were eliminated, which left Boerne as the only team to not have accumulated two losses. Otherwise, there would have been an "if" game the next evening on Monday at 8pm.

Game 4 Boerne @ Northern Little League (San Angelo), Friday, June 28th

It's another blisteringly hot evening in Ingram, and with the game starting at 6p, it still feels like we are on the red side of the sun. It won't cool off until 830 or so, when the sun finally gets low in the sky... And by cooling off, we mean dropping down to 98 or so!

Many folks will tell you that District "feels" much harder than the Section event. It's the first few games where the kids are truly tested, and so there is an incredible anxiety to it all. We celebrated each win, but we tempered it in talking with the boys that we have to remain laser-focused, because if we let any game momentum start to go against us, that can be a death blow. You are "living on the edge" throughout this entire series.

We arrive at Section now with these three wins behind us, and a consistent theme of each of our 12 boys executing in their respective moments. However, we have really not been "tested" defensively yet to this point, and on one of the defensive opportunities we had, we committed an error. We know these kids are 12 and so they will absolutely make errors, and we work very hard in practice to minimize those. However, we have some anxiety relating to seeing how the boys will respond against a team when they start to put the bat on the ball.

The Texas West Section 3 tournament has five teams in it as well, Northern LL from San Angelo, McAllister Park LL from San Antonio, Uvalde LL, Eagle Pass LL, and Boerne. This tournament starts on Friday, June 28th and it intended to finish by either Tuesday, July 2nd or Wednesday, July 3rd, if that second elimination game is necessary.

San Angelo is a really neat town in West Texas, in that it's the largest town without an interstate, and its home to about 120,000 people. In the 1900's, it was the "Wool Capital of the World," as it was a major stop on cattle drives in the American West. Angelo State University is now affiliated with Texas Tech University in Lubbock, and so there is a significant investment in education in the area. There is a strategic blend of history and modernization, all wrapped up with small-town charm and a "we know all our neighbors" feeling.

Game 4 highlights:

- Julian draws a walk
- Gray hits a single, draws a walk, and hits a double
- Kole records his first two-strikeouts pitching, hits two singles and his first home run
- Caden barreled up the baseball to keep the bats going
- Doc hits a single
- Cooper adds another six strikeouts to his pitching resume and hits a single
- Jett hits a single
- Aiden hits a single and hustles to get to first on an error
- Dylan draws a walk and has a 6-pitch at-bat that results in a single, scoring two
- Gage draws two walks
- Ben hits a single and a double
- Kaleb hits his first double
- Another no-hitter and run rule game

Boerne wins again 17-0! Northern got 0 hits in that game, 0 walks, and 8 strike-outs. They threw 117 pitches total. Colt Barker pitched very well at 71% strikes and Austin Epperson pitched 48% strikes. Boerne only threw 41 pitches with a combined 73% strike percentage. Cooper threw 79% (Boom!!!) and Kole threw 62% (well done)!!! Boerne had 14 hits, 4 walks, and 4 strike-outs. This is now Boerne's 4th game where we haven't allowed a single hit. This game sends Northern to the loser's bracket, where they have to play against Uvalde, who McAllister beat 15-0. This was also the 4th game where we run-ruled our opponents.

Recall the earlier conversation? We are trying to shut these games down as quickly as possible. It's a shame to some extent, because we mentally commit two hours for each game, plus the two hours of warm-up beforehand. Ending a game in the 3rd inning, or after about one hour of play, leaves us slightly unfulfilled. We feel like we blew through that game so quickly we didn't even get to enjoy it, and now it ended even faster than we planned. Obviously very positive for our team, but still a strange emptiness as well.

Game 5 Eagle Pass @ Boerne, Saturday, June 29th

We pack up and leave the Friday night game around 8pm, get home around 930p, and have to be back at Ingram the very next day, Saturday, for game 2 at 7p against Eagle Pass. Eagle Pass is a Texas border town about 130 miles southwest of San Antonio and has a bridge that connects to Piedras Negras, which is in the Mexican state of Coahuila. Every March there is an International Friendship Festival hosted to celebrate the shared culture and relationship of the two towns.

Having railroad tracks built in the late 1800's that connected Mexico with Galveston and San Antonio caused Eagle Pass to flourish. It is the fastest route between San Antonio and Mexico, also called "La Puerta de Mexico," which translates to "Mexico's Door." Laredo, TX is a larger town south of Eagle Pass that now is responsible for a lot of the tractor-trailer traffic between the two countries.

Game 5 highlights include:

- Julian rips a single, triple, and a home run
- Gray rips a single, draws a walk, and adds two strikeouts to his pitching profile
- Kole hits a line drive single scoring Cooper and moving Caden over
- Caden hits a line drive single
- Doc adds eight more strikeouts to his pitching profile, hits a single, and takes a hit-by-pitch
- Cooper hits two singles and a sacrifice fly
- Jett hits a ground ball and gets on first
- Aiden draws a walk and tags the runner out trying to steal second

- Dylan hits a single and takes a hit-by-pitch (we celebrate those selfless acts because we want to reinforce great teamwork!!)
- Gage watches a wild pitch that allows Jett to score
- Ben creates a 5-pitch at-bat and then draws a walk
- Kaleb creates a 7-pitch at-bat and hits a sacrifice fly to score Ben and move Jett over, and hits a fly ball to center who drops it

Boerne continues their dominating run with a win over Eagle Pass of 15-3! This is the fifth game now that we have run-ruled our opponents. Eagle Pass threw 140 pitches (54% strikes combined) in that game, and had to face our entire lineup three full times, 36 at-bats. That puts them at a real disadvantage, being down 1.5 pitchers.

Joseph Nino at 79 pitches (51%) is done for the next few days. D'Andre Daniel threw 37 (57%) so they are going to want to use him again, Richard Moreno only threw 17 (47%), so he can go again, and Robert Daniel III only threw 7 (86%).

They have to come back Sunday and play at 5p, and if they win, play again Monday at 7p, to then get to the championship game on Tuesday. They are looking at having to use at least two of those guys, if they could go complete games, which is unlikely, and then needing both D'Andre and another closer to play on Tuesday, if they can win their way all the way back.

Eagle Pass had 1 hit in that game, drew 4 walks, and had 10 strike-outs. After 4 games, Boerne finally allows 1 hit in the 5th game. That is an incredible accomplishment for our pitchers! Boerne had 14 hits in that game, drew 4 walks, and had 5 strike-outs. This sends Eagle pass to the loser's bracket. Northern beats Uvalde

15-6, so that earns them the right to play Eagle Pass, and they win that game 5-2.

Game 6 Boerne @ McAllister Park, Sunday, June 30th

The way the brackets worked out for the Section Tournament is that we played Friday night, Saturday night, and because we won, we get to play again on Sunday at 7pm, so three nights in a row we are back in Ingram. This is now the semi-finals game against an always competitive McAllister Park (MP) program. McAllister Park encompasses Northern San Antonio, so they have quite a pool of kids to pull from.

McAllister clenched invitations to Williamsport back in 2009, 2012, and 2016. They were state champions in 2013, 2014, 2015, 2017, 2018, 2021, and 2022. This program has a long history of excellence. With the first five games ending by run-rule, this is shaping up to be Boerne's first "real test." With McAllister Park having over 2,000 kids, technically they now have two charters, which means they have two different clubs, an American club and National club.

This is how we talked about it with the kids as well. We wanted them to be very focused and mentally prepared for an incredibly tough game. We believe we have a very strong team, however, the vast majority of these MP kids were initially selected for All-Stars at 10 years old and have been working diligently the last two years to get to this 12U All-Star season, so they can make another run at Williamsport.

Game 6 highlights:

- Julian adds eight strikeouts to his pitching resume and he goes the entire game, allowing only one hit, hits a single, and draws a walk
- Gray hits a fly ball to right field who drops it, and Gray becomes our leadoff runner, and then draws a walk
- Kole hits a double and a single
- Caden hits Boerne's first grand slam and then smashes another home run
- Doc hits two fly balls to the outfield to keep the bats going
- Cooper hits a single, draws a walk, and hits a double
- Jett hits a single and turns a double play
- Aiden rips a ball to center for a triple and draws a 7-pitch walk
- Dylan hits a ground ball and hustles to first, reaching on an error and draws a walk
- Gage draws a 7-pitch walk
- Ben takes a hit-by-pitch and hits a line drive single (way to go Ben!!!)
- Kaleb hits a sacrifice fly to right and scores Dylan

MP threw 93 pitches that game (52% strike percentage) and Julian only threw 51, with 34 of them being strikes (67% strike percentage). MP got one hit in the game and drew one walk. So, now we've gone 6 games and have only given up 2 hits total!!! Our 6th run rule game! Our pitchers and defense are incredible!! Boerne got 10 hits in the game and drew six walks. Perhaps even more impressive was that Boerne didn't have a single strike-out, whereas MP had 8.

This game sends McAllister Park to the loser's bracket, so they have to play Northern in the semi-final elimination game. Northern beats McAllister Park 3-2 in another nailbiter, and so that earns Northern the right to a re-match against Boerne on Tuesday!

We celebrate that victory because we just beat the team that many folks would have assumed was "the team to beat." Now we've got some confidence, and believe that we can take this Section tournament. However, as we are all painfully aware, anything can happen in baseball, so we celebrate with the boys and we prepare them to come back two days later and finish the job. This is the first glimpse that this could be something really special and we are excited to see how this ride turns out!

Game 7 Northern LL @ Boerne, Tuesday, July 2nd

Drama central! Here we go, we have been flawless through 6 games up to this point, and now we are in the Section Championship game trying to earn our way to Abilene and the State Tournament! Northern LL played their way back through the loser's bracket and so from their perspective, it's payback time, and from Boerne's perspective, we have to take care of business one more time!

It's Tuesday night, and two days before July 4, but everything rests on the outcome tonight! If we lose, we do get to play again Wednesday night. However, we sure don't want to put our backs up against the wall that way, so we want to get pressure on Northern early and never remove our boots (or cleats? 😊) from their neck!

Game 7 highlights:

- Julian hits two singles
- Gray hits two singles
- Kole hits a single and scores both Cooper and Caden
- Caden adds five strikeouts to his pitching resume and goes the complete game, allowing only three hits and hits a single
- Doc takes a hit-by-pitch and hits a single (way to go sir!!)
- Cooper hits a grounder and reaches on the error
- Jett hits a fly ball to center to keep the bats going
- Aiden catches a line out and hits two singles
- Dylan hits a fly ball to center and keeps the bats going
- Gage draws two walks and hits a triple
- Ben hits a sacrifice ground ball to score Aiden and smashes a home run

- Kaleb draws a walk and rips a line drive single

Boerne has done it!! We win 18-2 over Northern, and Boerne has earned a trip to Abilene for the State Championship! We run rule them after the 3rd inning as well, so this is our 7th run-rule game!

Northern got 3 hits in that game, 3 walks, and 5 strike-outs. Boerne had 15 hits, 3 walks, and only one strike-out. Northern threw 80 pitches with three different pitchers (cumulative 50% strike percentage) while Caden only needed 55 pitches, with 30 of them being strikes (55% strike percentage). We've now only given up 5 hits in 7 games, an incredible testament to the depth of our pitching lineup and our defense!

We have beaten the teams through both District and Section, and now it's time to pack up and get on the road to Abilene for the State Tournament. We expect that we are going to see some really intensive competition there, so we prepare the boys for things to simply continue to get much harder from this point forward!

The Boerne Star puts us in the newspaper again, and now we are starting to draw some attention and from around the country. We created our GameChanger app with an abbreviation so that our family/friends could find it but we didn't want any of the other teams around the country to be able to "follow" our team that closely. We are still in "stealth mode" because we have done well to this point, but at the end of the day, if you don't win State, you never get to go to Regional, and if you don't win Regional, you don't get to go to Williamsport. We were hoping that no one would know that this Boerne Freight Train was coming!

As you can see from these first seven games, every single one of our boys executed crucial plays in the moment to help our team secure these wins. This particular format, and we can't stress it enough, requires 12 really good, complete, baseball players.

Game 8 Boerne @ West Brownsville LL, Friday, July 12th

Winning that game against Northern meant that we got ourselves an invite to go to Abilene, TX in the middle of July for the State Championship Tournament. If you have ever been in Houston in mid-summer, when the temperature is 100 degrees and the humidity is 100%, yes, you know, it's miserable. If you drive west to San Antonio, it's 110 degrees but the humidity is around 70%. That means that you don't sweat if you are in the shade. If you drive to Abilene, which is north and west of San Antonio about 200 miles, or a 3.5-hour drive then you start to figure out what living on the sun is like. It's hotter and drier than San Antonio, oh and by the way, it's hotter and dustier too. Did I mention it's hotter?

Abilene is home to about 125,000 people and three universities, Hardin-Simmons, McMurry, and Abilene Christian University. There are a bunch of motels in Abilene that we were not interested in, and so we stayed downtown at the Doubletree Convention Center hotel. The Wylie baseball fields are on the south side of town, on the east side of Kirby Lake. Our Little League President Chris Carey is from Abilene, so he was quite excited to "return home."

We drove up early Friday morning because we wanted to get there early, have lunch, have time to loosen up after the long drive, check into the hotel, go get an early dinner, and then be at the Wylie stadium around 5p to start getting ready for our 7p game. We found Joe Allen's Pit BBQ, and ended up eating there 6 times in the four days we were there. A wonderful local BBQ restaurant that feels very homey, had a great food and great service, so that's why we kept going back. They served plain BBQ turkey, which is one of Kaleb's favorite protein-dense meals, and one of the meals we eat frequently before/after baseball tournaments and other sporting events. Let's get to the game, and of course, now all the parents are nervous and on edge!

There are four teams in this state tournament, Midland Northern, University (Fort Worth), West Brownsville, and Boerne. Midland beat University in a close game just before ours, 10-8.

We thought it was a long drive for us at 3.5 hours, but Brownsville is another 5 hours south of San Antonio, so for those families this was an 8-9 hour drive. Brownsville is a Texas border town, right next to Matamoros, Mexico, and is on the Gulf of Mexico, so it's right next to South Padre Island, a popular South Texas beach. 25 years ago, high school and college spring breakers would come party on South Padre Island, and then drive across into Matamoros where the legal drinking age is 18, but that's another story.

Game 8 highlights include:

- Julian hits a single, draws a walk, and rips a double
- Gray hits a ground ball to keep the bats going and draws a walk, and catches a fly ball in center field
- Kole records another pitching strikeout and hits a homerun
- Caden hits a single and a fly ball that is dropped
- Doc records another pitching strikeout, catches a line drive in center, and hits a grand slam
- Cooper adds six strikeouts to his pitching resume and draws a walk
- Jett grabs a ground ball at short and gets the out at second to end the inning and hits a single

- Aiden hits a ground ball to keep the bats going, a line out to center, and draws a walk
- Dylan hits two ground balls to keep the bats going
- Gage takes a hit-by-pitch (way to go Gage!!)
- Ben hits a ground ball and reaches on the error, draws a walk, and rips a double
- Kaleb just misses a fastball and pops out and then hits a ground ball out to keep the bats going

Whew... Boerne wins the game 11-0, but that 0 doesn't show how close they came to scoring several times! That game is also the first one that we went to the bottom of the 6th inning! Now that we've had to go all six innings, we are back to wishing we could have just run-ruled them by the third inning! See how crazy this becomes, and how our thoughts and emotions are all over the place?

Brownsville got 3 hits in that game, drew 3 walks, and struck-out 8 times. Boerne had 9 hits, 5 walks, and 6 strike-outs. Brownsville threw 105 pitches with a 59% strike percentage. Sebastian Hernandez threw an impressive 73% and Anthony Gonzalez threw 54%. Boerne conversely threw 97 pitches with a 63% strike percentage. Cooper threw 66%, Doc threw 59%, and Kole threw 61%.

Hopefully you are starting to see a pattern emerge here. The Boerne boys are really good hitters, which means they have plate discipline. If they get deep in a count, 2-0, 3-0, they'll watch another pitch or two to try to draw the walk. However, they are also swinging at strikes and trying to hit the ball hard. That is a learned skill, that takes years to develop (and is still developing) in these 12-year-olds. You don't get that by hitting balls once or twice a week. You get that through consistent 4-5-6 times per week hitting balls, practicing soft toss, and live batting practice. With baseball, it is almost always the same. You'll see a kid that becomes a pretty good defensive player first, then he'll develop his ability to pitch/throw strikes, and lastly, they will develop their batting skills so they become a good batter (meaning they bat over .400 consistently).

This is one of the reasons it's so important for Little League kids to get year-round practice, because you won't develop this as well if you are only doing it for 4 months per year. Jimmy Gonzales, a retired local MLB scout that owns Jimmy Gonzales Baseball Academy, says "hit every day. Even if it's just off a tee into a net in your backyard, hit every day."

We expected to see some better competition here at State, and some of the Brownsville kids showed us their batting ability! We've played several Rio Grande Valley teams before in other tournaments, and they hit the ball hard and they hit the ball a long way! We know these kids can hit, we've got to pitch well and when they do connect, we need to be solid on defense!

We send Brownsville to the loser's bracket, and they play against University (Fort Worth) on Saturday, and University wins 13-3 in four innings. So, with the double elimination, that means Brownsville goes home. University has to play their way back through the loser's bracket, so that means they will meet the loser of the Midland North v. Boerne game on Saturday. One more of those teams will be eliminated, and the winner will advance to the State Championship game.

Game 9 Midland @ Boerne, Saturday, July 13th

Midland has been a famous town in West Texas for a long time, given its rich history (...rich history, see what we did there? 😊) being located in the Permian Oil basin, the second-largest oil shale in the world. If you watch Billy Bob Thornton in the TV series Landman, much of that is filmed in Midland. Midland, and its sister town, Odessa about 40 minutes away, are home to thriving communities, have significant investments from a number of large international corporations, and The University of Texas-Permian Basin has a local college campus. Midland residents have the second-highest personal income in the United States (see, it really is "rich" history 😊).

Midland beat University 10-8 in their first game. We now face another unbeaten team! Our blood pressure shoots up again, ok boys, let's go!

Game 9 highlights:

- Julian records 13 strikeouts and hits a single
- Gray draws a walk and hits a double, scoring Gage and Julian
- Kole takes the hit-by-pitch and hits a homerun that scores two (well done Kole!)
- Caden adds two strikeouts to his pitching resume and rips a line drive double to left
- Doc hits a ground ball to keep the bats going and hits a single
- Cooper barrels up a line drive out to left to keep the bats going
- Jett scoops up a ground ball at short and gets the out, and hits a line drive to third to keep the bats going, and draws a walk

- Aiden rips a double, catches a line out at second, hits a ground ball and reaches on an error, and draws a walk
- Dylan draws a walk, hits a sacrifice ground ball to score Doc and move Aiden over, and hits a single
- Gage catches a fly ball in left for an out, draws a walk, and hits two singles
- Ben hits a sacrifice fly to right and move the runners over
- Kaleb rips a line drive to center and scores two and takes a hit-by-pitch (way to take one for the team!!)

The tense moment in this game was bringing Julian in to pitch. Caden was at 35 pitches (71% strike percentage) and so we brought Julian in to shut down Midland's offense. First of all, like all true champions, Julian wanted to pitch the Championship game the next day, and didn't want to have to come into relieve in this game and then not be able to throw in the championship.

However, the pitcher doesn't decide who pitches, the coaches do. Bert and Justin believed that Midland was the better hitting team and so we wanted to make sure we didn't lose control of this game. The format of these tournaments means that it can be very difficult to come back from a loss, and so we really focused on winning this game.

After that call, Justin didn't sleep for two nights and was concerned that all of us parents thought he was crazy for making that call. At the end of the day, we trusted in his decision and supported him do what he thought was best in the moment. The result is that Boerne advances to the State Championship with a win over Midland of 13-2!

Midland got 4 hits that game, 0 walks (that is HUGE!!!!!), and 15 strike-outs. We celebrate games where we don't walk anyone! Milkshakes for everyone!! They threw 127 pitches to Boerne

(49% cumulative strike percentage), resulting in 10 hits, 8 walks, and only 3 strike-outs. Winning this game meant that we sent Midland to the loser's bracket, so they had to battle University for the right to play us again in the Championship.

Remember, Midland beat University in the opening game, so this is University's chance at redemption. University does beat Midland 12-3 on Sunday, which is Midland's second loss so they go home. You could argue that after their 127-pitch game against us and them beating University the first time, they simply ran out of pitching, but they only scored 3 runs in that game vs University's 12, so their offense seemed to perform very similarly to the way it performed against us.

This is an important point and I don't want us to simply blaze past it for the sake of getting to the Championship game. It's very important to measure how your child and/or your team performs at their "average." Anyone individually or collectively can have a great game here or there. However, in baseball, and in any athletic activity, you have to compare your "average" play across a bunch of games so you can get a sense of how good you really are. That forces you to do the hard work of bringing the kids' average consistency up to whatever level you want to achieve.

Coach Nick Saban talks about there only being 5 "choices" in his philosophy on "The Process." It's a framework for achieving elite performance through consistent, disciplined, execution of small tasks. The five levels that athletes can operate at are: Bad, Average, Good, Excellent, and Elite. Getting to Elite status requires going beyond natural talent with special focus, intensity, commitment, choosing to focus on daily actions over outcomes, and fostering a culture of internal standards, self-discipline, and mental toughness.

When you measure your kid's performance and the team's "average" performance against these 5 levels, it requires the parents to swallow the pill that the child has not simply prepared enough yet and needs more practice. Many of the Boerne kids ask their parents, "Hey can we go hit?"

The parents would say yes, and so many evenings we would arrive at D-Bat Boerne (a local batting cage) and rent a cage for an hour or grab our membership card and go over to the machines to let the kids take batting practice. When any of us would show up on a random Tuesday, Wednesday, or Friday night, on evenings when we didn't have regular baseball practice, it was quite common to see 2-3 of the other kids and parents there, also putting in extra work.

That is the level of commitment it takes to get to Elite level, and it takes that sustained effort over a period of years to see that "average" performance move up those different steps. For our kids, free time meant there was time to go do more fielding/hitting/bullpen, which they enjoyed doing. Once you have developed the habits of hitting every day, after a couple years, the kids will come to you and ask to go hit. But don't expect them at age 7-11, if they are just learning, to always be the one to want to "initiate practice." Ok, off the soapbox, let's get to the next game!

That game against Midland was the second game where we played six complete innings. We did win both of the games by large margins, but you can see that our opponents are starting to stretch us deeper in games and we are having to go further into our bullpen. We explained to the boys about how this continues to get more difficult the deeper we get and so we simply have to focus on the play in front of us, execute in the moment, and let the results come as they will. We have to be "process-oriented" and if we execute our process, the outcomes will take care of themselves.

This win gives us an entire day off, Sunday, before we play again on Monday evening. We go jump in the pool that evening to let the boys cool off. We sleep in the next morning because this entire experience takes an incredible emotional and physical toll on your body, and so you look for opportunities to give your body 9-10 hours of rest. We also know that, given our kids are right in the middle of their growth spurts, they need the 10-11 hours of sleep every night to just to help their bodies recover from the growing they are doing, not to mention all the stress we are putting on them from an athletic perspective.

We go to a local batting cage there in Abilene, inside so that way we can appreciate the air conditioning, get some hitting in, and then go eat and relax some more before we get ready to go play again on Monday night.

Game 10 University LL (Fort Worth) @ Boerne, Monday, July 15th

Boerne has won 9 games in a row and, you could argue, quite decisive victories, outscoring our opponents 129-8. These have been the 9 most stressful games that all of our families have been a part of, and our kids have each played in hundreds of baseball games by this point, when you count both Little League and Select baseball games. And the stress just continues to build, because as we all know, anything can happen in baseball, and we are just hoping and praying that today is not the day that we stumble and fall.

We've got to say thank you to Chris Carey, President of the Boerne Little League, as he and his family were at every game cheering us on and doing more. This is one of those quick, behind-the-scenes moments. So, we've talked about it being hotter than heck in Abilene, and the boys have now played two games, so both jerseys and their pants are dripping wet with sweat, are smelly and nasty, as is common with 12-year-old boys. Chris, being the saint that he is, asks for everyone to deliver their uniforms on Sunday morning to him in the hotel lobby and he will go get them all washed before Monday night's game. So, we've got freshly washed uniforms ready for the next two games, hopefully only one is necessary.

Here we are, Day 4 in Abilene, and hopefully our opportunity to extend our summer playing baseball. University lost to Midland in the opening round, beat Brownsville 13-3, beat Midland 12-3, and now they are ready to come at us guns blazing to take another shot at the Boerne boys! They've had to manage their pitching too as this will be game four for them and is only game three, with a couple extra rest days, for us.

Two Fort Worth teams have been to Williamsport in the past, Northeast Optimist in 1960 and Westside in 2002. Westside battled Valley Sports from Kentucky in the semi-final game. This incredible game went six no-hit, scoreless innings being pitched by both teams!!! The game went to 7, then 8, then 9 innings! Both pitchers had to be pulled because back then the Little League rule was you can only pitch 9 innings. Alvey, the kid from Valley Sports threw 129 pitches and Kelly from Westside threw 118. The book titled Little Big Men, by Gary Yeagle, is an excellent read that talks about the Kentucky team winning the whole thing that summer.

Today, we look at those pitching numbers and we say, "that's crazy!" Recall the famous 1974 game when Nolan Ryan threw 235 pitches against the California Angels and then threw multiple 160+ pitch games in 1989 at age 42. We don't even come close to those types of pitch limits these days. The 10th inning comes and goes, and still, no score. The game finally ends 2-1, with Valley Sports emerging victorious in the bottom of the 11th inning! The game went 3 hours and 10 minutes, just short of the all-time longest game in 1998. During these 11 innings, 49 players were struck out! Valley Sports went on to win the World Championship that year. We say all that so that you can understand the history and context with these teams.

Everyone in Fort Worth Little League has been told that story 100 times. For years there are little kids dreaming of being able to take Fort Worth back to Williamsport and win the whole thing for their town! There was some controversy surrounding the Fort Worth Section tournament this year. Fossil Creek Little League beat University Little League 14-2 with Alex Padilla pitching, however, they didn't continue and so University moved on the State tournament.

Game 10 highlights:

- Julian takes a hit-by-pitch and hits two singles (thank you Julian!)
- Gray takes a hit-by-pitch and rips a double (thank you Gray!)
- Kole rips a double and a three-run homerun
- Caden pitches a complete game with 8 strikeouts, only allows three hits, hits a line drive single, and draws two walks
- Doc hits two singles, draws a walk, and catches a fly ball in center
- Cooper draws three walks
- Jett hits a single, rips a double, and executes two double plays at shortstop
- Aiden hits a ground ball to keep the bats going, takes a hit-by-pitch, hits a sacrifice ground ball, and fields a ground ball for an out
- Dylan hits a single and draws a walk
- Gage draws a walk, rips a double, and rips a triple
- Ben takes a hit-by-pitch, draws an 8-pitch walk, and hits a fly ball single (thank you Ben!)
- Kaleb draws a walk

They have done it! Boerne wins 16-2! The Boerne boys are advancing to the Little League Regional Championship in Waco! Boerne got 15 hits in that game, 10 walks, and had 9 strike-outs. University got three hits, 2 walks, and had 8 strike-outs. Caden had sole possession of the mound and only needed 78 pitches to get through their 20 batters, and threw a fantastic 68% strike percentage! University threw 167 pitches and averaged 49% strike percentage. The boys get their picture taken and are crowned the "Texas West State Champions."

We checked out of the hotel that morning, knowing that if we lost and needed a game two, we could check back in later that evening. Thankfully that wasn't necessary, so we drive home after the game, getting home after midnight that Monday night, thankful to be back in our own beds in Boerne. We know that we've got two weeks off before we have to play our first game in Waco on Thursday, August 1st.

The local newspaper, the Boerne Star reports on July 20th about our victory in Abilene, and for the first time, we start more significant fund-raising efforts. Now it gets very real! We are State Champions and we are one Regional Tournament away from the dream that is Williamsport!

We have to give a huge thank-you to Jeremy Affeldt, local business owner of Free Roam Brewery and a former MLB player who was drafted by Kansas City in 1997, and is a 3-time World Series Champion in 2010, 2012, and 2014 with the San Francisco Giants. He was very vocal and helped to organize various events with his downtown brewery being a very convenient meeting location, and we will be eternally grateful for everything he did for our team and our town. He held "watch parties" at his brewery, and so during all the regional and Williamsport games there was a large crowd in there cheering the boys' on! Or maybe they were just there for the suds? He'll argue, and we'll let him win, that they were there for both! ☺

There is plenty of drama that surrounds these tournaments. This Fossil Creek v. University story is just one example. You hear stories about various Little League teams and/or programs that bend and/or intentionally subvert various rules in order to get their teams to go further in these events. Rio Vista Little League was apparently disqualified for having one to two players they shouldn't have. The really famous case was Danny Almonte from the Dominican Republic in 2001, and there were reports of him having two birth certificates, one showing he was 12 and another showing he was 14. His team was disqualified after reaching the semifinals. The Jackie Robinson West Little League in Chicago was stripped of their 2014 accomplishments, including winning the US Championship tournament at Williamsport after it was found that they had ineligible players on their roster. Waterbury, CT had a protest filed against them as well for allegedly having some ineligible players as well.

Game 11 Texas West @ Arkansas, Thursday, August 1st

Waco...Welcome to the Little League Regional Tournament. For seven days every August, Little League players and families descend and take over the town. This baseball tournament provides a little over a $1.3 million economic boost to the town during this week. Even though we just played two weeks ago, it feels like it's been forever. The coaches wanted to get the boys to Waco a little early, so we drove up Tuesday, July 30th in the morning, even though our first game was not until Thursday at 10am.

Waco is famous for being the home of Texas Farm Bureau Insurance, Magnolia Market (from the Chip and Joanna Gaines Fixer Upper TV Show), Baylor University, Texas Ranger Hall of Fame Museum, Dr Pepper Museum, and the Texas Sports Hall of Fame. Now that we are 3 hours east of Abilene, the temperature fluctuated between 95-103 degrees, and the humidity is about 70%. Abilene is 45-50% average humidity, and so Waco is 20% more humid than where we were two weeks ago. In meteorological terms, the humidity comfort levels range from humid to muggy to oppressive to miserable. We didn't see any of the dry or comfortable days ☺ .

The Regionals tournament is different because the Little League actually takes over past the state tournament. Waco is home to the Little League Southwestern Region Headquarters, and so all games are played at the Marvin Norcross Stadium, which is right next to the Baylor University Equestrian Center and the Baylor University Golf Practice Facility. This stadium holds about 2,000 people, and one of the nice things about Little League events is that they are free to the public. This facility is immaculate! Many folks from around Texas and surrounding states make the journey every August to Waco to come watch these teams, in addition to the parents and extended family that come because their kids are playing that year. Many of the life-long fans of Little League try to come watch as many of these games as they can. Billy Martin showed up in Waco, and then he also came to Williamsport to watch the tournament. He was the Houston pitcher who threw the first no-hitter in tournament history in 1950! He was recognized as a "Diamond Moment" in the 75-year history of the LLWS!

There are seven teams in this tournament, Arkansas (Junior Deputy Baseball LL from Little Rock), Louisiana (Greater New Orleans LL), Mississippi (Clinton Baseball Association LL), New Mexico (Roadrunner White LL from Albuquerque), Oklahoma (Tulsa National LL), Texas East (Lamar LL from Houston), and Boerne, which is now Texas West. Mississippi sent their Hub City LL from Hattiesburg to the LLWS in 1977. Oklahoma had teams make it to Williamsport in 1964 and 1988. We'll talk about Arkansas, New Mexico, and Louisiana as we play them.

All the boys and coaches were provided rooms courtesy of Little League in the La Quinta hotel downtown. Many of the parents booked in the Aloft Hotel that shares the parking lot with the La Quinta, that way we can walk back and forth. That also means you have all 7 teams staying together in one hotel, 84 kids plus 21 coaches, so the La Quinta was a madhouse every day and a really great opportunity for the boys to bond and get to know each other! La Quinta cooked breakfast for the boys, and then Little League provided gift cards to the coaches that were to be used for the lunches and dinners for the boys. We also have to give a Texas "thank you" to Rudy's BBQ, a Texas BBQ chain that graciously supplied breakfast tacos to the boys on multiple mornings. Kaleb's favorite breakfast food is bacon & egg tacos, so he says that his great play was a direct result of Rudy's breakfast tacos.

The boys also got a further taste of what stardom is like. Axe bats provided each of the boys with a complimentary bat. The more interesting thing though, for the boys, was that each of these games are televised live on ESPN+. The competition continues to improve to, so, while Boerne has gone undefeated in its first 10 games to get to this point, each of the other programs have also won 8-12 games to get to this point. This takes on a whole new level of stress and anxiety for the families, as now, every pitch, every swing, and every error, is seen by thousands, if not millions of folks around the world, and the boys are now only one step away from realizing the dream which is to get to the Little League World Series in Williamsport.

Arkansas has been to Williamsport three times; National Little Rock in both 1952 and 1953, and Burns Park in North Little Rock in 1979. Arkansas comes to Williamsport with big dreams to take their state back to the grand stage! This is what makes Little League World Series incredibly popular, but also an emotional rollercoaster, because you've got these twelve kids now representing an entire state, and doing their absolute best in every play for the millions of people back home!

The team gets a good breakfast in them, arrives at the batting cages around 8a for batting practice, and then they head to the field for a second hour of warmup and getting ready.

Game 11 highlights:

- Julian adds three strikeouts to his pitching profile, hits a single and a double, and gets intentionally walked
- Gray hits two singles and makes a catch in center field
- Kole adds one strikeout to his pitching profile, executes a good play at 3rd base for an out, hits a single, and draws a walk
- Caden hits two singles
- Doc draws a walk
- Cooper adds two strikeouts to his pitching profile and hits two singles
- Jett barrels up a curveball to keep the bats going and makes a barehand grab from Aiden to get a double play
- Aiden makes a good spin move at second after fielding a ground ball to get the lead runner out going to second base and hits a hard grounder for a single
- Dylan hits a single and barrels up a curveball to keep the bats going
- Gage hits two singles
- Ben hits two deep fly balls to keep the bats going
- Kaleb hits a single and then hits a fly ball to keep the bats going with the new Axe bat

PHEW!!!! A 7-2 victory over Arkansas, and they held Boerne to only 11 hits, 7 runs, 3 walks, and 2 strikeouts. Boerne's pitching was able to hold them to 7 hits, 3 walks, and 6 strike-outs. Boerne continues its pitching accuracy with a 71% strike percentage on 103 pitches. Arkansas pitched well too at 65% for their 96 pitches.

Texas West and Arkansas broke the record for double plays in a Southwest Region Tournament game with five. That is the first game we have scored fewer than 11 runs, and the closest game we have had yet. That puts us on edge, knowing that the rest of this Regional tournament is going to be a really tough test, but at least we get to celebrate today! We left the stadium, went to go find a good lunch, refuel and rehydrate, went to go relax the rest of Thursday afternoon, and get to bed early that evening so that way we would be ready for New Mexico first thing in the morning.

Game 12 Texas West @ New Mexico, Friday August 2nd

Winning on Thursday against Arkansas meant that we got to play again the next day, Friday at 10a again against New Mexico. Arkansas got sent to the loser bracket and they would face Texas East on Saturday, who won Thursday against Mississippi, but then lost on Friday to Louisiana, and so that was an elimination game for both of those teams. New Mexico got the bye, with there being 7 teams, so their first game was against us. New Mexico has appeared in the Little League World Series one time in 1956, where the Lions Hondo team won the whole thing! This New Mexico team arrives with the hopes to take their state back to Williamsport as well!

It's another beautiful day in Texas, not a cloud in the sky, and it's going to be a hot one! In our first 11 games, there have only been three games where we have failed to put points on the board in the first inning. This game we didn't score until the 4th inning!! (page 254 if you want to go play-by-play)

Game 12 highlights:

- Julian adds three strikeouts to his counter, draws a walk, and hits a home run
- Gray takes a hit-by-pitch and hits a double (well done Gray!)
- Kole hits a ground ball to advance the runner and makes a catch at 1st base
- Caden adds three strikeouts to his counter and draws a walk
- Doc adds two strikeouts to his counter, hits a curveball to get on base, and makes a sliding catch in right field
- Cooper hits a sacrifice fly to score Dylan and hits a single

- Jett hits a single, makes a catch in shallow left, and catches a line out
- Aiden hit the curveball to keep the bats going, draws a walk, turns a double play with Jett and Kole, and then throws a grounder home to Julian to tag the runner and keep a run from scoring
- Dylan draws a walk
- Gage hits a single
- Ben hits the curveball to keep the bats going and draws a walk
- Kaleb creates a 9-pitch at-bat and gets on top of a fastball to keep the bats going
- We got our first taste of "live replay," just like in MLB games

Boerne beats New Mexico 5-1!! Gray taking the hit-by-pitch was really important, because in this game, it was scoreless through three innings! Dylan got walked, Julian got walked, and Gray took the hit-by-pitch to load the bases with one out! Cooper, our next batter, hits a sacrifice fly to score our first run! Had Gray not taken that HBP, we wouldn't have scored there! That was the only run we scored in the 4th inning, and then they score one in the bottom of the fourth!

New Mexico had 5 hits, two walks, and had 8 strike-outs. They held us to 6 hits, gave up 5 walks, and 5 strike-outs, so those three walks and our slightly better strike percentage (66% vs. theirs of 61%) were difference makers. We were also fortunate to have some timely hitting, but our bats didn't show up today like the normally have. We need to go have a word with that Axe sales rep! 😊

Prior to today, our lowest was 9 hits against Brownsville. How many times have we already seen in the 12 games we've played thus far that you need 12 good hitters, because several of these games will come down to what your #9-12 batters can do for you at the plate! It's almost inconceivable to believe that it is only noon on Friday, most of the real world is working, and we've been at a baseball field for the last 4 hours, but seems like much longer. That game was so tense!

Winning on Friday meant that we earned a day off and we would not play again until the semi-final game on Sunday, August 4th at 3p. We took the boys for a good lunch and then some went swimming to offset the 100+ degree heat. We'd get together for a practice on Saturday, definitely do plenty of hitting, but keep things pretty low-key so everyone can be at 100% for the game Sunday. After what we have just experienced in these first two games, we're going to need to bring our A-game!

Our two "go-to" restaurants in Waco end up being Terry Black's BBQ and Texas Roadhouse. Since we won Friday night and wouldn't play again until Sunday, we had all day Saturday off. We took Kaleb to the pool for a while and then took him back to the hotel and dropped him off after dinner.

The boys figured out that our Aloft hotel had a pool table in the lobby, so whenever they were simply hanging out at the hotel, many times we'd find them in our lobby as opposed to theirs.

Saturday evening Betty and I were able to make our way to Melody Ranch, a local country dance hall, and spend a bit of "adult time" together while Kaleb was getting his much-needed rest for Sunday's game. Melody has live music every Saturday night. Betty and I typically get to these country dance halls around 8p, dance to the first set or two of the band, and then head back home, or in this case, to our hotel. That gives us 2-3 hours of dancing, but then we still get a good night's sleep before all this baseball drama continues the next day!

Louisiana beats Texas East later on Friday 3-0, so that puts Louisiana in the semi-final game against us for Sunday. Do you see a "theme" in these scores? Many of the scores at District, Section, and even state had teams scoring 10-20 runs, and here we are at Regionals and there was only one blow out game, and the rest of the games have been decided by 1-4 runs. New Mexico's loss sends them to the loser's bracket so they had to play Saturday at 2p (really, 2p on Saturday afternoon when it's 1,000 degrees outside?) against Oklahoma, who lost to Louisiana in the first round, but was able to beat Mississippi 10-0 in the first loser's bracket game. Mississippi played Texas East on Thursday in the first round, and Texas East beat them 4-0, so Mississippi didn't score a run in the Regional tournament. They will take that information back home and re-tool for next year. New Mexico would beat Oklahoma in a nail-biter 1-0 game, and then ultimately lose to Texas East in another nail-biter game 3-2 on Sunday before our first game against Louisiana.

Game 13 Texas West @ Louisiana-Greater New Orleans, Sunday, August 4th

Louisiana did something unique this year. The Greater New Orleans (GNO) Little League partnered with the Jefferson Parish Parks & Recreation Department (JPRD) to extend the opportunity to play Little League to the kids in Jefferson Parish. This partnership allowed nearly 1,000 kids with more accessible and more affordable opportunities to play baseball. They charged just $25 per family, which got kids their jersey, hat, and all the registration fees.

This is such a great example of the importance of Little League and local community partnerships around the world, where else could you play baseball for an entire season for just $25? GNO-JPRD has a population of around 800,000, so they have quite a pool to select the best players, versus our 22,000 in Boerne.

Louisiana has sent 9 teams to Williamsport in the past, with Eastbank (River Ridge) LL winning the World Series Championship in 2019 against Caribbean! They lost their first game against West, and then won the next 6 games in a row to come back from the loser's bracket to win it all!

For this Regional Tournament, they beat Oklahoma 4-1 and Texas East 3-0, and so here we are in the winner's side of the bracket, in for the proverbial fight of our lives! A proven Louisiana program vs the "upstart" team from Boerne. Let's go!! We love our underdog stories!

Game 13 highlights:

- Julian adds two strikeouts to his counter and hits a ground ball to keep the bats going
- Gray hits a single and catches a line drive in center field

- Kole hits a double and catches a line drive in left field
- Caden adds five strikeouts to his counter, hits a single, and is robbed of a home run, yes I said robbed (you have to go watch it on YouTube or read about it on page 268)
- Doc draws a walk and throws the ball to 3rd base to tag the runner trying to do a delayed steal
- Cooper makes a catch in left field and hits a single
- Jett hits a fly ball to keep the bats going, makes an out at shortstop, and makes catch to end the game
- Aiden makes a catch at second base, fields three ground balls for outs, and hits a single
- Dylan hits a single
- Gage hits two ground balls to get on base
- Ben hits a ground ball to keep the bats going
- Kaleb rips a single to right field and that Axe bat continues to perform

That game was dramatic!!! Boerne wins 4-1!! Louisiana had 6 hits, 3 walks, and 7 strike-outs to get their one run. Boerne had 6 hits, 3 walks, and only 1 strike-out to get our four runs! Caden's 59% strike percentage and Julian's 63% strike percentage, combined with their velocities 68-74 mph, were crucial to keep Louisiana's bats quiet. For Louisiana, CJ threw 61% and Ben threw 64%, so they did well too, but the depth of Boerne's hitters really showed here. Thanks for your pep talk and making sure your bats performed, Mr. Axe bat rep! ☺ Total pitch count for both teams was Louisiana at 98 v. Boerne at 94!

Wow!!! How many times have we seen the guys in the bottom of the lineup come through at crucial times? This means Louisiana gets sent to the loser's bracket and they have to play again in 21 hours against Texas East.

Game 14 Louisiana-Greater New Orleans @ Texas West, Tuesday, August 6th

Here we go!!! Regional Championship game on Tuesday, August 6th at 6p, and we have to re-match Louisiana!!! Louisiana narrowly beat Texas East yesterday 6-5 at 2p in the afternoon, so here they are having to play another game 26 hours later. Meanwhile, Boerne has been off since Sunday around 5p, so we've had 48 hours between games to get ready to play tonight! I would say that we went for massages, went for spa treatments, lounged at the pool, but the only truth in those statements is the pool time we did take advantage of to escape the Waco heat and humidity! Louisiana had to manage their pitcher lineup too, because this is their 5th game in 6 days.

Game 14 highlights:

- Julian adds 11 strikeouts to his counter, draws a walk, and hits a ground rule double
- Gray takes a hit-by-pitch (team player!!)
- Kole hits a hanging curveball for a ground rule double and a single and makes the game-ending play at third base
- Caden hits a single
- Doc adds two strikeouts to his counter and hits a grand slam
- Cooper hits a single and makes an out playing 3rd base
- Jett hits a line drive to 3rd and reaches on the error, makes a good play at shortstop for an out, and catches a line drive for an out
- Aiden hits two fly balls to keep the bats going and makes a good play at second base
- Dylan was a tough out twice at the plate
- Gage hits a ground ball to keep the bats going

- Ben was a tough out twice at the plate
- Kaleb draws a walk

Boerne has done it! We win 6-3!!! The boys are going to Williamsport!!! The crowd in Waco erupts! The boys rush the mound, they throw their gloves high in the air, they shake Louisiana's hands, and then they hoist the championship banner in victory!!!!

Boerne threw 95 pitches in that game with a combined 71% strike percentage. Louisiana threw 94 pitches in that game with a combined 62% strike percentage. We only walked one of their batters and they walked two of ours. We had seven hits to their four hits. You see how tight and close these games have become? Talk about on the edge of your seat the entire game!!

We finish the game around 8pm and shortly thereafter, the fans empty out of the stadium, and so the families are the only ones left. The field is eerily quiet as dusk settles in and the Little League officials call the Boerne family together in the stands for a meeting.

We sit down and they tell us, congratulations on a great tournament. Guess what, your boys will be on a 6am flight on Friday morning from San Antonio airport to Newark, where they will board a bus and be shuttled to Williamsport, PA. There are on-campus dorms in Williamsport; Little League takes care of everything, but there are a few things you are going to need to pack for them and then you are basically turning your kids over to us for the next three weeks. You don't need to worry, we run this like a well-oiled machine, and they will be in good hands.

They also said that they recommend us getting on our phones while we are sitting there and figure out where we want to stay, because there are only a few hotels in Williamsport and they book up fast. What???

We are sitting there trying to absorb the fact that we just won the Regional Championship, listen to what is going to happen at Williamsport, while we are also having to frantically search on our phones to get hotel reservations. First world problems, yes, we are aware, but after two months of hot summer baseball, we are realizing the dream has come true, and that it's not over yet, we are now signed up for three and a half more weeks of baseball craziness to a place that none of us have been before.

Stunned by the speed with which this is all happening, we pack up, grab some dinner in a drive-through, and drive home to Boerne, getting home again around midnight, knowing that we've only got two days to get them ready and then they'll take off.

This is a significant strain on the families, as we have been in four different cities for basically almost 5 days each already in the last 7 weeks, and now we are facing another three-week stretch in Williamsport. Thankfully Ingram was within driving distance, but both Abilene and Waco required week-long stays. Several of our team members were juggling work commitments with their spouses, and some of our folks that were able to work remotely, were doing work as possible from the hotels at the odd times they were able to grab some screen time and taking calls from the parking lot. Yes, I know these are first-world struggles, and it's a wonderful thing to face this type of challenge, and we wouldn't change it for the world.

It also speaks to the generosity of the Boerne and Kendall County community, because without their support, this would not have been possible. Each family was already on the hook for about $4,000 in expenses from just from Abilene and Waco, and for the upcoming 3-week stay in Williamsport, you are looking at close to $10,000 per family when you factor in flights, hotel, rental cars, and food. For 12 families, that works out to roughly a $180,000 investment to get all the way there. Little League pays for the flights to get the kids to/from their respective cities, boards the kids in Williamsport, and takes care of feeding the boys for the entire time, but the families' expenses are all on the families. For the international families, those flights are even more expensive, so thank you, thank you, thank you to anyone that has ever donated to any team for this Little League dream, because you want both the kids and the families to thoroughly enjoy this experience, and not be inhibited by financial restrictions if at all possible.

We are also reminded of how grateful we are to have it so good in the USA. We were told a story about one of the Little League teams from a Latin America country (we won't say the name because we don't want to embarrass them), and they were interviewing one set of parents of one of the kids, who had two other kids beside their baseball player, and they were talking about making the decision on which two kids were going to get to eat that day, and which one was not. That was just utterly heart-breaking, but we know, especially in the many impoverished nations around the world, that is a daily fact of life. Our prayers, hearts, and donations go out to those families.

Friday morning arrives at 2a, yes you read that right, 2 o'clock in the morning, and we meet in the nearby HEB Fair Oaks parking lot. Have I mentioned yet all the late nights and the early mornings? Hopefully you don't like to sleep very much because there is plenty to keep you awake during all this baseball. We have police cruisers and several shuttle vehicles to take the boys in a police escort to the airport. Little League, true to their word, emailed the coaches later that Tuesday evening a list of exactly what the boys would need, and so we've been able to pack appropriately. It's a surreal experience though, turning your 11- and 12-year-olds over to your three coaches and knowing that they will be halfway across the country for the next several days before we all get up there to see them again.

The boys get to the airport and the local San Antonio TV news crews are there to interview them about the upcoming trip and get some video. They make a stop at the airport Starbucks, and Kaleb gets introduced to a double-smoked cheddar bacon egg sandwich and a pink drink, and he now asks for those on every road trip. Peer pressure at 12 years old, good grief! That was his first caffeine drink. He's never drank a coke in his life. He lives on milk, protein shakes, water, lemonade, Gatorade, and now, the occasional (like once every other month) pink drink.

Kaleb takes the team mascot, a stuffed fish appropriately named the Boerne Bass, and shares that with the reporters. They have explained to us that the boys will be very busy, because they will be getting uniforms, equipment, being interviewed, moving into their dorms, meeting the 19 other teams that have made it to the tournament, and doing some practice as the coaches put together a schedule.

I recall my dad taking me to college nearly 30 years ago and it was the only time I've ever seen him cry. This is very similar, except now I'm the parent in this situation. I'm scared to death to turn over my 11-year-old, but I've got full confidence that he is independent enough that he will be fine, and I've got a lot of faith in our coaches, because they are all incredible men and fathers, and I know that they will take the best care of our boys during this entire trip.

The Lead-In to Williamsport

The boys arrive Friday, August 8th late morning into Newark, are loaded onto a charter bus, and then driven a couple hours out of town and they stop at a Chik-Fil-A for lunch. They boys all have money given to them by their parents, so they load up on chicken sandwiches, milkshakes, and fruit cups. They get back in the bus and drive the second half to Williamsport, where they are met by their "Dorm Uncles," (thank you Chris Long and John Blachek for taking such good care of our boys!!!) the volunteers that will be watching over them for the next three weeks. They have just arrived at the "Disneyworld" of baseball. This place is truly magical! This is a heavenly place that was designed for and serves only one purpose. Letting 240 12-year-old kids come together once a year in August and play 38 games for a World Championship Trophy!

Williamsport was originally a massive lumber center, as it sits in the middle of the mountains of central Pennsylvania and on the banks of the Susquehanna River. In the 1870's, the town claimed to have more millionaires per capita than any other city the US, and those families built many large Victorian-era mansions along West 4th street (dubbed Millionaire's Row). Lumber declined around the turn of the century, and so the city shifted to more manufacturing. In 1939, Carl E. Stotz founded Little League baseball, and from the humble beginnings of only three teams in a single league, it has grown to what it is today.

The vast majority of the staff at Williamsport are volunteers. These are people that give up 3 weeks per summer to drive to Williamsport and help run this event. Just like all the local volunteers that run the local Little League clubs, it's an incredible collaboration of a lot of really good people to celebrate the achievements of these kids. They help them get luggage out of the bus and get into their dorm rooms. Lake Mary (Florida) had punched the first ticket to Williamsport and so they were already there, and we punched the second ticket, so our team was second to arrive. The Uncles, Chris and John, show our boys the cafeteria, game room, and outdoor sport court. The game room included ping pong, car racing simulator, pinball, and two TVs with Playstation's MLB The Show hooked up to them. The gameroom was also where all the pin trading occurred for the majority of the teams. They issue all the boys their identification cards that they have to wear at all times. These lanyards give them the ability to have the run of the entire Little League complex. It's already late Friday afternoon, so after a good dinner and some games, the boys call it a night.

Saturday they wake up, eat breakfast, and get to play with the Lake Mary kids all day, while everyone else was busy getting home from the Regional tournaments and packing their kids to ship them off to Williamsport. Sunday was a very busy arrival day as the majority of the teams came in that day.

The dorms were divided into quads, and ours consisted of Latin America (Venezuela), Japan, Mid-Atlantic, and Team Southwest. It was an incredible experience for our boys to use their phones and Google Translate so they could talk to both the Venezuela and Japan teams! Tomoki Watanabe, #22, the catcher for Japan spoke some English, and so he and Kaleb became good friends! Tomoki would be the translator for his team whenever the boys would get together and play wiffle ball or something else on the sport court. They came up with a nickname for Kaleb that sounded like "Cookie."

Monday was a very special day for the boys because they received their head-to-toe new uniforms from Adidas! Now they were officially Team Southwest! They got jerseys, pants, belts, socks, cleats, and new hats! They then walked into the Easton tent and were able to pick up their new backpacks, bats, gloves, catcher gear, helmets, batting gloves, and elbow guards. They had a batting cage set up so the boys could test various bats and see which one they liked the best. The other thing that happened on Monday was all the kids had pictures and videos taken, and all were interviewed, so now they really do feel like professional athletes! Thank you to Alison Guerrero and Marchon Eyewear for the Nike sunglasses for all the boys! Kaleb adds an Easton Hype Fire to his bag along with his Axe bat. Bruce Bolt, a local company in Austin, TX founded by a kid in 2017, sent all the boys new batting gloves! They are the best batting gloves that we have ever used!

The coaches were able to orchestrate a practice for Tuesday late morning. There are six fields on the other side of Mountain Avenue where the boys practiced. There are three fields that were reserved for game-day practices and those are inside the complex right next to the batting cage building, between Mountain Avenue and Champion Drive. Tuesday, August 13th is the Grand Slam Parade, live from Williamsport at 5pm. This is the official kick-off of the Little League World Series program. All the boys get on floats, the entire community of Williamsport shuts down and comes out and lines the streets, and the boys throw out candy, sign autographs, take pictures, and just enjoy being celebrities!

Wednesday, the boys got up for breakfast, had a morning practice, and then were given the afternoon to go watch the two opening games, play wiffle ball or pickleball on the sport court with the other kids, or just chill out. There used to be a swimming pool but it was replaced by the sport court a few years ago.

Jeremy Affeldt, the local Boerne owner of Free Roam Brewery and 3-time World Series Champion, sends the boys a video, saying that he is super-pumped that we got to Williamsport, and that he wants the boys to take the Boerne fire and go have a great time and do their best! Juan Soto of the New York Yankees also sends the boys a video message!

After months of hot, hot baseball all over Texas, here we are in the mountains of Pennsylvania, where the temperature during the day can get up to a hot 85-90 degrees, but then in the evenings drops into a quite refreshing 55-65 degrees. They get plenty of rain in this part of the country and so all the Kentucky bluegrass is incredibly lush. When you look out over Lamade and Volunteer stadiums at the Little League complex, there is not a blade of grass out of place, the infield/outfield grass has perfectly mowed, striped strips, and the mound dirt and batter's box dirt are all perfectly compacted orange clay, with clean, crisp, bright white painted lines. Lamade can seat 10,000 fans, with space for over 40,000 on the hill behind the outfield. Volunteer seats 5,000 fans, with space along the fence and outfield for additional fans.

The US teams all play each other in Lamade Stadium in the "National Bracket," and all the International Teams play each other in Volunteer Stadium in the "International Bracket." Only one team from each side will meet for the World Championship game on Sunday, August 25th at 3pm. The two teams that lose their prior games, the US National Championship game and the International Championship game, play a consolation game for 3rd place on Sunday, August 25th at 10am.

The fences are a uniform 225' from home plate, and so there is a perfect symmetry to the fields that the boys will be playing on shortly! During the day it looks spectacular and at night, when the lights come on, it's lit up like a Christmas tree! This is baseball heaven and it truly is a magical place!

As if this three-week trip wasn't enough, we find out that ESPN is filming for a documentary that will be released the following year, called Big Dreams: Little League World Series 2024. ESPN cameras and reporters are all over the complex the entire three weeks, taking video, interviewing players, coaches, and parents, and ensuring they catch all the content they want for the movie they are making the next year.

Game 15 Southwest @ Mid-Atlantic, Thursday, August 15th

This is a new environment, here in Williamsport. The stadium seating is a whole lot bigger, the crowds are much larger, and news crews are running around everywhere. It feels just like an MLB game. Our first game, we are playing the "hometown team" as Council Rock Newtown LL is only a 3-hour drive, and they are the Pennsylvania team, now Mid-Atlantic, in this event. The vast majority of the fans in the stadium are cheering quite loudly for PA, and so Boerne has stepped into a very respectful, yet hostile environment.

This particular group of boys finished 3rd in the PA state tournament when they were 10 years old. The next year, at 11, they finished 2nd. This year, as 12-year-olds, they finally captured the state championship. They then went and won the Mid-Atlantic Regional Event, and they arrive in Williamsport undefeated, just like Boerne. Coming into Williamsport, they are hitting a collective .442 and feature a 1.26 ERA. Given how closely the Regional tournaments were decided, everyone expects this to be a nailbiter!

Thankfully, we had nine days since the win against Louisiana so that our nails have grown back, just in time for us to gnaw them off again! We did get a video message from Marcus Semien, shortstop of the Texas Rangers wishing Boerne good luck in the game today, so that pumped the boys up!

Don Renninger, a "Corporal" in the Ushers that help manage the crowds in the stands, is in charge of our section. He is an incredible artist and he provided hand-drawings of a collage to all the families as simply a gift, because he loves to share his work! The umpires all have special coins as well to show their participation, and they have several handfuls that they hand out to the boys as well! It's just an incredible outpouring of love, appreciation, and excitement as we get into this tournament!

Saverio Longo is the starting pitcher for Newtown and Julian leads us off. He watches a slider out over the outer half for strike one, watches three balls in a row, watches strike two, fouls off strike three, and then turns on fastball middle of the plate to send a rocket out to the left center gap all the way to the wall for a stand-up double to start us off! Gray watches strike one, watches balls one and two, and then connects on a high outside fastball to hit a line drive to shallow left that their fielder is able to make a sliding grab and come up with the catch. Cooper gets jammed and sends a grounder to first that the first baseman picks up and tags the bag for out #2, and Julian is able to get to third. Kole watches ball one, fouls off strike one, watches ball two, watches strike two, and then goes down swinging on a 71-mph fastball on the inside corner for strike three. A 17-pitch inning for Saverio and he keeps the top of our lineup from scoring!

Caden is on the mound for Boerne and Dean Hamilton steps in the box. He watches balls one, two, and three, watches strike one, watches strike two, and then watches a fastball catch the outside corner for strike three. Brayden Peiffer fouls off strike one and then watches four balls in a row. Tyler Neeld watches strike one and then hits a ground ball between third and short. Jett is able to backhand it, but Tyler gets to the bag when the throw across the diamond arrives and is just called safe, so one out, two runners on.

After an official review, call is confirmed safe. Saverio watches ball one, watches strike one, watches ball two, and then hits a grounder to Jett at short, who turns it to Aiden at second and he flips it to Julian to get the bang-bang double play and end the inning! After another official review, they overturn the call at first, saying his foot barely beat the throw! Greyson Gage watches strike one, watches strike two, the runner steals second, and then Greyson goes down swinging on Caden's really good slider that just keeps running away for strike three! Ok, good job boys, getting through the top 5 hitters and no runs, so we breathe a little. A 20-pitch inning for Caden and now we've got to get those bats going!

Another interesting tidbit is that Julie Foudy, former US women's soccer team captain and ESPN broadcaster, would be in the stands during every game, doing impromptu interviews with the parents. They would come to our section, and they would ask us to identify each of the dads and moms, and they would develop a quick reference seating chart, so when Jett flips the double play, they would run to the Matthews' and ask them a couple questions about Jett. When Julian would strike someone out, they would run to the Hurst's and ask them a few questions. Also, as you probably saw on ESPN, when any of the kids would make some sort of play, they would do a close zoom-in of the parents. For the first couple games, it was a bit disconcerting, simply because we weren't used to it, but after a while, it became routine and they got to know who each of the parents were as we continue in the tournament.

Caden watches ball one, watches strike one, watches strike two, watches ball two, and then swings and misses at a good curveball down and away for strike three. Doc fouls off strike one, and then watches four balls in a row to draw the walk. Gage fouls off strike one, swings at a curveball strike two that gets past the catcher and allows Doc to advance to second base, watches ball one, and then watches strike three. Aiden watches balls one and two and then hits a hard ground ball bouncer down the first base line that bounces off the glove of the first baseman and allows Doc to score! Boerne takes a 1-0 lead! Dylan watches ball one, watches ball two get past the catcher and Aiden advances to second, watches strike one, swings at strike two, and goes down swinging for strike three. Sav's 4th strikeout of the game, a 22-pitch inning, and this is a dogfight!!

Gavin Caudill fouls off the first two pitches, watches ball one, and then rips a line drive right back into Caden's glove for out #1. Rocco DaBronzo swings at strike one, fouls off the next two pitches, and then hits a grounder between Caden and Kole at 3rd, so Caden rushes to it, and turns and throws it high over Julian's head, and so that gives Rocco second base. Brody Gage watches balls one and two, swings at strike one, watches ball three, fouls off strike two, and then watches Caden's really good slider start inside and come back right over the plate for strike three! Ryan Uhl watches ball one and then lances a line drive right to Gray in center field for an out #3. Ok, a 16-pitch inning for Caden, so let's go! We've let them get runners on twice now, but we've been able to still keep them to no runs, so let's go pour some on!

Jett watches balls one, two, and three, watches strike one, swings at strike two, fouls off three pitches in a row, and then gets a fastball in on the hands that he hits a grounder between Sav and 3rd, Sav rushes to grab it, but similar to Caden, throws it high, and so Jett turns left into the field of play with the thought of going to second, but the right fielder throws the ball back to 1st, they tag him out. Kaleb watches ball one, watches strike one, watches ball two, watches strike two, and then swings and misses at a fastball for strike three. A 14-pitch inning for Saverio and he is doing his job well!

Saverio got to 52 pitches and so Newtown decides to pull him and brings in Dean Hamilton to pitch. Ben watches two balls in a row, watches strike one and two and then turns his shoulder into an inside curveball for ball three and it just brushes his jersey sleeve under his lead arm, so he is awarded first base on a hit-by-pitch. Julian watches strike one, fouls off strike two, and then is able to hit an inside pitch to shallow right field for a line drive single.

When Gray was asked who his favorite athlete is, he said Jace LaViolette. Gray and his family are Texas Aggies fans. So Gray gets up to bat tonight in the top of the 3rd inning, his favorite athlete is flashed on the bottom of the screen. Well, the real Jace takes a picture of it and posts it above one of his photos where he is rounding the bases after he hit a home run and he tweets, "This is for sure one of the cooler things I've seen in my life!" Gray watches balls one and two and then is able to turn on an inside fastball to hit a hard grounder between 3rd base and shortstop to load the bases for Boerne with two outs!

Cooper watches ball one and then watches the next pitch come right in and stands there to take the hit right on his left hip! That hit-by-pitch scores a run and makes it 2-0! If there is ever a bigger reason to show kids why they need to practice "taking the hit" than seeing this play on ESPN in front of millions of fans, I don't know what it is!! Kole watches strike one, fouls off the next two strikes, and then hits a high fly ball to right field for out #3. A 17-pitch inning for Dean but we scored two! Let's go!

Caden had gotten to 36 pitches so Boerne brings in Julian to relieve and see if we can shut down this game and take the win. If we win this game, we play again on Monday, August 19th (4 days' rest) but if we lose, we have to play Saturday, August 17th (2 days' rest). Wes Esteves, their #10 hitter steps into the box and watches strike one, watches ball one, swings at strike two, fouls off strike three, and swings and misses at a nice curveball to the outside corner for Julian's first strike-out in Williamsport. Will Siveter watches the first two pitches for balls, fouls off strike one, watches ball three, swings at strike two, and then watches ball four to draw the walk. Ok, well, at least it's not the leadoff batter, but we can't afford to have any unforced errors here.

Tyler Wexler watches strike one, fouls off strikes two and three, watches balls one and two, and then watches Julian throw a heater in there at 71 mph for strike three. Dean returns to the plate and fouls off strike one, watches balls one and two, watches strike two, and goes down half-heartedly swinging at Julian's nasty curveball for the final out! A 22-pitch inning for Julian and we keep the lead!

Caden is patient, sits back and waits for a slider that hangs a little and hits a rocket over the left fielder and over the left field wall for Boerne's first home run of the World Series and the first home run of the 2024 World Series! A no-doubter and now a 3-0 lead!!

Newtown wastes no time and swaps out Tyler Neeld for Dean at pitcher. Dean threw 65% strikes. Doc watches ball one, watches strike one, fouls off strike two, and then turns on a high slider inside to hit a hard grounder to bounces over the 3rd baseman's glove and into left field for a hit. Gage watches ball one, fouls off strike one, watches ball two, and then lines out to center field for the first out. Aiden watches strike one, watches ball one, swings at strike two, watches ball two, and then watches a slider start inside and curve back over the plate for strike three. Dylan watches ball one, swings at strike one, and then watches three balls in a row to draw the walk and get two runners on base. Jett watches strike one, fouls off strike two, watches ball one, and then watches a high pitch just catch the top of the zone for strike three. Tyler minimizes the damage with a 22-pitch inning and no additional runs.

Brayden watches ball one, fouls off strike one, watches balls two and three, swings at strike two, and then watches Julian's nasty curveball for strike three and started to 1st like it was a ball, but the ump rings him up. Tyler watches strike one, swings at strike two, and then swings and misses at that nasty curveball dropping in him for strike three and Julian's 5th strikeout today! Sav watches balls one and two, swings at strike one, and then watches balls three and four to draw the walk. Greyson watches strike one, fouls off strike two, and then goes down swinging for strike three on another nasty curveball. A 17-pitch inning for Julian and he's looking good!

Kaleb watches strike one and then takes a high pitch inside on his shoulder for a hit-by-pitch and the leadoff runner for Boerne is aboard!! Way to take one for the team! Ben fouls off strike one and then is able to reach and get to an outside pitch for a line drive up the middle that is just missed by shortstop as he dives for it and it gets to center field for a hit! Now we have 2 runners on and no outs! Julian hits a ground ball chopper up the middle to center field to load the bases!

Gray swings at strike one and then watches four balls in a row to walk in a run!!! Had Kaleb not taken that HBP, that run doesn't score there! Cooper watches ball one, fouls off strike one, and then check swings for strike two, but hits a grounder back to the pitcher who grabs it and throws home to get the lead runner out. Kole watches balls one and two, swings at strike one, and then sends a rocket homer over the center field wall for a grand slam on a hanging curveball!

Boerne blows it open with a 8-0 lead!!! Kole gives a heart sign with his hands to his Mom in the stands and she is holding her sign "We LOVE KOLESLAW!" Caden fouls off strike one and two, and Tyler gets one in on the hands that he hits a ground ball to second for out #2. Doc watches balls one and two and then hammers a home run down the left field line that clears the bushes and reaches the fans sitting on the "iconic hill" that surrounds Lamade Stadium's outfield! 9-0 Boerne!

Newtown swaps out Tyler for their lefty, Will Siveter. Tyler threw well at 54%, but they are now thinking about having to play back through the loser's bracket, and they are going to need their arms. Gage watches ball one, fouls off strike one, watches strike two, watches balls two and three, and then watches strike three cross the outer third of the plate. A 28-pitch inning for Newtown and our bats are showing up!

Gavin C pops out to Julian just between the mound and first base for out #1. Rocco fouls off strike one, watches strike two, and then swings and misses for strike three with his nasty curve again, and his 7th strike-out of the evening. Brody watches strike one, watches ball one, fouls off strike two, watches balls two and three, and then watches his heater come in there at 71 mph for strike three to end the 5th inning. A 10-pitch inning for Julian and he looks to be in complete control!

Aiden watches strike one, watches ball one, fouls off three pitches in a row, watches ball two, and then hits a line drive over the second baseman into right-center for a single. Dylan watches ball one, swings at strike one, swings at strike two, fouls off strike three, watches ball two, fouls off strike three, and then flies out to Rocco in left field. Jett stripes a single into deep right-center gap and Aiden gets to third. Kaleb swings at strike one, swings at strike two, watches ball one, Jett takes second base on defensive indifference, Kaleb fouls off strike three, fouls off strike three again, watches ball two, fouls off strike three, watches ball three, fouls off strike three, fouls off one more pitch, and then watches ball four to take his 11-pitch walk to load the bases with one out! Ben fouls off strike one and two and then swings and misses at a high fastball for strike three.

Julian watches ball one, fouls off strike one, watches ball two, and then hits a ground ball to short and they make the play at first to end the inning. Come on boys, three outs away from our first win at Williamsport!!! A 33-pitch inning that we just created, and we are forcing their pitchers to reach deep!

Ryan, their #9 batter, watches ball one, swings at strike one, watches strike two, watches ball two, and watches a nasty slider that he thought was going to hit him slide back over and cross the plate for strike three. Wes fouls off strike one, watches strike two, and then grounds it back to Julian just off to his right and Julian is able to grab it and throw it to first for out #2. Will watches three strikes, with the final one being his heater right down Broadway to end the game! An 11-pitch inning to finish it, 10 strike-outs for Julian to start the LLWS and a 9-0 win for Boerne!!!

Newtown got 2 hits in that game, had 3 walks, had 13 strikeouts, and 20 at bats. Boerne had 12 hits, 4 walks, and 9 strikeouts, and 30 at-bats (we got into our lineup for the 3rd time, so we accomplished our goal). Sav threw 58%, Dean threw 65%, Tyler threw 54%, and Will threw 68%. Caden threw 61% strikes and Julian threw 65% strikes. Even though the score doesn't reflect it, that was an incredibly tight game for several innings and now we can take a relaxed breath! Really good pitching by Newtown kept this entire game on edge!

Justin took Doc, Kole, and Julian to their first-ever ESPN after-game interview. The boys were all given little notecards with one word written on it, and the boys were given the option to say that word at some point during the interview. Kole was the first one to talk about his first grand slam ever, and to do it in Williamsport was very special.

They asked Julian about his 10 strike-outs. Julian said he has always loved pitching ever since he starting playing baseball and that he just wants to induce soft contact. Kole makes fun of Julian by saying, "that's a big word." Kole said that he simply thought in his head that the entire Pennsylvania crowd was actually cheering for Boerne. They ask Doc about his home run. He said that he is just trying to hit line drives and be a tough out, but sometimes you get under it and it can go far. He said he knew it was fair the whole way. Kole jokes again with him saying that he thought it was foul! Julian said he feels like he is seeing the ball here very well and he is just trying to hit hard-line drives.

Kole, at the end of the interview, asks if he can keep the Little League placard in front of him with #13 as a keepsake, and he gets a "no" from both the crowd and his dad. You can see the whole 5-minute interview here. (Game 8 Southeast Presser, August 15, 2024)

The boys gather at the physical bracket board that is outside the stadium in the main square of the complex, and they get to place their Southwest placard in the next open spot in the winner's bracket, which is a game on Monday, August 19th. The game tomorrow, Friday, is with Northwest v Southeast, and the winner of that game determines who plays us on Monday. We now have the entire weekend off, Friday-Sunday, before we play again on Monday night.

On Sunday, August 18th, the boys were put on buses and taken out to the local Williamsport airport. They greeted the Detroit Tigers as they disembarked from their private plane. The Tigers and the Boerne boys all piled back into the buses together and rode back to the complex.

The MLB players spent their time in the stands with the boys and/or walking around the complex signing autographs, taking photos, and being interviewed. The Mountain team met the airplane for the New York Yankees and rode back to the complex with them. Aaron Judge walked up to the press box and put on headset for a while with the ESPN announcers there during the Northwest v Mid-Atlantic game. Gerrit Cole talks about his time in a LL jersey and now he gets to come back and spend time with the kids. One of his comments was he felt like he was one of the Beatles, with the energy and all the fans so excited to see him, get an autograph, take a picture, etc. A handful of the MLB players slid down the iconic hill on cardboard boxes with the kids, including Will Vest, who ultimately pitches later that evening for the Tigers and is able to punchout both Juan Soto and Aaron Judge.

Later that evening, the MLB puts on the Little League Classic, where the Yankees and the Tigers battle it out at the Historic Bowman Field in downtown Williamsport. This is a minor league stadium, home to the Williamsport Crosscutters, that seats approximately 2,300 people. The boys were bussed out to Bowman field, had specific sections for each of the teams, and then the parents filled in the stadium seating past the 1st and 3rd bases. One kid from each team lines up in a straight line from home plate to center field, and they relay the first pitch ball from center to home. It's a night of traditions and history-making, and the boys enjoyed every moment! It's incredible to be able to watch an MLB game from this close.

Tarik Skubal starts on the mound for the Tigers and pitched really well. Marcus Stroman started off on the mound for the Yankees. For Matt Vierling of the Tigers, this was like coming home as he was a Crosscutters player during 2012-2014. He was mike'd up while playing left field, so it was fun to go back and watch that game and be able to listen to his commentary with the ESPN announcers. He has to go on the run and catch a deep fly ball in the corner and slams into the wall while he is chatting with the announcers.

Gleyber Torres scores the first run for the Yankees with a passed ball by the catcher in the top of the 6th inning. In the bottom of the 9th inning, the Detroit rookie Jace Jung hits a hard ground ball to left for a single that scored Colt Keith, after his double to the left field corner just earlier. He gets to share his first MLB RBI with all the boys at the stadium! It was a nailbiter game as well, going to 10 innings, the Yankees' DJ Lemahieu scoring one run, and then the Tigers scoring 2 to ultimately win 3-2 with Parker Meadows hitting the walk-off single!

Fireworks shoot off to end the game and then the boys get shuttled back to the dorms! It's a late night for them, as that game didn't end until after 11pm. However, they are living their dream here in Williamsport and going to bed early for school the next day is the furthest thing from their minds!!

Kaleb showed me his new Easton Hype Fire bat, and it was a 30". For his current size, he really needed a 29" bat, but the shortest they had was 30". We ran to the Easton tent to see if there was any way to exchange it for a shorter one, but they checked their inventory, and they didn't have any other 29" in stock. I asked them to check their state-wide inventory, at all the different stores they sell to, and unfortunately, no one in the entire state of PA had a 29" drop 8 Hype Fire bat. I was texting back and forth with our good friend and hitting coach, John Gump and he asked me if I wanted him to overnight one to us from Texas. I thought that might be a little bit over the top, so I made the "dad" decision that Kaleb could just work with what he had. That 1" shorter bat gives him better barrel control, and he can get it through the zone just a little faster than with the slightly longer version. With these kids throwing heat, that split second can be the difference between barreling up the baseball and a swing and a miss. I'm still kicking myself for that decision...Shame on Dad!

Game 16 Southeast @ Southwest, Monday, August 19th

Metro, Mountain, Mid-Atlantic, and Southwest got the byes in Round one, so this is our second game. Southeast (Lake Mary LL from Florida) played Midwest on Wednesday, August 14 and beat them in a nailbiter 2-1, and then played two days later on Friday against Northwest, beating them 6-1. This is their 3rd game in 6 days.

Florida steps in here with plenty of confidence, as they won the regional games by a total score of 35-8, culminating in their decisive victory over Tennessee of 11-0 (Boerne won 22-7, but who's counting?). Florida has a long history of sending teams to the LLWS, as they have been here 23 times in the past, and they have reached the championship game 8 times, but have yet to be able to win. All the boys slept in this morning after a late night at the MLB classic game, but then got up mid-morning for breakfast and to start to get ready for this all-important game Monday night! This is going to be the greatest baseball battle we have seen yet!

Julian's on the bump today and Chase Anderson, the 5'4" son of the Lake Mary Coach Jonathan Anderson, is leading off. Chase is a lefty hitter and watches Julian's 71 mph fastball for strike one, watches strike two, fouls off strike three, watches ball one, fouls off two more, and then goes down swinging on Julian's nasty curveball that bounces off the plate for strike three. Chase starts to run to first but an easy throw by Caden to Kole records the first out. JJ Feliciano, Florida's 5'6" star pitcher is next up. He watches ball one, watches strike one, watches ball two, fouls off strike two, and then connects on a 73-mph fastball for a ground ball just out of reach for Jett and to Doc in center for the first hit of the ballgame. DeMarcos (DJ) Mieses, the 5'4" first baseman watches ball one, watches strike one, and then hits a chopper ground ball that bounces over Dylan's fully outstretched glove at the top of his jump at third base and runs down the left field line. Cooper is over to scoop it up, but it's good for a double and scores JJ. Florida takes an early 1-0 lead!

Landon Bono, their 5'5" infielder watches balls one and two, swings at strike one, watches ball three, fouls off strike two, and then watches Julian's 72 mph fastball come over the inner third of the plate for strike three looking. Garrett Rohozen, their 5'8" utility player fouls off strike one, watches strike two, watches balls one and two, and then hits a ground ball back up the middle, Jett comes over and scoops it up and makes it look easy, the third out and Boerne now gets to bat. Our hearts are in our throat as now we are losing! A 26-pitch inning for Julian but they scored 1!

JJ Feliciano is pitching for Lake Mary and Julian fouls off strike one, watches ball one, swings at strike two, watches ball two, fouls off strike three, and then watches a 74-mph fastball just catch the lower outside corner for called strike three. Gray watches strike one and then sees a curveball come up and in, stays in there to take the hit on his upper left arm, and takes his base! Cooper watches ball one and then he lances a hard-line drive over the first baseman that keeps cutting back into the right field corner. The fielder has a little trouble grabbing it as Gray is reaching third, and then he throws to his second baseman cutoff, so they wave Gray home. The throw is not in time, and Boerne has just tied the game at 1-1!

Kole watches balls one, swings at strike one, swings at strike two, and then just misses a 73-mph fastball for strike three. Doc watches strike one, watches ball one, swings at strike two, watches ball two, and watches a 74-mph fastball over the outside half for strike three. Ok, breathe, we just tied the game, and now let's go keep playing! A 19-pitch inning for JJ! Julian and JJ, two titans slugging it out in the Coliseum!

Jacob Bibaud, the 5'3" OF/1B swings at strike one and then hits a hard-line drive just past Kole's outstretched glove at first into right field for a single. He tries to do a delayed steal but Julian flips the ball to Aiden, who tags him out at second. The rule in Little League is that until the pitcher is on the rubber, it's a live ball and runners can steal. Once the pitcher's foot is on the rubber, the runner has to have their foot on their base.

Liam Morrisey, their 5'8" center fielder fouls off strike one, watches strike two, and swings and misses at Julian's nasty curve just dropping off the table for strike three, and his 3rd strikeout tonight. Luis Calo, the 5'3" OF/RHP watches balls one and two, watches strikes one and two, watches ball three, and then swings and misses at a high 73 mph fastball at the top of the zone for strike three. A really good 11-pitch inning for Julian!

Caden watches strike one, swings at strike two, watches ball one, and then swings and misses at JJ's curveball for strike three. Jett fouls off strike one, watches strike two, fouls off the next two pitches, watches balls one and two, fouls off the next pitch, watches ball three, and watches a 75-mph fastball go by for strike three. An incredible 9-pitch at-bat for Jett, and he is doing his job helping our team to rack up JJ's pitch count. Aiden bends over to let an inside pitch brush by his waist, but it still catches his hip, and so he'll take his base. Gage watches balls one, two, and three, swings at strike one, watches strike two, and then swings at misses at a 72-mph fastball at the knees for strike three. A 20-pitch inning for JJ, and you can see that every pitch matters, as these very minor differences in each inning may decide the outcome of this game.

Teraj Alexander, 5'3", swings at strike one, watches strike two, and then watches Julian's 72 mph heater over the outer half for strike three. Christopher Chikodroff, their 5'3", 135 lbs. lefty fouls off strike one, watches ball one, swings at strike two, fouls off strike three, and then swings and misses at Julian's filthy curveball for strike three. Lathan Norton, the 5'6" RHP, fouls off strike one, swings at strike two, and then swings and misses at that same filthy curveball for strike three, Julian's 7th strikeout of the game and an 11-pitch inning!

Kaleb watches balls one and two, watches strike one, watches strike two, and then watches balls three and four, the last one being the 72-mph fastball just a little low, to draw the walk, and our leadoff runner is aboard! Dylan watches balls one and two, watches strike one, watches strike two, and then goes down swinging on an inside half 72-mph fastball for strike three. Ben shows bunt and then pulls back as a hard 72-mph fastball comes inside and hits him on his left shoulder, and he takes his base. Way to take the hit Ben! 2 runners aboard and one out!! Lake Mary pulls JJ at 56 pitches (52% strike percentage), and brings in Luis Calo, 5'3" to pitch. Julian watches strike one, watches ball one, watches ball two as it's a curveball way outside in the dirt that gets past their catcher, and that advances the runners.

Now we've got 2 runners in scoring position and one out! They intentionally walk Julian to load the bases! Gray watches the first pitch get thrown behind him, and Kaleb takes advantage of the wild pitch to get home and put Boerne up 2-1! Ben and Julian move up a base on the same throw. Gray watches a low outside curveball into the dirt get by the catcher and get stuck in the backstop. Ben is awarded home to make the score 3-1, and Julian goes to third. Southeast pulls Luis at 7 pitches (1 strike) and brings in Jacob to pitch. Gray watches Jacob's lefty curveball come in and down and hit him in the foot, and he takes his base! Way to stand there like a statue and take the hit! Cooper swings at strike one and then sends a chopper ground ball to third, who grabs it and quickly throws it home to prevent the run, but Julian is able to get back to third base without getting in a rundown because the shortstop didn't shift over to cover the bag.

Kole watches ball one, swings at strike one, fouls off strike two, watches balls two and three, and then watches a fastball over the inner half of the plate for strike three. Doc fouls off strike one, swings at strike two, then swings at a fastball in and turns on it to rip a line drive between third and short into left field for a single, scoring Julian, and Boerne takes a 4-1 lead! Caden swings at strike one and then flies out to shallow center field to end the inning. Ouch, bases loaded. At least we took advantage of their errors and scored 2 runs on wild pitches, and another run on Doc's single to left. A 33-pitch inning for Florida and we were able to stretch them a bit!

Hunter Alexander lays down a bunt back to Julian and it's an out at first for one down. Chase watches strike one, fouls off strike two, and then grounds out to Aiden at second for a quick flip to Kole at first. JJ watches ball one, swings at strike one, watches strike two, fouls off strike three, and then doesn't catch up to Julian's 71 mph fastball at the top of the zone for to end the inning! A 9-pitch inning for Julian!

Jett starts off the bottom of the fourth inning with a line drive shot into center field for a single! Aiden hits a ground ball to the left side, the 3rd baseman dives but misses it, JJ Feliciano gets there and is able to flip it to second base to get Jett out. Gage hits a curveball on the ground to second, who flips it to JJ at second base for the second fielder's choice out. Kaleb hits a line drive that is caught by JJ at short to end the inning. Shoot, a 4-pitch inning for Jacob! It's a dogfight!

DJ watches balls one and two and then gets under a fastball to hit a sky-high fly ball to Jett in shallow left. Landon watches balls one and two, fouls off strike one, watches strike two, and then gets the barrel to an outside fastball but it's a fly ball to deep center and Doc is there to make the catch. Garrett's back up and watches ball one and then lines out to Jett who makes a leaping grab at short to end the inning. Jett congratulates Garrett on his hard-hit line drive and Garrett congratulates Jett on his nice catch as both boys make their way back to their respective dugouts. This is an absolutely incredible display of great sportsmanship and reminds us of the simple joy of just getting to play this game and doing their best! A 10-pitch inning for Julian and could this game be any more back-and-forth?

Dylan watches ball one, watches strike one, fouls off the next two strikes, watches ball two, fouls off another strike, and then swings and misses to the lefty Jacob's slider that keeps running outside for strike three. Lake Mary pulls Jacob off the mound at 26 pitches (73% strike percentage) and brings in Lathan to finish the game. Ben fouls off strike one, watches strike two, and then watches a fastball top of the zone for strike three. Julian watches balls one and two and then flies out to deep right field and Luis Calo makes the catch to end the bottom of the 5th inning. A 13-pitch inning for Florida and these guys have a fantastic bullpen!

Jacob, their #6 batter starts off the top of the 6th. He gets on top of a 71-mph fastball to hit a ground ball to Jett at short and he makes the throw to Kole at first for out #1. Liam fouls off strike one, swings at strike two, watches ball one, and then swings and misses at Julian's filthy curveball for strike three. Luis is their last hope and he watches strike one, watches strike two, watches balls one and two, fouls off strike three, and then swings and misses at a low fastball for strike three!

An 11-pitch inning, Julian's 10th strikeout of the game, and Boerne wins 4-1! Julian threw 78 pitches, went the whole game, and threw 56 strikes, an incredible 72% strike percentage on our biggest stage yet! Lake Mary collectively threw 89 pitches at a 60% strike percentage. Lake Mary got 2 hits, 0 walks, while Boerne had 3 hits, had 2 walks, and also 10 strike-outs. On the smallest of margins these games are won and lost... This was a new "low" for us. Against New Mexico we only got 5 hits, and in two other games against Louisiana we got 6 and 7 hits. You better believe that we didn't breathe for the last two hours...WHAT A GAME...

Justin took Julian, Jett, and Ben to the ESPN after-game interview. Justin said he has watched Jett hit line drives and play great baseball since he was 5-6 years old. Julian was asked about this being his 3rd game with 10 strike-outs, and only one other pitcher has been able to achieve that this season, and Julian's response was that he is focused on throwing strikes. He had a 72% strike percentage, which was an all-time high for him, so he was very excited about that accomplishment. Jett said that picking up that hot grounder was very exciting. They asked GM Justin if they had caught the earlier game in person, and he said, no, they watched it on TV. He said that the coaches needed to be with the boys, because they are 12 years old, and if you leave them alone, they wouldn't be relaxing, they would be playing wiffle ball or hanging from the rafters. You can see the whole 8-minute interview here. (Game 24 Southwest Presser, August 19, 2024)

Justin Anderson's interview, he talked about if JJ Feliciano was doing well, they'd let him go 85 pitches today. However, he got to 50 pitches and would be available again on Thursday, and had struggled with the last couple batters, so they decided to change to Luis, and today was a day he didn't have it, and so they moved to Jacob, who did a good job cleaning it up. He said they ran into a really good pitcher in Julian and he held them down. Justin commented they might need JJ again available for Texas on Thursday.

He said that Julian's curveball to his left-handed batters' back feet was very difficult for them, and they weren't picking it up well out of his hand. He said that JJ just wasn't controlling his curveball very well today. He said they need their bats to wake up, as they only got 8 hits in game 1, then 4 hits in game 2, and then 3 hits in this last game against Texas. He said that is not what Lake Mary has done to get to Williamsport. You can listen to his interview here.

The way the brackets work out in the Little League series is that you might play between 5-8 games in total over the 11-day stretch, from August 14th through championship Sunday August 25th. Since we got a bye in round one, if we lost that game, we would have had to win the next seven games in a row to get back to the World Championship game. However, since we won, we are now only one win away from the US Championship game and two wins away from the World Championship game. The boys visit the bracket board out in the square and place our placard on the winner's spot for the next game!

Game 17 Mountain @ Southwest, August 21st

Time really does stand still in Williamsport. It's hard to believe that is has already been two days since the game against Southeast, the boys have already been in town for 13 days, and they are excited to continue their historic run! Similar to Joe Pit's BBQ in Abilene, we have found a fantastic restaurant in Williamsport with good food and a great salad bar called Hoss' Steak and Sea House, and so we ate there probably ten times in two weeks. We also took full advantage of the Williamsport YMCA to work out at whenever we could find the time early in the morning before baseball consumed the rest of the day.

This is Nevada's third trip to Williamsport and the first for Paseo Verde LL. Mountain (Paseo Verde LL) lost their opening game in Regionals to Montana, 7-1, and then had to play back all the way through the loser's bracket to get to the championship. They beat Wyoming 24-4, then got to rematch Montana after Colorado sent Montana to the loser's bracket in a hard-fought game 18-7. Nevada beat Montana this time with a 6-0 victory, then beat Colorado 4-0, and finally beat Utah in a close 2-0 game on Friday, August 9th.

The Mountain team had a first-round bye here at Williamsport. They then proceeded to beat the Metro team (New York) 9-1 on Thursday, August 15th and then beat West (Central East Maui) in a nailbiter 3-2 game during the Monday, August 19th game at 3pm.

That was a huge win for them because West is a consistent force here at Williamsport. West had beaten New England 3-1 in the opening game on Wednesday, August 14th, beat Great Lakes 5-0 two days later on Friday, and then lost to Mountain on Monday, August 19th. Arizona has been to Williamsport 6 times, California has been 50 times, and Hawaii has been 16 times, including this year. We feel somewhat fortunate that Mountain knocked West to the loser's bracket, but now that means that since they beat them, this is going to be a really tough test for us! Both of our teams played Monday and are now playing against each other Wednesday at 3pm.

Caden is on the mound for Boerne and Caleb Gomez watches strike one, watches balls one and two, watches strike two, and then swings and misses at Caden's fastball for strike three. Rusell McGee watches ball one, watches strike one, fouls off strike two, and then flight out to Gray in right field. Wyatt Erickson watches strike one, swings at strike two, and then rips a line drive to left field for a single. Oliver Johnson watches strike one, watches a wild pitch down outside in the dirt for ball one and Russell advances, and then Oliver rips a hard ground ball to left field for a single, and we've now got runners on the corners with two outs. Noah Letalu watches ball one, fouls off strikes one and two, and then hits a ground ball to Jett, who makes it look routine for out #3. A 19-pitch inning for Caden and now we get to bat!

Wyatt Erickson is on the mound for Mountain and Julian watches strike one, watches balls one and two, watches strike two, watches ball three, and then rips a line drive double to the left field corner for a standup double! Gray fouls off strike one and then hits a hanging curveball inside for a line drive to left as well, putting runners at second and third with no outs! Cooper hits a sacrifice fly ball to deep center, allowing Julian to tag up and score the first run for Boerne! Kole watches balls one and two, watches strike one, swings at strike two, and then watches a pitch go over the outer third of the plate for strike three. Doc fouls off strikes one, hits a grounder into the infield and is thrown out, but the umps review it and it hit his foot, so it's a foul ball strike two, and he takes full advantage of getting another chance in the box and hits a line drive past second into center and scores Gray to put us up 2-0! He gets to second on the throw home. Caden fouls off three in a row and then flies out to shallow right.

Parker Soranaka hits a ground ball just left of second base, Jett sweeps over, and it's an out at first. Dominic Laino swings at strike one, watches balls one and two, swings at strike two, fouls off strike three, watches ball three, fouls off another pitch, and then watches ball four to draw the walk. Jimmy Foss watches ball one, fouls off strike one, watches strike two, watches ball two, fouls off the next two pitches, and then hits a grounder down the first base line that Caden goes to grab but can't get the ball to first in time. Luke Lentz watches ball one, watches strike one, and then watches balls two, three, and four to draw the walk and load the bases for Nevada! Liam Sparks watches ball one, fouls off strike one, watches ball two, watches strike two, and then watches balls three and four, and that walks in a run for Nevada, so now it's 2-1!

Boerne decides to pull Caden and put Kaleb on the mound. This was another controversial decision that Bert and Justin made to send Kaleb into relieve in this all-important game. Kaleb was the only 11-year-old on the team and didn't throw as hard as the "Big 5" pitchers we had (Julian, Cooper, Doc, Caden, and Kole).

Prior to this game, he hadn't pitched in a single Little League All-Star game all summer. However, the coaches had seen him throw strike after strike after strike in our live batting practices all summer, against our really good hitters, and Kaleb was able to get strike-outs on our 12-year-olds. He can locate his 4-seam and 2-seam fastballs and he's got a really good curveball and changeup that throws hitters timing off.

He had pitched in two high profile baseball tournaments that summer. He pitched at both the Perfect Game World Series in East Cobb (Marietta, GA) in June and in Southaven, MS in the Perfect Game Invitational that July. In the PG World Series, he faced 38 batters over 7 innings, gave up 13 hits, 3 walks, and 3 strike-outs with a 62% strike percentage, and in the PG Invitational, against both Knights Knation 11U Dean and USA Prime Houston North 11U Ireland (both Top 30 select teams in the country), and against the latter, faced 14 batters and allowed 5 hits, no walks, and 4 strike-outs, throwing a 71% strike percentage. He batted .600 in Georgia and .500 in Mississippi. The timing worked out perfectly because the Kaleb flew to Georgia, played in PGWS June 13-18, and then flew home in time to be ready to play in the Little League District tournament on Friday, June 21st. The Little League boys played in the Section Tournament in Ingram that ended July 2nd, Kaleb flew to Memphis, played in PGI from July 5-11, and then flew home and went to Abilene to play in the Little League State Tournament July 12-15. For his other teams, he is "the" pitcher that is always put in during the "big moments," so he has plenty of history to draw on the confidence that he showed in Williamsport.

Gunnar Gaudin watches ball one, watches strike one, watches strike two, fouls off strike three, watches ball two, fouls off two in a row, watches ball three, and then watches Kaleb's fastball come in over the outer third for strike three. Kaleb's first strikeout of the Little League World Series and a huge out to get to two outs with bases loaded! Gunner Beranek watches strike one and then hits a grounder off Kaleb's good curveball to shortstop but Jett can't get there in time and he makes it to first, to tie the game. Caleb Gomez returns to the plate and watches strike one, watches strike two, and then lines out to Gage in right for an easy out #3. 27 pitches for Caden and Kaleb needed 14 pitches, so

Mountain did a great job forcing a 41-pitch inning! Really great job by Kaleb to limit the damage to only the one run! There is no higher pressure situation in baseball than to be the lone pitcher coming into a bases loaded situation and getting those crucial outs for your team!

Jett watches strike one, watches strike two, and then swings and misses at a nasty slider that kept sliding to the outside for the first out. Aiden flies out to right field. Kaleb watches strike one, watches strike two, and then lines out to the third baseman who catches it over his shoulder as he is running back to his right. A quick 7-pitch inning for Wyatt.

Boerne brings Cooper into pitch. We thought about letting Kaleb go longer as he had good command (79% strikes for those 14 pitches), but the coaches wanted to bring the higher velocity against this team and be as difficult to hit as possible. Russell fouls off strike one, watches ball one, fouls off strike two, watches ball two, and then hits a ground ball to Dylan at third who makes a great stop, regains his balance and makes the laser throw to Kole at first for out #1. Wyatt watches strike one and then watches four balls in a row to take his base. Oliver watches balls one, two, and three, watches strike one, and then hits a high fastball deep to center field but Doc gets under it for out #2. Noah watches strike one and then hits a line drive to shallow center field for a single and gets two runners on with two outs. Parker watches balls one and two and then flies out to Gage in left to end the inning. A 20-pitch inning for Cooper, we've held them, and now we get to go hit!

Dylan watches strike one, swings at strike two, and swings and misses at a fastball outside corner for strike three. Gage hits a fly ball to shallow left center that drops perfectly in the gap between the three converging defenders for a single. Ben lays down a great bunt that just dies in front of home plate, and the catcher grabs the ball and throws to the shortstop who had moved over to second, but is not in time because you had Gage, greased lightning, running as soon as that bunt was laid down.

Julian watches strike one, watches balls one, two, and three, and hits a deep fly ball to the right center gap that gets down, and loads the bases. The throw comes into home, but is offline to the left, almost next to the dugout, so the catcher moves over to block it, and Bert sends Gage streaking for home to slide in and take a 3-2 lead for Boerne! Gray watches ball one and then rips a line drive into the left field corner and scores Ben! Cooper fouls off strike one and then hits a high fastball sacrifice fly to center field to score Julian and Gray gets to third base! Kole watches ball one and then flies out to the second baseman running into right field to end the inning, but Boerne has now taken a 5-2 lead on a 16-pitch inning for Mountain!

Dominic fouls off strike one and then Cooper throws a great pitch in on the hands and up in the zone to get a pop out right back to him for out #1. Jimmy turns his shoulder and takes the ball in his back to take his base. Luke swings at strike one, watches ball one, fouls off strike two, and then swings and misses at Cooper's heater for strike three. Liam watches balls one and two, watches strike one, and then pops out to foul territory by Kole is able to go make the catch by the wall. A great 12-pitch inning for Cooper!

Nevada decides to pull Wyatt at 45 pitches (78% strike percentage) and bring in Noah to close the game. Doc fouls off strikes one and two, watches one, and then gets on top of one and hits a grounder down the third base line and is at first base so they don't even throw it. Caden watches ball one, fouls off strike one, watches ball two, fouls off strike two, watches ball three, and then hits a hard grounder to shortstop and they get Doc out going to second. Jett catches it out on the end of the bat and lines out to shallow right center. Aiden hits a ground ball to first base that pulls him off the bag, but Noah hustles over to accept the toss and tag the base for out #3. A 12-pitch inning for Mountain!

Gunnar hits a ground ball to Aiden for a quick throw to Kole and the first out of the top of the 5th inning. Gunner watches strike one and grounds out to Jett at shortstop. Caleb watches ball one, swings at strike one, and then flies out to Gray in right field. Another great pitching inning for Cooper with only 7 pitches needed!

Kaleb watches strike one, watches ball one, watches ball two, watches strike two, and protects for strike three but hits a pop out just behind the first baseman that the second baseman is able to come over and catch. Dylan swings at strike one, swings at strike two, fouls off strike three, and then swings and misses at a high pitch for strike three. Gage smokes a line drive over Gomez's head in center field that gets to the wall and he turns on the jets and turns it into a triple! Ben flies out to center field to end the inning. An 11-pitch inning for Noah! Let's go, boys, 3 outs away!!!

Russell, the #2 hitter in their lineup, watches ball one, watches strike one, watches strike two, fouls off strike three, and pops out to Jett at shortstop. Wyatt watches ball one, watches strike one, watches strike two, fouls off strike three, watches ball two, and watches a strike come over the inside corner of home for strike three. Oliver watches balls one and two, watches strike one, watches strike two, and then hits a ground ball to Jett, who has been so pure at shortstop all summer long, scoops it up and fires it to Kole at first one more time and that's the ballgame!

A 16-pitch inning to end it! Nevada got 5 hits, 4 walks, and had 4 strike-outs in that game. Wyatt and Noah both pitched fantastic too, with Wyatt throwing 78% for his 45 pitches and Noah throwing 74% for his 23 pitches. Nevada only needed 68 pitches for that game. Boerne got 9 hits, had no walks, and 4 strike-outs. Caden threw 57% strikes on 47 pitches, Kaleb threw 79% strikes for 14 pitches, and Cooper threw 62% strikes on 55 pitches (116 pitches total).

Very similar to what we saw with Southeast, the Mountain boys can pitch and it turned on a few timely hits by Boerne! With that win, Boerne secures a spot in the US Championship game, to be played three days later on Saturday at 330pm!!!

Justin took Doc, Cooper, Gage, and Kaleb to the ESPN after-game interview. Kaleb said he was just focused on throwing strikes, if they catch barrel, fine, but he was focused on no walks. Justin said that even though Kaleb is like the "younger brother" on the team, he is 10-feet-tall and bulletproof. He's got a very high confidence in himself and said that Kaleb is always ready. Justin said he just felt like he was the right kid for that moment. Cooper said he felt really good in the second inning, and he said that pitching in the game was just so much fun. Justin said that Cooper was well into 60%+ strike percentage and because Cooper throws high 60's and can touch 70 mph, that the velocity was going to be really tough for the opponent, especially with a number of 11-year-olds in their lineup. Gage got to talk both about him getting home on the passed ball as well as his double that he turned into a triple. Doc said that he was able to block out the noise of the crowd and just focus on executing in the box.

He said he was nervous to swing, because we had not been down in many games before. You can see the whole 11-minute interview here. (Game 30 Southwest Presser, August 21, 2024)

Paseo's manager was very complimentary about our Boerne team and was simply re-iterating to his team that they need to enjoy this. He said their hits were good, but they left 8 kids on base, and that they were only a couple hits away from a different result. His interview is here. The boys visit the bracket scoreboard in the plaza and place their placard again on the winner's line, which is now playing in the US Championship Game!!!! Holy cow, we did it!!!

The local San Antonio news was following our progress very closely, and so after this win, you see all the sports reporters with the local newspapers and TV stations, San Antonio Express-News, WOAI, KSAT, and KENS5, all scrambling to grab plane tickets and get to Williamsport in time for the upcoming game. We recall seeing Mary Rominger of KSAT, Bill Taylor of KENS5, and Don Harris of WOAI all shooting short Facebook videos in the airplane seats at it took off, and then interacting with them at the stadium once they arrived! We appreciate Victoria Lopez of MySA.com and Tom Robinson of San Antonio Express News covering our summer as well! This is crazy!! The hype, the energy, the air is electric! Let's go Boerne!

Game 18 Southeast @ Southwest, Saturday, August 24th

Jamie Flick, one of the Pennsylvania state representatives invited both Canada and Southwest to his house one evening for some really good food and fellowship. His house is on the bank of the Susquehanna River, and so the boys had a great time playing in the backyard, throwing the football, playing cornhole, and simply relaxing. They chowed down on some thick steaks that Jamie cooked up for them. Our boys really enjoyed playing with the Canadian kids, Xavier Cabalfin, Rye Precioso, Raymon Dhasi, Moose Kluth, Kayden Krestanovich, Riley Suvilai, Jozef Young, Blake Anderson, Ronan Bobiles, Joshua Hernstedt, Eric Popovich, and Ben Wegwitz. Canada had a really tough draw as they drew Asia-Pacific in the first round on Wednesday and lost 8-0. AP would go on to win the International Championship bracket. Then Canada had to play Mexico on Sunday, and they got beat 8-0 in that game as well. Both the AP and Mexico teams are always really tough.

A few of the days we had free they encouraged us to check the boys out of the complex and return them late that night. We grabbed Kaleb and made the drive up to Niagara Falls, about 3 hours away, and then also made the shorter drive to Hershey, PA, where they have the chocolate factory. Needless to say, all the Boerne boys loved the snack bags that Kaleb brought back. He slept the entire way up and the entire way back.

The constant attention, the constant crowds, and the fact that you have 240 kids all jammed together behind locked fences from all over the world at some point does start to become mentally and physically exhausting, so it was great to give him some down time with family and catch up on his rest. Anyone that has experienced a college freshman dorm at 18 years old for their first semester can relate to the experience.

We stopped at Dick's Sporting Goods and bought a bucket of baseballs, so on our down time, we would go find a baseball field nearby, get a few swings in, and then return him to the dorms. The Pennsylvania community has baseball fields all over, many don't have outfields, and they all have L-screens adjacent to the field, so we were very grateful to borrow the facilities for an hour or so. In many of our communities around Texas, all our baseball fields are surrounded by high fences and locked gates, so it's nice to experience a part of the country where everything is wide open and available.

It was quite surreal the outpouring of support by the Texas community for this whole trip, and every win, just kept amplifying the support and well-wishes of everyone back home. We had everyone in our region rooting for us too, as we heard from people in Louisiana, Arkansas, and Oklahoma that they were cheering us on. This is the biggest difference with Little League vs. Select ball. You represent a town, a community, a region, and every citizen that lives in that area is rooting for you to do your best and represent "the community" well.

In select, you have is 10-12 players on a roster and you likely don't even go to school with over half of them, because they are made up of the better players from a larger geographic area. In the case of a few select teams, including TBT National White, they fly in talent from all over the country for the bigger select tournaments, such as Perfect Game World Series in GA, Beast of the East, Houston 1000, and more.

One kid that Kaleb has practiced with in Austin is Ethan Palacios, who is the same age as Kaleb, but is already 5'4", 125 lbs, throws

74 mph, and hits the ball about 300', so he is a frequently called player for those big events. If you can assemble 12 of those nationally best players at this age, then you would expect to be able to be incredibly competitive, and TBT has shown that by being generally in the Top 3 teams, and many times, the winner, in a large number of national tournaments.

The boys were supported with words of encouragement by many high-profile athletes and coaches, including Jim Schlossnagle, head baseball coach of the University of Texas Longhorns. His words for the boys on Thursday before the US Championship game were "wish you the best of luck this weekend. You guys are built for this. You've trained for this. Just do what you do and have all kinds of fun. The entire state of Texas is behind you, Coach Newson and your entire staff. Hook 'em!" Michael Earley, the Texas A&M Head Baseball Coach sent the boys a personal video message. Brandon Beckel of the Philadelphia Phillies sent the boys a personal video message. McLennan Junior College and their Head Coach Tyler Johnson sent a personal video message. Coach Whitting, Head Baseball Coach of the University of Houston sent a message. Theo Gillen, 1st round pick for the Tampa Bay Rays sent a message. Kayson Cunningham, USA Gold Medal Winner, MVP for Team USA & Perfect Game Player of the Year sent a video message. Cole Philips of the Mariners sent a video message. Coach Trout & Rashawn Galloway of Texas State University sent a video message. Hunter Brown of the Houston Astros sent a video message.

It's hard to believe that this summer-long run is almost over. It's really hard to believe that we've already been in Williamsport nearly three weeks, especially because we've only played three games. It's already the final Championship Saturday, and no matter what happens, from this point, the boys play only two more games and then everyone goes home. However, this tournament is not over yet, and while the Boerne boys arrive here with 17 straight wins, we know it's going to be a tough test again today. Florida had to battle back through the loser's bracket to get to this game, so they have played 6 games in the last 11 days. Boerne, conversely, had played in just 3. Florida played Metro on Tuesday, August 20th, the day after they lost to us, and they were able to beat them 6-1. The next day, Wednesday, they played West and beat them in a nailbiter 4-3. The following day, Thursday, they played Mountain after we sent them to the loser's bracket, and they beat them 6-3. So Florida is looking for a second chance and Boerne is looking to continue its historic run. From roughly 600+ clubs and 2.4 million kids around the world, we are down four teams with a total of 48 players: Venezuela, Asia-Pacific, Southeast, and Southwest.

Before the US Championship Game kicks off there is a very special event called the Little League Challenger Exhibition. Saturday morning at 1030a all the boys came to the stadium to assist special needs kids with playing in a baseball game designed to be fun and be respectful to their specific challenges. This is just another example of how deeply rooted in "community" Little League is. The boys get to participate and serve these other kids! Kaleb pushed a kid in a wheelchair so he could "run" the bases, and all the kids are screaming and yelling with delight! It'll make you tear up real fast and it also makes you incredibly proud of your kids to watch them serve others in such a gentle and gracious manner!

It's now 330pm in the afternoon, and after the national anthem and Little League Pledge, Julian is back on the mound for Boerne and Chase is at bat. Didn't we just watch this a few days ago? Chase fouls off strike one, watches balls one and two, swings at strike two, watches ball three, fouls off two more pitches and then watches ball four. Crap... okay, let's get control back. JJ fouls off strike one, watches balls one and two, swings at strike two, and then hits a ground ball back to Julian, who spins, throws it to Jett, who tags second, and throws to Kole at first, for a double play! Ok, great recovery boys!!! Garrett watches strike one, watches ball one, and then flies out to Doc in center to end the inning. A 17-pitch inning for Julian, so let's go hit!!

JJ's back on the mound for Southeast, and Julian swings at strike one, watches strike two, watches balls one and two, and then hits a hard grounder between second base and the second baseman for a leadoff single. Gray watches strike one, fouls off strike two, watches ball one, fouls off strike three, watches ball two sail high over the catcher, and Julian gets to second. Gray fouls off another pitch, watches ball three, and then watches a fastball on the outside corner for strike three. Cooper watches strike one and then watches four balls in a row to draw the walk. Doc fouls off strike one, watches ball one, watches a fastball down and outside in the dirt that lets the runners advance, swings at strike two, and swings and misses at a 71-mph fastball top of the zone for strike three. Kole watches ball one, watches strike one, fouls off strike two, watches ball two, fouls off strike three, watches ball three, and just misses a 74-mph fastball for strike three. A 23-pitch inning for JJ, and no runs yet! Let's go play defense!

In the top of the 2nd inning, Landon hits a ground ball to Aiden at second and he makes the out to Kole at first. Julian throws a great pitch to DJ, gets it in on his hands, and DJ hits a ground ball to Jett and he is out at first for two outs on two pitches. Jacob watches strike one, fouls off strike two, and then is out in front of a filthy curveball from Julian for strike three! A 5-pitch inning for Julian! Great work boys, keep it up!!

Caden watches strike one, watches strike two, and watches a fastball grab the outside corner for strike three. Jett watches strike one, watches ball one, watches strike two, then hits a chopper ground ball between the second baseman and second base for a hit! Aiden watches ball one, but Landon (catcher) misses the catch and so Jett gets to second. Aiden watches ball two, fouls off strike one, watches strike two, and then watches balls three and four to put two runners aboard with one out. Gage watches strike one, watches ball one, swings at strike two, and then watches balls two, three, and four, and now Boerne has the bases loaded!!! Kaleb shows bunt but the throw is down and outside, so it gets past Landon, Jett scores, and the runners advance! Boerne takes a 1-0 lead! Kaleb watches strike one, watches strike two, fouls off strike three, fouls off another pitch, and then hits that outside corner fastball away for a ground ball that gets underneath the first baseman diving for it, picked up by the second baseman, and JJ makes it to first to accept the throw and tag the bag. Kaleb does his job and scores Aiden, and Boerne takes a 2-0 lead! Dylan watches strike one, fouls off strike two, and then watches an inside fastball for strike three to end the inning. A 25-pitch inning for JJ, so he's at 48 pitches in two innings!

Liam watches strike one, fouls off strike two, and swings and misses at Julian's inside fastball for strike three to start off the third inning. Luis watches strike one, watches strike two, watches ball one, and swings and misses at a 71-mph fastball for strike three! DJ fouls off strike one, swings at strike two, watches balls one and two, and then throws him the heater for a swing and miss strike three and Julian's 4th strikeout in a row! A 12-pitch inning for Julian! Let's go hit!!

Ben watches strike one, swings at strike two, watches balls one and two, fouls off strike three, and then watches that outside corner fastball for strike three. Julian watches ball one, fouls off strike one, and then hits a chopper grounder between third and short into left field for a hit! Gray watches balls one and two, fouls off strike one, hits a line drive to foul territory in right field right next to the wall that Luis can't come up with, and then watches balls three and four. Cooper fouls off strike one and then hits a curveball line drive to shortstop for out #2. Doc watches ball one watches strike one, swings at strike two, and then hits a line drive to left field who dives for it and can't quite get there, and so it's a double for Doc and he scores two, to put Boerne up 4-0! Kole fouls off strike one, fouls off strike two, watches ball one that hits the catcher's leg gear and bounces away, so Doc gets to third. Kole swings and misses at that low outside 72-mph fastball for strike three to end the inning. A 27-pitch inning for JJ, now at 75 pitches in three innings, and Boerne is exerting as much pressure as they can!

Against Julian in these two games so far, Florida has batted .107 so far with only 1 run, and for their 5 other games, they batted .272 and had 24 runs total. Halfway through this game and we've got a 4-0 lead!!

Christopher watches ball one and then hits a ground ball to Jett, who is deep, and the runner just barely beats the ball to first. Florida's first hit in this ball game, and now they have their leadoff runner on in the top of the 4th inning. Hunter watches ball one inside and high, getting by Caden, and so Christopher advances to second. Hunter swings at strike one, watches ball two, fouls off strike two, and then swings and misses at a fastball inside corner for strike three. Chase watches ball one, watches strike one, and then hits a hard ground ball up the middle for a single, and now Florida has runners on the corners. JJ watches ball one, swings at strike one, fouls off strike two, fouls off strike three, and hits a line drive to shallow center field for a single and scores Chris. 4-1 and we haven't taken a breath in this game...It's too close.

Garrett swings at strike one, watches ball one, fouls off strike two, and then watches that fastball for strike three and two outs. Julian's 6th strikeout today! Landon swings at strike one, watches balls one, two, and three, fouls off strike two, swings and misses at strike three, but it's a passed ball, and Caden is able to recover it and get him out at first to end the inning. Whew. A 25-pitch inning for Julian, the most yet, but we held them to only 1 run. Let's go hit and win the inning boys!!

Caden watches balls one and two and hits a ground ball to short and he is out at first. Southeast brings Landon into pitch as JJ hit 78 pitches. Jett swings at strike one and then flies out to left field who makes a nice running catch toward the line. Aiden watches balls one and two and flies out to deep right field and Luis Calo makes the catch as he's running toward the fence. An 8-pitch inning for Southeast. Come on boys, just two more innings!!!

DJ watches strike one, watches strike two, and then hits a high fly ball that just gets over Doc's head into center field onto the warning track, so DJ gets a double! Now we have their leadoff runner aboard again! Jacob hits a hard-line drive to left for a single, DJ advances to third, and now they have two runners aboard! Liam watches strike one, swings at strike two, but the ball catches Caden's leg gear and bounces away, so Jacob gets to second. Now we have both runners in scoring position with no outs!

Jacob fouls off the next pitch and then hits a hard grounder to Jett at short who is able to get him out at first, but DJ scores, so now it's 4-2! Luis watches balls one and two, swings at strike one, watches ball three, swings at strike two, fouls off strike three, and then watches ball four to draw the walk and we have runners at the corners with one out!

Julian is grabbing his shoulder and motioning like it hurts and so Boerne pulls him at 74 pitches with a 68% strike percentage and puts Doc on the mound. Hunter watches balls one, two, and three, swings at strike one, and then hits a line drive to the right center gap to the wall and scores Jacob, moving Luis to 3rd. Hunter moves to second on the throw. Chris watches strike one, watches ball one, and smokes a line drive right back at Doc and hits him in the leg and bounces off. Doc pounces on the ball, but Luis scores to tie the ballgame at 4-4! Doc is down and hurt.

Kole comes into pitch, and Chris looks at strike one, fouls off strike two, fouls off strike three, and then swings and misses for strike three, and a huge out for Boerne! Come on boys, one more out! While Kole is walking back to the rubber and Caden is looking at the dugout, Tarej takes off and is able to get home before we can catch him, so now Southeast takes a 5-4 lead! Chase watches ball one, fouls off strike one, watches strike two, watches ball two, and swings and misses for strike three. Southeast forces a 32-pitch inning on Boerne! A couple timely hits, unfortunate injuries to both Julian and Doc, a bit of inattention, and just that fast, the game flips.

In the bottom of the 5th inning, Gage watches balls one and two, and then rips a hard grounder that bounces off Hunter's foot at third base and goes into the outfield, so Boerne has our leadoff runner on! Kaleb fouls off strike one, watches ball one, fouls off strike two, and then swings and misses at the fastball at the top of the zone and can't catch up to it. Sorry, bud, I'll take responsibility for that one! Should've got him the 29"! Dylan watches strike one, watches ball one, fouls off strike two, and then goes down to get a low strike and send it to center field for a line drive hit!

Southeast brings Luis in to relieve Landon and try to change the momentum starting to go Boerne's way. Ben tries to lay down a bunt but pops it up and Landon at catcher is able to step forward and make the catch. They throw four sliders to Julian, perhaps trying to hit the outside corner or just be close enough to entice him to swing, but he watches all four balls and takes his base. Bases loaded, two outs! Gray watches ball one and then rifles a hard ground ball up the middle to center and scores Gage to tie the game at 5-5!

Cooper watches ball one, watches a wild pitch go outside and in the dirt that passes by the catcher to allow Dylan to score, fouls off strike one, swings at strike two, and then swings and misses at strike three. However, the ball comes inside and bounces off the catcher so Julian scores and Cooper gets to first on the dropped third strike! It was an inside pitch to Cooper that just went under his hands and missed the catcher's glove and so it's 7-5 Boerne!

Since Doc was injured on that hard hit ball back to the pitcher, they have rotated him out of the hitting lineup, so Kole hits a ground ball to JJ at shortstop for a flip to second to get Cooper out and end the inning. A 23-pitch inning for Florida! 3 more outs boys and we won't even need to hit again, let's go!!!

Kaleb is brought into pitch in the top of the 6th inning. We are on our feet and we rocking back and forth we are so nervous! Our 11-year-old is up against their best hitter! Now it's David v.

Goliath but in reverse! JJ watches four fastballs in a row. Oh gosh, come on kid, you can do this! Garrett watches strike one, fouls off strike two, watches ball one, fouls off strike three, and then rips a line drive to left center field! Gray's running flat out, gets to the warning track and makes a leaping grab for the ball, but it just bounces off his glove and down onto the warning track while Gray slams into the wall. Gray may have just saved that from ball from being a home run, and the hit is good for a double. Landon watches balls one and two, fouls off strike one, watches ball three, fouls off strike two, and watches ball four to draw the walk. He throws a good pitch to DJ and gets it in on his hands, and he pops out to Cooper at first. Landon had come off the bag and Kaleb came over, so Cooper throws it to Kaleb but he can't quite squeeze it, and so it drops for what would have been a double play.

Jacob watches balls one and two and then hits a ground ball up the middle and JJ jumps over the ball while Jett is going for it and then it takes a hop and gets into center field to load the bases with one out, scoring JJ. Liam watches strike one, watches balls one, two, and three, and then flies out to Gage in right. Garrett tags up and scores to tie the game at 7, and Gage throws it high and over Caden's head, so the runners advance on the overthrow. Luis watches balls one and two, fouls off strikes one and two, and then hits a line drive in the right center gap for a double, scoring both Landon and Jacob, so now Southeast flips the game again and it's 9-7.

Hunter watches ball one, watches strike one, swings at strike two, and watches balls two, three, and four. While he is jogging to first, Luis takes off stealing third. Caden sees him steal, throws the ball to Dylan at third, but the ball bounces off his glove and goes behind the bag, so he has to go get it and by the time he throws it back home Luis has scored, and now Florida is up 10-7. When he throws home, Hunter rounds second and he tries to go to third, but Caden throws again to Dylan who makes the catch and tags Hunter out for the third out. A 36-pitch inning for Kaleb, and now we need 3 runs to tie!

Caden swings at strike one, swings at strike two, and then swings at Luis' curveball down and away for strike three. Jett fouls off strike one and hits a ground ball chopper to third base, who grabs it and then overthrows first base, so Jett is safe on the error. Aiden hits a ground ball up the middle, JJ comes over to grab it, tags second and then throws to first and ends the game with a double play. Southeast wins 10-7.

Heartbroken...We let out our breath that we've been holding for the last two hours, and in some respects, for the last three months.

Florida got 10 hits in that game, 5 walks, and 9 strikeouts. Boerne got 7 hits in that game, the same 5 walks, and 10 strikeouts. It took Boerne 126 pitches to finish that game, a record high. Julian threw 68% strikes for his 73 pitches, Doc threw 50% for his 8 pitches, Kole threw 78% for his 9 pitches, and Kaleb threw 44% for his 36 pitches. For Southeast, they threw 123 total pitches. JJ threw 60% for his 85 pitches, Landon threw 58% for his 19 pitches, and Luis threw 63% for his 19 pitches, for a total of 123 pitches. Everyone knew they had just seen two giants battle it out for the last two hours and leave it all on the field. This was a battle against two really good teams that came down to just the smallest of margins, a few errors and a couple timely hits.

This game aired on ABC, was also streamed on ESPN+, FuboTV, and YouTubeTV, and averaged 3,016,000 viewers. It was the most-watched game since 2015 and up 19 percent year-over-year. The broadcast peaked with 4,436,000 viewers at 615pm. The 50,000 people in attendance in person pales in comparison to the online viewership, but every seat was taken and all eyes were on this game to see which of these two really good teams would emerge victorious.

The dorms where the kids stayed is called the "International Grove." There was a special tent section set up next to the buildings on the hill overlooking the complex where the families could gather in the evenings after the games to spend time with the boys before they headed back inside. This was gated and away from the crowds where everyone could just relax and take it all in. Once the boys would head in, the parents would make the quiet walk down past the stadiums, still all lit up in beautiful white lights, down the hill to Mountain Avenue, and across into the parking lot to get into our rental cars and return to our hotels and/or AirBnB's. That was a very special walk every time, because the complex had emptied of people, and so for just the ten minutes or so it took to make the walk, the complex felt like your own personal baseball heaven, you could smell the moist fragrance of the grass that already had sprinklers turned on, you could smell the food that had been cooked earlier that day, and you heard the amazing silence and stillness unlike anywhere else you will ever experience. Disney is magical, but you are always there with a million people. In this quiet moment, late at night around 10-11pm, you are by yourself, with only a handful of family members and/or staff within 1,000 yards of you, and you slowly breathe in and out to capture the magic of the moment.

Boerne had won 17 games in a row starting on Wednesday, June 19th and the season comes screeching to a halt two months and six days later in the US Championship game. If we had lost the prior game, it would have still been under the double elimination rules. However, both the US Championship game and the World Championship game are single elimination. We beat Florida one time earlier that week on Monday and they beat us on Saturday.

Unfortunately, there is no tie-breaker game. We always say that anything can happen in baseball, and, for that day, it was Southeast's day to emerge victorious. Southeast wins the US National Championship and plays Asia-Pacific in the World Championship the following day, Sunday at 3pm. Southwest goes to the consolation 3rd place game and plays Venezuela, that Asia-Pacific beat 4-1 before our game on Saturday.

There are no words. Our kids were stunned, dejected, and so disappointed to have come so close, but not get all the way there. There were a lot of tears and hugs that night. It was a very quiet evening as the boys returned to their dorms for dinner and to get ready for bed.

Game 19 Southwest @ Venezuela, Sunday, August 25th

The coaches dragged the boys out of bed and headed straight to the field. Kaleb called us and said he was hungry because the coaches didn't wake them up to eat breakfast. We rushed to a local diner and had them whip together three egg sandwiches, which we delivered to him in time for him to wolf down before the game started at 10am. Both teams huddled together in one big circle for a prayer before the game. This is the consolation game, competing for 3rd place overall in the tournament. Both the Venezuela and US national anthems were played before the game, so that is a cool experience for the boys!

Willian's Mora, 5'9" was on the mound for Venezuela and faced off against Julian. Julian swings at the first pitch and hits a high fly ball that drops into right field for a hit. The defense was playing back almost at the wall, and it almost looked like he didn't see the ball until it was too late. Gray, on 3-2 count, hammers a 70-mph fastball as a hard-line drive straight to the first baseman, who knocks it down, picks it up and throws it to second to get the lead runner out, but then they don't have time to get it back to first. Cooper, on an 0-1 count, waits on a curveball to come in hanging and he rips a line drive to left field for a single and puts two runners on.

Doc, thankfully is able to come back into the lineup, hits a 73-mph fastball ground ball back to Mora, who grabs it and overthrows third base into the booth, so both Gray and Cooper will turn past third and score to take an early lead 2-0! The umps review the play, and confirm the two runs. Kole is at bat and watches ball one go by, and get by the catcher, so Doc comes sliding into home for a 3-0 lead! Kole chases a slider out over the outer corner for strike three and out #2. Caden gets to a 3-2 count and watches a fastball over the middle of the plate for strike three to end the inning.

Caden's on the mound for Boerne and Luis Yepez, 5'7", hits a hard-line drive into right field for a single. Jesus Diaz, 5'4" hits a line drive through the gap into right field as well. Gage bobbles the ball a little and so Luis will take third base, and we've got runners on the corners with no outs. On a 1-2 count, Caden throws a hard fastball inside and Jhonson Freitez, 5'9", can't pull his hands in to get to it. The pitcher Mora, on a 1-1 count, hits a ground ball up the middle that Jett can sweep up, tag second and throw to first for a double play and ends the 1st inning.

Jett, on a 2-2 count, hits a ground ball off the end of the bat to third base and is out on the throw to first. Gage, on a 2-2 count, goes down swinging at a fastball for strike three. Aiden, on an 0-2 count, hits a curveball line out back to Mora, who catches it for the third out. Mora has a 13-pitch inning against Boerne, but they are still chasing!

Samuel Carrasquel, 5'6", hits a ground ball to Dylan at third, that drops out of his glove, he picks it up and throws to first but not in time. Jose Perez, 5'4", watches an inside pitch for ball one get away from Doc, and Sam will advance to second. Then a second pitch down in the dirt and away gets past Doc, and Sam will take third. On a 2-2 count, Jose hits a grounder to Kole at third, who quickly checks the runner and throws hard to Julian at first for the first out. Diego Biarreta, a big 5'7" lefty hitter, rips a line drive to the left center gap all the way to the wall and gets a stand-up double, scoring Sam, and Venezuela chips away at the lead, 3-1.

Abraham Lucena, 5'7", gets to a 3-2 count and then watches a pitch that just misses inside for ball four and he draws the walk.

Santiago Bello, 5'5", on a 1-1 count hits a fly ball to right field, but Gage is playing deep and so it drops for a hit to load the bases. Simon Vicheria, 4'11", on a 1-2 count gets jammed by Caden and hits a ground ball to Aiden at second, who flips it to Jett and they get Santiago out, but Diego scores to make it 3-2 Boerne. Joshua Duran, 5'8", on an 0-1 count, hits a ground ball to Julian at first who tags the base to end the second inning.

Dylan, on a 1-2 count, swings and misses for strike three. Kaleb, on a 1-2 count, swings and misses for strike three. Ben, on an 0-1 count, flies out to right field. A 10-pitch inning for Mora.

Jonathan Landaeta, 5'0", on a 3-2 count, watches ball four and takes his base. Beiker Zarraga, 5'2", shows bunt but pulls back and the ball goes up and bounces off of Doc's catcher's mitt and that allows Jonathan to advance to second. Beiker, on the 1-1 count, lays down a bunt, Caden grabs it but the throw it wide and goes past Julian at first, allowing Jonathan to score and tie the game at 3. Luis, on an 0-1 count flies out to Kaleb at left who throws it to Dylan at third to hold Beiker at second.

Jesus hits a perfect fly ball to right center, and there is a communication error by Kaleb, Aiden, and Gray, so they let it drop between them. Jhonson takes a pitch up and in on his shoulder to load the bases. Mora, on a 1-2 count, hits a pop fly behind first base that Aiden calls and makes the catch for out #2. Sam, on a 3-2 count, watches a close pitch on the corner called ball for ball four, a run walks in, and Venezuela takes the lead 4-3. Jose, on a 1-2 count, swings and misses at a good slider to the outside corner to retire the side. A 27-pitch inning for Caden.

Julian, on a 3-2 count, lines out to the first baseman. Gray, on a 1-0 count, hits a ground ball to second for a routine out at first. Cooper, on a 1-0 count, hits a hard-line drive that bounces just short of the second baseman, who slides, backhands it, and throws to first to get the out. Another 10-pitch inning for Mora and Boerne needs to get something going!!

Diego, on a 1-1 count, hits a ground ball to Jett at short and he gets the out at first. Abraham, on a 0-1 count, hits a ground ball up the middle to center field for a single. Santiago, on a 3-2 count, hits a ground ball to Aiden at second, who flips it to Jett, who bare-hands it and throw it to first, but Santiago narrowly beats the throw. Jett has had 17 opportunities at short and has not committed an error in Williamsport. Joshua, on 2-2 count, watches ball three get by Doc and so Santiago takes second.

Caden misses with the next pitch so it's a ball four walk for Josh. Boerne pulls Caden at 86 pitches and puts Cooper into pitch. Jonathan hits a hard grounder that bounces up and over first base and they send Abraham, who slides under the tag at home, and Venezuela is now up 5-3. Upon review the call at home is overturned and that ends the 4th inning, 4-3.

Doc, on an 0-2 count, hits a hard grounder that pulls the first baseman off the bag, and he is able to beat the throw back to the pitcher. Kole, on a 1-2 count, swings and misses for strike three. Caden, on a 1-0 count, hits a ground ball back to Mora, who spins and throws out Doc going to second. Jett, on a 1-0 count watches a ball way outside get past the catcher and so Caden advances to second. On the 2-2 count, Jett hits a ground ball to the third baseman, who misses it and gets into left field. Jett runs for second and just barely beats the throw, so we have runners on 2nd and 3rd with two outs. Gage, on a 2-2 count, tries to check swing, but they call it a swing and miss for out #3.

Jonathan, on a 2-0 count, gets hit right on his elbow guard, and he takes his base. Beiker, on a 1-0 count, lays down a bunt that

Dylan is able to grab and get him out at first. Jesus, on an 0-1 count, watches a high pitch get away from Caden and Jonathan advances to third. Jesus takes a hit on the elbow for his base, and now we have runners on the corners. Jhonson hits a ground ball to Aiden at second base, who rolls it to Jett, and he throws to 1st for a double play to end the bottom of the 5th.

Aiden tries to keep the run alive, with a 1-2 count, hits a line drive in the right center gap for a single. Dylan, on a 2-2 count, swings and misses for strike three. That is the 8th strikeout for Mora, and he is at 85 pitches, so they bring in Sam to relieve. Kaleb gets to a 3-1 count, and watches a high pitch for ball four and draws the walk. Ben gets to a 2-2 count and he swings and misses for strike three. Julian is patient during an 8-pitch at bat and he draws the walk to load the bases. Gray gets to a 3-1 count and then hits a line drive right to the second baseman for the out.

Venezuela takes 3rd place and Team Southwest will take home 4th place back home to Boerne!

Chapter 20 Statewide Heroes return home

It was a sad ending, but that sometimes happens in baseball. Whenever you get to a championship game, one team will win, and that also means that one team will lose. We are incredibly proud of these boys, as they played with toughness, grit, guts, and great sportsmanship all summer! Even through that loss, the kids embodied the Little League spirit, which was, "...win or lose, I will always do my best." What did we learn? We simply learned that we can't control the outcome. We have shown Kaleb the quote from Michael Jordan: "I've missed more than 9000 shots in my career. I've lost almost 300 games. 26 times, I've been trusted to take the game-winning shot and missed. I've failed over and over and over again in my life. And that is why I succeed." And he is considered to be the best basketball player of all time. The boys did their best, they left it all on the field, and for that, we say that they are winners in life. They can also use the pain of this loss, to fuel them going forward, continue working, and if you never quit, at some point you will win.

Southeast beats Asia-Pacific on Sunday 2-1 to win the Little League World Series and they take the championship home to Lake Mary, FL. Disney threw them a grand parade and celebration and the politicians of Florida gave all the boys two years' worth of in-state college tuition to say thank you.

Losing those last two games was absolutely heart-breaking, but there is very little time to sit and reflect on the last three months. The Venezuela game was Sunday morning, and many of the parents were able to get flights home that evening back to San Antonio. The boys climbed back in the buses for the 4-hour drive to Newark on Monday, and then caught the direct flight back home to San Antonio. They visit Starbucks again and Kaleb takes advantage to get another double-smoked bacon cheddar egg sandwich and pink drink! When they are out of your control and out of your sight, they make the decisions! The boys arrive to a hero's welcome!

San Antonio airport's firefighting staff meets the plane with what is called a "shower of affection," where they have two fire trucks on either side of the airplane and they are shooting a shower of water from each side that rains down on the airplane. The Delta pilot came on the intercom and said that in 35 years of flying, he had never experienced that type of "welcome home reception." The local news was there to film them arriving back home in San Antonio!

Tim Tadlock, Texas Tech Head Baseball Coach, sent the boys a note congratulating them on their great play.

Thank you San Antonio, Boerne, and Texas, for everything that you did for our kids and families. The boys climbed into a procession of vehicles, supplied by local car dealerships, and got a police escort straight to Boerne, where the entire community came out to a parade through downtown Boerne that was set up in honor of the boys' achievement. The parade culminated at Boerne Main Plaza, where the mayor and other elected officials provided some words of appreciation and recognition. The boys were beset on all sides by thousands of fans, who wanted their autographs on balls and the baseball shirts designed for the event that were purchased at local stores.

The boys were the guests of honor at a San Antonio Spurs basketball game a couple months later. They boys were the guests of honor at a Republican party meeting, (thank you Ellen Troxclair, Donna Campbell, Chip Roy, and Ted Cruz) where they raised a few thousand dollars to cover the outstanding expenses of the trip for all the families. The boys were invited to the Capitol in Austin, and each received an American Flag and a Commemoration by the Texas Elected Officials recognizing them for their efforts on behalf of a grateful state. Texas Senate Resolution No. 561 is a permanent record of the boys' accomplishments. Dr. Emmanuel Alfonso and Dr. Emerico Gomez of Boerne Orthodontics & Pediatric Dentistry graciously offered "free braces" as a congratulations for all the boys, so when you see their perfect smiles, you know who is responsible! ☺

Since the Venezuela game was on Sunday, August 25th, the boys had already missed two weeks of school. Tuesday, August 27th when they arrived at school for their first day, the entire school lined the halls of the three Boerne middle schools that the boys are split between, and so the boys participated in another parade through the halls with the high school baseball team members, cheerleaders, and high school drum line providing an escort. The schools had been live broadcasting the games on a screen in the cafeteria so the entire school could watch and cheer the boys on! Even a year later, none of the boys can go anywhere in town without being recognized, and, even when they go play in baseball tournaments in Austin, Dallas, or San Antonio, many of the kids and parents stop and tell them how much they enjoyed rooting them on and watching them on TV.

It was very exciting to host the opening day of Boerne Little League Spring Baseball 2025, and see the special plaque that is hung above field 5, commemorating the trip to Williamsport. There is a banner hanging on the softball field fence when you first drive into Northrup Baseball Park that says "Congratulations," and so, for the twelve members of this 2024 team, Northrup will always feel like home and will forever hold a very special place in our hearts. On any given day, it's not uncommon to find one or several of the team practicing on the public access field or one of the private fields.

There were a number of requests for the boys to attend various events, but we had to draw a line somewhere. They are 6th and 7th graders after all, and since many of them are multi-sport athletes, they are already two weeks' behind in 7th grade football practices, and there are specific UIL rules that have to be followed before they can dress in full pads and join the team in the regular practices. So, we declined a few invitations, got the kids focused on going back to school, getting back in their routines, and continuing their development both as students and athletes. However, every player still routinely gets stopped and asked for their autograph, and they are always very excited to provide it. This has been an experience these 12 boys and families will never forget.

We hope that this book is used as a training guide for future players and parents on how to develop your athletes and how to build a competitive league and program. We fully believe that Little League and Select can live together in a very symbiotic relationship. Our hope and prayer is that future Boerne Little Leaguers will be inspired by what we were able to accomplish and will work really, really hard over 5-7 years in order to put together more Boerne All-Star Teams and make a run for Williamsport. It's not finished, we were able to get there, but until a Boerne team can bring home a World Championship trophy, we've all got something to reach for. We hope that you can stand on our shoulders and finish what we started. One of the things that Little Leagues parents/coaches can do, is to have this conversation with a bunch of the 6- and 7-year-old kids. This can be the first time for them to create and work for a multi-year goal. Some Little Leagues already do this, as both 10- and 11-year-old All-Star teams finish at the State level. You saw this level of focus and discipline with both McAllister and the Mid-Atlantic team, and how they work diligently for three plus years to accomplish their goal of getting to Williamsport.

Both programs become "tribes" and you will develop great relationships with the families involved in both programs. Little League is typically 1-2 games per week. Select allows kids to play 3-7 games in a weekend, which allows a bunch of kids to get reps on the mound, in the batter's box, and at various positions in the field. Little League, in some areas, is now building an "Elite Program" that provides similar benefits with some additional games on the weekends. It comes down to a decision for each family on what level of time/finance can you commit to the improvement of your child? It's difficult, as most families have multiple children involved in multiple activities and so parents, and sometimes grandparents, get stretched thin. As you increase in skill level in Select, it can become increasingly difficult to find good competition locally, and so you will see many select teams travel to Austin, Houston, Dallas, Baton Rouge, or even nationwide where they host some larger tournaments and that draws the more competitive teams.

Having the benefit of being in both programs for years, in a perfect world, you would do it like a sandlot format, you'd have your top 20 kids in the city show up at a field every weekend, they would blind draw for teams, and they'd play 4-6 games a weekend. Allow each kid to get reps on the mound, allow kids to rotate between infield and outfield positions, and have every kid get at least some work in at catcher, because it's a very difficult position, and it helps to teach you so much about the game and be focused, because you are involved in every play. Your team would lose a lot and win some, and so the kids could get really comfortable in all types of environments. It's amazing how quickly kids get better when they play 50-60 games per year.

Just for an example, when you think about two of the really good teams we faced, here is how many of their kids play both Little League and Select ball. The Lake Mary roster looks like this:

- Chase Anderson plays select for the Central Florida Suns
- JJ Feliciano plays for RT Scout select team
- DJ is a member of the TBT National White select team and that team was the #1 team in the country for a few years for that age group
- Landon Bono also plays for the Central Florida Suns
- Garrett Rohozen also plays with RT Scout
- Jacob Bibaud plays for Hit Dogs Florida select team
- Liam Morrissey also plays for RT Scout
- Luis Calo also plays for Central Florida Suns
- Teraj Alexander plays for CFL Pride Makos
- Christopher Chikodroff plays for the Jersey Devils Nationals
- Lathan Norton plays for GSB Prospects
- Hunter Alexander plays for Wow Factor

If you look at Louisiana's roster, the overlap with select looks like this:

- Dominic Barranco plays for Louisiana SWAG
- Zayne Barrett plays for Louisiana SWAG
- Kole Cao plays for Louisiana SWAG
- Brandt Deeke plays for New Orleans Renegades Black
- Benjamin Florane plays for New Orleans Naturals Blue
- Sayid Jabbar plays for NOLA Hurricanes
- Cy Kirklin plays for Louisiana SWAG

- Chase LeBlanc plays for Traction Canes National
- Kamren Lew plays for Louisiana SWAG
- Christopher Newsome Jr (CJ) plays for NOCA American
- Lane Pastor plays for Louisiana SWAG
- Landon Valladares plays for Traction Canes National

The US All-Star Team was comprised of the 11 hand-picked players from 2024. The list includes Julian and Doc (who we talk about in the Profiles in the following pages), as well as these players:

- Evan Tavares, Hawaii (Pitcher), allowed zero earns runs during the summer in more than 40 innings pitched and had 101 strike-outs
- Matthew Yang, Hawaii (Catcher), hit .556 and .600 OBP
- Wyatt Erickson, Nevada (Infield), hit .571 and .636 OBP, and pitched a complete game 5-hitter, winning 9-1
- Noah Letalu, Nevada (Infield), hit .444 with a .500 OBP
- Teraj Alexander, Florida (Infield), batted .417 in seven games and a .523 OBP
- Chris Chikodroff, Florida (Infield), hit .500 and .615 OBP
- Kellan Goodwin, Illinois (Outfield), was able to get a hit against Evan Tavares and played great defense
- Dean Scarangelo, New York (Outfield), hit .571 and .625 OBP
- Dylan Degaeta, New York (Utility), hit .625 and had 5 hits in a 3-game stretch at Williamsport

What we want families to take away from our experience is that we had a really good team of 12 great athletes and a great group of families that all committed themselves to this effort. In baseball, to win 17 games in a row against tough competition, especially at both State and Regionals, takes all 12 kids putting forth 100% effort and doing the best that they can do in that spot. Did we make some errors, sure. We expect that, because these boys are 12 years old. However, did the training and practice that they have received for over six years lead up to them performing better in those moments? Absolutely.

Even though the media like to showcase a single individual, in baseball, and in this format, it takes a team of 12 to actually create consistent victories across a large number of games. All of our kids executed many crucial plays at various points in time throughout those 19 games, and had they not executed, we would not have been there at the end. Every single member of our team was absolutely crucial to our success and we are so thankful that they and their families made the decision to work hard all through the spring and summer of 2024 to take that journey with us.

Several of us have gone to Cooperstown during the summer of a kid's 12U season, which is basically the "personally financed" version of Williamsport. It's a beautiful facility, both Dreams Park and All-Star Village. The boys enjoy staying in the dorms, meeting new people, and playing baseball at odd hours, since it seems to rain, sleet, and bake you all in the same week in northwestern New York. However, it will never have the magical aura of Williamsport, because you can't buy your way there. It has to be earned, and it's earned in the blood, sweat, tears, and years of practice by young athletes, who join together to compete and represent their local community.

Many of the Cooperstown teams are local teams from around the country whose parents want to give their kids a very memorable 12U baseball summer experience. Some are select teams that travel there as part of the calendar they build for the spring season, and a couple are built by coaches that want to put together a "dream team" and win the whole thing at Cooperstown. Whatever your motivation, we would definitely recommend going there at least once, as the entire place is steeped in history and, especially for those of us in the south, the climate is a welcome respite in June or July from the 100+ degrees in Texas. You see similar locations pop up around the country and advertise (Slumpbuster in Omaha during College World Series, Cal Ripken Experience, Baseball Parks of America, Diamond Nation, etc.). Just like with anything else in life, you can spend as much or as little as you want in pursuit of giving your kids fun experiences and opportunities to improve.

This is an experience unlike any other and nothing even comes close. We hope that this book was able to encapsulate some of the emotion that we experienced during those three months and we hope that this inspires you to help develop the next generation of kids who would absolutely love to have this opportunity. In the following pages, we have provided details to the boys' playing histories, that way you can get an idea of the work and development that we have put into them over the years, so it can a point of reference for you as you build a program for your individual kids and collective teams.

Julian Hurst

Julian Hurst is a 2030 grad and a right-hand pitcher (RHP), catcher, and third base/first base. He is 6'0", 160 lb, and he has now gotten his velocity up to 83 mph. He has worked with a number of great instructors and true professionals of the game, including pitcher Jake Arrieta (Orioles, Cubs, Phillies, & Padres from 2010-2021).

According to his Perfect Game (PG) statistics, he has played in 41 events and received 31 awards. Generally All-Tournament Hitting award is given for those kids that bat .500 or better with at least 10 at-bats. All-Tournament Pitching award is a more complex algorithm that we have yet to figure out, but if you have a very low ERA and no/few walks, then you generally receive that award as well. He has played for Lone Star Baseball Club (LBC) Central French, LBC National 13U, Houston Wildcatters Elite 14U, and Texas Twelve Maroon.

Julian made the US All-Star Team, a selection of the 11 best US Players in 2024. He won Player of the Year in his Williamsport debut! He had a 2.09 ERA, striking out 27 in 14 1/3 innings. He hit .667 with a .733 OBP.

Doc Mogford

Doc Mogford is a 2030 grad and a RHP and a middle infielder/outfielder. He is 5'10" and 140 lbs, and can throw 83 mph. He has played in 75 events and won 23 awards. He has played for Cinch Red, Corpus Christi Crew, Texas Twelve, and LBC.

Doc also made the US All-Star Team, hitting .600 and was named one of the series best hitters!

Cooper Hastings

Cooper Hastings is a 2031 grad and a Right Hand Pitcher/third base/first base. He is 5'6", 150 lbs., and he has gotten his velocity to 72 mph. Cooper earned the highest Contact Percentage at 94.74% for the team. He has played in 67 events and won 27 awards. He has played for Texas Twelve, LBC National, Canes, and the Texas Sun Devils.

Kole Newson

Kole Newson is a 2030 grad and is now 5'11", 135 lbs. Kole earned third in QAB for the team! He has gotten his velocity up to 69 mph. Kole started baseball like most kids at his local Little League. His first season was Tee-Ball at Boerne Little League when he was 4 years old. He was hooked from day one and has played every spring and fall since. He also plays football and excels in the classroom.

He was around 9 years old when he got the nickname "Koleslaw". And it has stuck with him ever since. It is a very active and heated debate on if it was Bert Munoz or his wife Lorina that first called him that (Aiden's parents). ☺

Kole has grown to be a very versatile player and plays every position on the field and a reliable bat in the lineup that hits for power and contact still to this day. He started getting weekly lessons for Coach Jason Marshall at around 9 years old at D1 in Boerne.

He normally hits in the top half of every team he's been on and has had the privilege of playing on some pretty talented and special teams. Being a part of the first Boerne team to make it to the LLWS in Williamsport has been the highlight of his sports career so far.

According to PG, he has played 58 events and won 19 awards. He has played on Texas Sun Devils, Texas Twelve, LBC South, and LBC Central.

Caden Guffey

Caden is a 2030 grad, RHP/3B/1B/C/OF, and is 5'9", 155 lbs. He can throw 76 mph. He has played in 66 events and won 24 awards. He has played for the San Antonio Kings, Texas Twelve, LBC Central, and the Central Texas Wildcatters.

Gray Collins

Gray is a 2030 grad, 5'8", 135 lbs, and has touched 71 mph. Gray earned the highest line drive percentage rate for the team at 51%. Gray and Ben tied for the most "hits" by pitch with 5. He has played in 43 events and won 16 awards. Gray has played for the Fair Oaks Falcons and Texas Twelve.

Aiden Munoz

Aiden is a 2030 grad, 5'6", 140 lbs., and has touched 67 mph. Aiden tied for the most 6+ pitch plate appearances at 9 of 46, or 20% of the time! Really good plate discipline and patience! He has played in 41 events and won 5 awards. Aiden has played for Texas Twelve and LBC South.

Aiden began playing sports at just three years old, with soccer as his first introduction to athletics. Soon after, he added baseball and basketball to the mix, but by the age of six, it was clear that baseball had truly captured his passion. With both parents having played at the collegiate level and his paternal grandfather having played professionally in Guadalajara, Jalisco, Mexico, sports run deep in his blood.

In Spring 2022, Aiden faced a significant setback during his very first tournament of the season. In a freak accident, he swung at a high inside fastball that deflected off the bat and struck him in the face. The impact resulted in a fractured lower orbital, nearly collapsing the orbital floor, as well as a concussion. He underwent plastic surgery to repair the damage.

Returning to the field was not easy. Aiden faced uphill battles at the plate as he worked to rebuild both his physical and mental comfort and confidence. However, through determination and perseverance, he gradually found his rhythm again.

His hard work paid off in a big way during the Spring 2024 season with his Boerne Little League team. Over the course of the regular season, Aiden recorded 42 plate appearances without a single strikeout, an incredible testament to his resilience, discipline, and growth as a player. He also played a key role in his team's defensive success, contributing to a record setting number of double plays during the Southwest Regional Tournament.

Aiden will forever remember and cherish every person and moment from the 2024 Little League World Series run. He has since continued his youth baseball career and looks forward to competing at the high school level.

Jett Matthews

Jett is a 2030 grad, 5'9", 120 lbs., and can throw 70 mph. He has played in 41 PG events and won 9 awards, and by his dad's count, he has played in over 400 baseball games since he was 5. Jett has played for LBC, Twelve, and Fair Oaks Falcons.

Gage Steubing

Gage is a 2030 grad, 5'5", 115 lbs, and a middle infielder. Gage led the Boerne team in walks for the Summer with 9 over 42 plate appearances. Excellent plate discipline! He can throw 68 mph. He has played in 12 events, won 1 award, and has played for Texas Twelve. In addition to baseball, as you read about throughout the book, he is incredibly fast. He also runs track and has set personal records of 17.74 for the 100m hurdles, 45.34 for the 300m hurdles, and a 16'11" long jump.

Ben Burkhart

Ben is a 2030 grad, is 5'9", and bats right and throws right. Ben earned the top spot for being able to draw out the most additional pitches after two strikes with 18.6%. Excellent plate discipline and patience! Ben and Gray tied for taking the most "hits" to get on base, with 5 each. In addition to being an athlete, he has been highly involved in academic competitions his entire school career. He attends the Geneva School in Boerne. He has received awards for Cum Laude in Logic School on the National Latin Exam (NLE) as well as Reading/Math awards.

Dylan Burke

Dylan is a 2030 grad, 5’3”, 120 lbs., and has touched 67 mph. Dylan earned the highest pitches seen/plate appearances at 4.136, showcasing his excellent plate discipline and patience! He has played in 26 events and won 3 awards. He has played for Texas Sun Devils and the Canes.

Kaleb Christ

Kaleb is the sole 11-year-old on the team and a 2031 grad. He is 4'11", 92 lbs. Kaleb was #2 in Quality At-Bats (QAB) at 65.12% for his team for the entire LLWS run, an incredible accomplishment, meaning that he is incredibly smart and did the right thing in the vast majority of his at-bats.

Kaleb got his first introduction to sports through Soccer Shots at daycare. From age 2 on, his parents introduced him to many athletic sports including: flag football, soccer, basketball, teeball/baseball, golf, tennis, ping pong, swimming, running, biking, and triathlons. When he was 4, he started playing organized sports with Catholic Youth Organization (CYO). He played fall flag football, winter basketball, spring baseball, and summer basketball. After 3 years, he started playing more competitive flag football through Under Armor Sports & Nike Flag Football, competitive basketball through Cornerstone Sports Academy & Standard of Athletics, select baseball through Perfect Game, NCS, and FiveTool, competitive golf with Southern Texas PGA Little Linksters and US Kids, and competition swimming/running through Jewish Community Center, YMCA, and USAT. He played Little League for Helotes Little League for a season and then played Boerne Little League for the historic Spring/Summer 2024 season. At Voss Middle School, he is quarterback and kicker of the 7th grade "A" team in football, a runner in Cross Country, and is a shooting guard for the basketball team. His select baseball career includes playing with the Fair Oaks Falcons, San Antonio Kings, San Antonio Tigers, Medina Valley Blackcats, Showtime, Canes, Banditos, South Texas Sliders, CTX Wildcatters, Twelve, and Lake Travis Outlaws.

He has received excellent instruction in all aspects of baseball from a number of great instructors including, but not limited to Jason Marshall at D1 Training in Boerne, Mark Trimble at D-Bat San Antonio, John Gump, Ben Van Ryn (drafted by the Expos in 1990 and played for the Angels, Cubs, Padres, & Blue Jays in 1996-1998), Jesse Garcia (Orioles, Braves, & Padres in 1999-2005), Martin Maldonado (former Astros and current White Sox player) Catcher Camp, Jimmy Gonzales (26-year MLB scout for Washington Nationals), Noah Miles, Marco Palacios, Jake Arrieta, and collegiate preparatory baseball camps such as UTSA, Texas A&M, and University of Texas. He has also done a number of sports camps for his other sports as well, football, basketball, golf, etc.

Based on his Gamechanger statistics, from the Fall 2019 through the Summer 2024, he has played in 362 games, has had 954 plate appearances, 794 at bats (meaning he has been walked 129 times, has been hit by pitch 28 times, and has had 3 sacrifice flies). His career batting average is .523, with an on-base percentage (OBP) of .600, and OPS of 1.408. He's had 415 total hits (262 singles, 94 doubles, 44 triples, and 15 homeruns). He has struck out 61 times and struck-out looking (K-L) 23 times. He has stolen 188 bases and has a 92.6% stolen base percentage. He has seen 2,783 pitches and averages 2.9 pitches seen per plate appearance.

He has pitched 233 innings in 96 games, starting in 51 of them, faced 1,145 batters, and thrown 4,162 pitches. He has allowed 239 hits, 162 earned runs, walked 175 kids, struck out 233 of them and 91 strike-out looking. He has hit 17 kids (HBP). His WHIP is 1.774 and he has picked off 33 runners. His opponents' batting average is .252. He averages 17.8 pitches/inning, and lifetime strike percentage is 57.7%. Of his 233 innings, 126 of them he didn't walk anyone, and he averages .750 walks/inning. He has only walked the leadoff batter 37 times, and 22 of them scored. His strikeout/walk ratio is 1.331.

In his Perfect Game profile, he has played in 102 events to date and has 26 awards.

We do want to say a special thank-you to the Facebook "Little league district 22" New York author, as he did a great job covering the games with a bunch of social media posts. We were humbled to hear that his most popular post was the one about Kaleb, with over 3 million views, "The Do it all, Kid...He was inches from the win, a bad hop away, a catch in the outfield away, and even after all that he sent his team into the dugout only down by two runs with a chance, he gave his team a chance. It's kids like this that the LLWS was created for. They are champions in every way." In addition to the Boerne team, Kaleb was an underdog in this story, and Americans love gritty underdogs. We are humbled by your kind words and we thank you!

Chapter 22: The Road Ahead

Many of the families are laser-focused on high school sports for the boys. They have 1-2 years of middle school left to go through puberty, grow, get bigger/stronger/faster, and play middle school sports in preparation for high school. Boerne has two high schools, Boerne High and Champion High, both of which are very competitive in the vast majority of their sports.

Both high schools are now classified as 5A high school programs for UIL. Boerne Champion's Baseball Coach, Ben Woodchick, has been incredibly supportive of the boys and came out to some practices for us during the summer. Ben has been successful at getting Champion's team to 13 playoff rounds in the last 3 seasons. Boerne High Baseball Coach Geoff Curtin is excited to get several of the boys to his school and see if he can take them to State, as Boerne High did win a State Championship back in 2004 against the always competitive Calallen High School (near Corpus Christi), in a nailbiter 2-1 game.

Jason Marshal, owner of D1 Training in Boerne, and former UTSA Head Baseball Coach, continues to provide instruction to a number of our athletes on various aspects of the game. Jason traveled to Williamsport to cheer on the team, and we greatly appreciate his focus, instruction, and dedication to our athletes. We also greatly appreciate the local D-Bat Boerne, for all your support and having your doors open to many of us continuing to practice there on almost a nightly basis. Stay tuned for what's next and it would be our honor to meet you at a future baseball game or other sporting event in the future!

All of the boys are very good at the various components of baseball. We continue to develop their skill work with drills and practices going forward. However, the difference maker, for the boys that have aspirations to play in college versus only playing in high school, will be the intentional work they put into the gym. They have to get incredibly strong, and there is no "easier" time in their lives than high school when their system is flooded with growth hormones. 3-4 times per week they will be in the gym, and we "hope" to see 10-20 pounds of additional muscle being added to their frame every year. Right now they weigh 92-150 pounds, many can't do a single pullup, some can squat 200 pounds, and the most any of them can bench is about 125 pounds. Benching 225+ by senior year for at least 10 reps is the goal. Squatting 2-3x of their body weight by their senior year is the goal. Being able to do 15 unassisted pullups, or do 1 pullup with an additional 50 pounds of weight hung around their waist, is the goal.

Dr. Josh Heenan was interviewed on the CoachU Podcast, and he talks about the scientific way to achieve throwing 90 mph. He says you have to be able to deadlift 400 lbs for one rep. You need to long toss 300+ feet. You need to be able to do a chin-up with 250 lbs of weight. You need to be able to do 10 back barbell reverse lunges with each leg with your bodyweight on the bar (bodyweight is calculated as height in inches multiplied by 2.75-3.25, so, for a 6' high school junior, you want to work up to 198-234 lbs.). Just as with anything, this is "directional" in nature and not an absolute. There are kids that can't do the above that can throw 90 mph. There also may be kids that can do all these exercises that can't throw 90 mph. However, they are good Big Hairy Audacious Goals (BHAG's by Jim Collins) to put on your whiteboard and strive to achieve over a 4-year high school career, if your kids have dreams of playing in college.

Chapter 23: A Blueprint for Developing Young Athletes

As you have read about in these profiles of the boys' above, all were introduced to athletics at very early ages. In any athletic endeavor, it's incredibly important for kids to develop athleticism first. They need hand-eye coordination, they need great footwork and explosive jumping ability, they need balance, they need speed and maneuverability, and they need as much strength as they can possibly get for their size. In any sport, then they also need great fundamentals and great mechanics. For baseball, they need to be great at fielding and throwing. For pitching, they need to have really good mechanics and a clean delivery. For hitting, they need to have good balance on their back foot, good timing, and then really good bat path and eye tracking through contact. Then they also need the intellectual Intelligence (Baseball IQ) about the game. What do they do with the ball when it's in their hands? None of this comes naturally. It is all learned. All of it only comes with good instruction and LOTS of practice.

As a team, we batted .413 for the entire LLWS. That is an incredibly impressive statistic and is a great example of what 12-year-old boys can achieve with an extensive amount of batting practice over multiple years. Julian led the team with a .622 avg, Gray batted .500, and Cooper/Doc/Gage/Kole all batted over .400. Kaleb had our lowest batting average at .273, but because of his baseball IQ, his on-base percentage (OBP) was .395 and he was #2 in Quality At-Bats (QAB). In Major League Baseball, for OBP anything above .340 is good, .360 is very good, and .400+ is elite. Remember when we said that it takes 12 really good hitters? When your #12 kid is still getting on base 4 times out of every 10 at-bats, and/or driving in RBI's/moving kids on base over/generally doing the right thing in the moment, you are going to do well. We had a total of 564 plate appearances with 462 at-bats. We had 191 hits, including 23 home runs, 195 runs, 72 walks, 86 strike-outs, 33 strike-outs looking (great opportunity for us to continue to improve), we were hit by 23 pitches, and our team average QAB was 55.50, with an average of 3.4 pitches seen per plate appearance. For the 19 games, our overall run totals were Boerne 195, opponents 34.

For pitching, we threw 1,505 pitches and faced 371 batters. We allowed 56 hits, walked 41 kids, had 163 strike-outs, and an overall Earned Run Average (ERA) of 1.978 and Walks + Hits per Inning Pitched (WHIP) of 1.054. We threw an average of 4.057 pitches per batter faced (P/BF) with an overall team strike percentage of 64.25%. Out of 92 innings, in 60 of them we didn't walk anyone. We gave up three homeruns. Our opponent batting average was .174 for the entire series. In Williamsport alone, our opponent batting average was .213. The league average in the MLB often sits in the low to mid- .240s. Julian threw the most pitches, 510, with Caden a close second at 438. As you saw throughout our series, we needed 7 pitchers in total, and collectively they threw 64.25%. We have some other kids that were also good pitchers and they didn't even get to see the mound.

Many of our kids couldn't catch a fly ball over their shoulder at 7 years old. If they have gotten a solid foundation of baseball by age 7, then you can really ramp up the training practice for the next five years, and you can get them to this type of elite performance by 12 years old.

As you read about in the games, we were very solid defensively. We made a few errors, which everyone expects a few at this age, and so our fielding percentage was .973. Hopefully this allows you to set some goals, that you now know are achievable by a group of 12-year-olds, measure your kids' current status, and develop a practice plan to get them to meet/exceed our numbers.

If you listen to the Westside Barbell podcasts, a fantastic resource for strength training and injury prevention for athletes, they talk a lot about the origins of their program. They studied Russian athletes who dominate in many Olympic games and all the kids started doing athletics at age 2-4. They all start weigh training at 8 years old, and then focus intently on developing sports-specific movements from ages 12-22. In baseball, one of the reasons you see so many international athletes is that many of those kids play baseball a lot, starting from very young ages, and so they are better at it by the time they get to college-age than some of their US peers. So you see things like IMG Academy, where they accept kids starting in middle school to do a very programmatic combined academics and athletic program, that are trying to build a program to better help families put their children in the best possible position to succeed.

Doing athletic activity has to become the "default." When a kid asks, what are we doing today? The answer should be at least 1-2 hours of some sort of athletic activity, and there is absolutely nothing wrong with there being 5-8 hours' worth of athletics in any given day. Kids can go play pickup baseball/basketball with their friends and easily consume 2-3 hours, if not all day long. That type of conditioning is built up over time, but it has to be an intentional goal of the parents to provide their kids with this type of environment where they can get the necessary practice in to allow them to excel in the games. If you listen to any of Kobe

Bryant's interviews, that is what he talks about as well, that putting in an extra daily practice and after 4 years, you have put in thousands of hours more than your peers, and then at some point, your peers have no hope of ever catching up with you, because there is not enough time for them to practice on top of what you are already doing together in order to log the miles you have already logged.

My favorite quote is that "we don't practice until we get it right, we practice until we don't get it wrong." In any sport, you can figure out "the math." If you go hit balls on a field or in a cage, for every 100 swings, how many were solidly hit line drives? Until that number is 95+ consistently over 3-4 weeks' of hitting balls 4-5 times per week, they have not had enough practice. Until they hit .350+ in games consistently over entire seasons, they have not had enough practice. Until they can pitch 65% average strike percentage for multiple games they have not had enough practice. And once you reach those particular milestones, then you set new and higher targets. You are never "there," you are always chasing perfection, which we know is unachievable, but if you are disciplined and fortunate, you get to live with excellence.

We watched Jamarquis Lawrence, Nebraska basketball player practice for over 3 hours each on two different days when we were in Salt Lake at Lifetime Fitness. He set up three barrels in a triangle, and was working on his shooting and dribbling. Kaleb was practicing at the other end of the court so I was able to watch his practice out of the corner of my eye. In 20 minutes, he might have missed 1-2 shots. It was absolutely incredible to watch. It's that repetitive practice, it's loving the process, that ultimately separates the great from the good.

It's incredibly important to establish a baseline of where your kid is currently at, and then set intermediate goals that you can work collectively to achieve. Set a hitting goal for the end of the season average, and then break it into monthly goals, and every game goals. Measure each of them, did they hit that goal or did they not? Do we need to adjust the goal, or was something else off? Did they get the necessary practice in (5-10 hours per week outside of their regular practice)?

To give an example outside the world of baseball, we have played golf with a kid when Kaleb shot his best ever round, which was a 75 on 18 holes (3 over par) from the women's (red) tees at Lady Bird Johnson Golf Course in Fredericksburg, TX. In that same event, we played with Dawson Dial, a very good junior golfer from Austin, who shot 64 (8 under par). Dawson, a golf friend of Kaleb's, won the US Kids World Championship Golf Tournament in Pinehurst, NC for the 9-year-old division, and then won the Drive, Chip, & Putt Championship at Augusta, GA in 2025 for the Boys' 10-11 division. Texas Terry, another golfer friend of Kaleb's, won the US Kids Championship at 8 years old and then won the Drive, Chip, & Putt Championship for his age group in August 2024.

There are kids in every sport, some that only focus on one particular sport, that are absolutely incredible at that sport by 8-13 years old. When we say they are really good at their sport, we are talking about, like they are in the Top 5-10 best players in the world. That is an extremely high bar, and takes 8-10 years of consistent, intentional coaching and development work to achieve. However, the nice thing about starting early is that if you can develop your child to an elite level by 12 years old, then they simply get to continue their development from there, where there really doesn't become anyone that is in "real" competition with them after a certain point. What we have tried to do with our kids is to "reach" the top skill level by 12 years old, and then we can take advantage of puberty and the years in high school to continue their development in preparation for collegiate sports or whatever aspirations they have beyond high school.

What you want to figure out as a parent, is how good is your child at that sport? Are they a top-ranked player in their city? In their state? In the country? Around the world? It takes an incredible amount of planning, focus, effort and practice, but if you can help your child become a true "world-class athlete" by age 12-14, then you have a real chance of them being a highly competitive athlete in high school and then being able to be a competitive athlete in college. The vast majority of PGA & LPGA Tour golfers were shooting scratch golf as freshman in high school.

When you ask 100 random MLB players how long they have been playing baseball, 90+ of them will tell you they have been playing the game since teeball. That does mean there are 9-10 of the 100 that picked it up later in life, but for the most part, a higher likelihood of success is from early athletic development and a continued passion and focus over decades.

The big differentiator in high school is that those athletes have to live in the workout facility and be very intentional about gaining weight. They all have to lift weights and work to put on 40+ pounds of muscle between their freshman year and their senior year, in addition to continuing to get better at the mechanics, the mental game, and the execution of whatever sport they play.

For any sport, a little bit of research provides you the framework for what your goal can be. For baseball, a high school senior that is 6'0" (and hopefully going to grow 1-4 more inches), 185 lbs (hopefully can put on another 20-40 lbs in college), that can throw a baseball 90 mph with 65% strike percentage, and that has a batting average of .400+, is a very desirable recruit for college.

One of the things we found in Little League at 12 years old, is that many of the batters were simply not prepared to hit 70+ mph pitching. When you have those kids like we mentioned earlier, including Luis Yepez from Venezuela, Antonio Guerrero from Mexico, or Lin Chin-Tse from Taiwan, that throw 78-82 mph, then you have to develop your kids early and prepare them to actually succeed when they face that speed, and not simply be reactive. In order to prepare kids for that, many of our kids have played "up" in several tournaments where they play against 12-, 13-, 14-year-olds while they were still a year or two younger. Many of the Boerne kids were watching 70-74 mph come at them from the pitching machines at D-Bat Boerne when they were 10 years old and from hitting batting practice against the other kids.

You have to prepare them in advance to succeed. I have always told Kaleb, if you ever encounter a situation in a game that we haven't practiced, then I failed. I want you to have worked on every situation hundreds of times in practice or in recreational games, so that when you encounter it when it matters, like the Little League World Series, High School Baseball games, National Select tournaments, or other, that you can be very confident because you know you are prepared. We love listening to Patrick Jones Baseball podcasts while we are traveling to/from practices and/or games, and one of his guests is Giuseppe Papaccio, Associate Head Coach at Seton Hall, and his comment is "Separation is in the Preparation."

We recognize that this level of commitment is not for everyone. It's reserved for the few who are willing to take the hard road. We play sports instead of video games, although we have gotten to a very high level on Baseball 9! Our kids go run around with the neighborhood kids some nights until it gets dark, because, after all, they are just kids, and mindless play is important for any kid growing up! It's important to be balanced.

However, we do dedicate, with intention, time to practice, and then practice some more. We believe that we have given them the tools to succeed at a very high level in all aspects of their life. They hold themselves to a very high standard and they will have developed the habits and mental fortitude to be able to hopefully withstand even life's hardest lessons.

For any other parents and/or kids that are willing to take this journey, you are welcome to come practice and workout with us. Monday nights, Friday nights, Saturdays/Sundays with no tournaments, or hit nights at Jimmy Gonzales Baseball Academy, you will generally find us doing some sort of athletic activity. On vacation, you will see us carving out a bit of time and finding a local D-Bat batting cage or a local baseball field. We'll find the local Lifetime Fitness and take an Alpha class and/or take advantage of the basketball court and shoot a couple hundred shots/layups.

It's the work that you do when no one is looking that really matters, and we have all dedicated ourselves to giving our children every opportunity to succeed in their chosen endeavor. If you listen to Mike Boyle's interview on Eric Cressey's podcast, he talks about a lot of these same principles for long-term athletic development and in-season training.

Some books we've read that you might find useful:

Nolan Ryan's Pitcher's Bible by Tom House

Faster Higher Stronger by Mark McClusky

The Science of Baseball by Will Carroll

The Physics of Baseball by Robert Adair

Movement over Maxes by Zach Dechant

Play College Baseball by Karen Murphy

The Unstoppable Athlete by Andrew Simpson

The Next Pitching Star by Terrence Armstrong

Win the Next Pitch by Dr. Curt Ickes

Pitch Like a Pro by Leo Mazzone

The MVP Machine by Lindbergh Sawchik

Swing and a Hit by Paul O'Neill

Unleash Your Pitching Velocity by Dr. Chris McKenzie

Full Count by David Cone

Explosive Power and Jumping Ability for All Sports by Starzynski and Sozanski

Children and Sports Training by Dr. Jozef Drabik

Thank you for taking the time to read this book and we sincerely hope that we have inspired you, entertained you, and provided you with a true insider's perspective into our world and our experience during the 2024 Summer. May God bless you and your family the way He has blessed us.

APPENDIX GAME PLAY-BY-PLAY

Game 1 Boerne @ Ingram

There are five teams in this District tournament, Fredericksburg (the famous wine town that is becoming the Napa Valley of Texas), Ingram, Kerrville, Medina Valley, and Boerne. Every Little League game starts off with the Little League Pledge:

I trust in God, I love my country, and will respect its laws. I will play fair, and strive to win, but win or lose, I will always do my best."

Our first game is against the Ingram All-Stars team. Ingram is located on the banks of the Guadalupe River in the Texas Hill Country, and is known as "Rock Town," because of a 2/3 replica of Stonehenge (like the one in the United Kingdom). Ingram is home to a number of very popular summer camps for kids. We take a brief pause of remembrance for the tragedy that occurred at Camp Mystic and the local area, with over 135 people losing their lives in the pre-dawn hours of July 4, 2025.

The Guadalupe has a long history of flash flooding going back over 100 years. Little did we know it at the time, in the summer of 2024, but these would be some of the last Little League All-Star games played on these fields, before they were destroyed in the flooding. The community has rallied with donations to rebuild the fields, and our prayers continue to be with them as they move forward from this terrible tragedy.

Ingram beat Kerrville 13-3 in the Opening Game of this District Tournament two days earlier, on Monday, June 17th. Gio Garza is on the mound for Ingram. Julian Hurst, "King Julian," as our team came to call him, looks at strike one and then leads us off with a ground ball to the left fielder for a single. Doc Mogford comes to the plate, watches balls one and two, watches strike one, watches ball three, Julian steals second with the count 3-1, and then swings at strike two and swings and misses at strike three. Cooper Hastings comes to the plate, fouls one off, watches ball one, and then hits a ground ball single to the third baseman. Julian advances to third on the throw. Kole Newson, son of the General Manager Justin Newson, bats fourth. He watches ball one, swings at a strike, lets ball two go by, and then swings at strike two. It's a passed ball and Julian scores for Boerne's first run of the game, while Cooper advances to second.

Kole hits a grounder, the catcher pops up to grab it, but Cooper is already at third by the time he makes the throw. Caden Guffy comes up with two out. He sends a rocket out to left field, a double, and Cooper scores to put Boerne up 2 runs! Gray Collins, son of our first base coach Jonathan Collins, comes up, looks at strike one, and then lines out the center fielder to end the Top of the 1st. A 19-pitch inning for Garza and a great start for Boerne!

Cooper Hastings starts things on the mound for Boerne, Ryan H is the leadoff for Ingram, and he strikes out on three pitches. Cooper is a stocky 12-year-old that throws hard, and it's quite intimidating to see this big kid throwing a missile at you that comes in about 70 mph from 46 feet. Jessen Bruinsma watches strike one, swings at strike two, watches ball one, and then watches strike three. Ruger Hensley comes to the plate, watches strike one, watches balls one and two, fouls off strike two, watches ball three, fouls off three pitches in a row, and ultimately draws a walk on ball four. Patrick Carpenter watches strike one, fouls off strike two, ball one, and then a swing and miss strike three to end the 1st inning! A 20-pitch inning for Cooper and we won the first inning!

Aiden Munoz, son of our Pitching Coach Bert Munoz, is the first to bat for Boerne, he watches four straight balls and takes his base. Jett Matthews watches ball one and then pops out to the second baseman. Kaleb Christ comes to the plate, watches ball one, fouls off the next pitch, and then watches balls 2-4, so he takes his base. Now we've got runners on 1st and 2nd. Ben Burkhart comes to the plate, watches strike one, and then rips a double to the center fielder, scoring Aiden and sending Kaleb to 3rd base! Dylan Burke comes to the plate and continues the aggressive plate performance by watching balls 1-3, swinging at strike one, fouling one off, and then smoking another line drive to the center fielder, scoring both Kaleb and Ben!

Gage Steubing, batting 12 in the lineup for Boerne comes to the plate, watches balls one and two, swings at strike one, allows Dylan to steal 3rd, watches ball three, swings at strike two, and then draws the walk with ball four. Julian returns to the box for the second trip through the lineup, watches ball one, and then hits a sacrifice fly to the right fielder. Dylan scores and Gage advances to 2nd. Doc grounds out to the second baseman to end the top of the 2nd inning, and Boerne has taken a 6-0 lead! A 28-pitch inning for Garza, good job boys!!

Cooper returns to the mound and Gunner Tatsch leads off, looking at strikes one and two, and strikes out swinging at the 3rd pitch. Eli Rodriguez watches two balls go by, fouls one off, swings and misses at strike two, fouls another one off, and then pops out to Julian at first base. Gio Garza, the pitcher, comes in and looks at strike one, swings at strike two, watches balls one and two, and then goes down swinging for strike three. A 14-pitch inning for Cooper and he is in total control.

Top of the 3rd inning and Cooper is leading off. Cooper sends his first pitch out to right field on a line drive for a single! Kole is back in the box, watches ball one, lets Cooper steal second, then fouls off the next pitch, then watches ball two. The fourth pitch comes inside so Kole turns his shoulder and takes the hit, and he takes his base. Caden comes to the plate and sends a rocket over the left field wall for Boerne's first of many home runs, scoring 3! Gray comes in right behind him and sends another rocket over the center field fence for back-to-back home runs!!

Ingram swaps out their pitcher and brings Eli Rodriguez in. Aiden continues our aggressive batting and singles on a ground ball to shortstop. Jett comes in, looks at strike one, Aiden steals second, and then Jett hits his own "Jett rocket" over the left field wall for Boerne's third homerun of the first game and scores 2! Kaleb comes in, watches ball one, and then singles on a ground ball to the third baseman. Ben watches ball one, Kaleb steals second, swings at strike one, watches ball 2, swings at strike 2, and then hits a fly ball to the center fielder that results in a double play, getting Kaleb out at second because he had started to go to third thinking it was a hit.

Dylan swings at strike one, fouls one off, watches ball one, and then singles on a grounder to the center fielder. Gage rips the first pitch on a line drive to the center fielder for a single and advances Dylan to second. We always tell the boys, if we can get into our batting lineup for a 3rd time, we have an excellent opportunity to win the game. That is our offensive goal. With six innings, that is 18 outs that the other team has to get, so that means worse-case-scenario that everyone bats once, but then only the top half of your lineup bats a second time, so that means you got at least 7 hits/walks in order to get your leadoff hitter to the batter's box for a third trip. Julian's back at the plate, swings at strike one, watches balls one and two, and then rips his own home run over the center field wall, scoring three more runs! Doc comes to the plate, watches ball one, fouls off strike one, and then swings and misses at the next two to finally end the inning for Ingram. Boerne has taken a commanding 15-0 lead after the top of the 3rd inning and a 29-pitch inning for Ingram.

Boerne swaps Cooper out for Gray to pitch, and Gray, who is 5'5", 115, and can touch 65 mph with his fastball, comes in to pitch. Vasquez swings at strike one, watches ball one, swings at strike 2, and watches strike 3. Alejandro Gonzalez swings at strike one, watches balls 1 and 2, fouls one off, and then also watches strike 3. Jase Adams watches balls one and two, looks at strike one, swings at strike two, and then he watches strike 3.

A really important point about baseball in general, and you'll see that the Boerne team can continue to improve in this area, is that you see a wide difference in player IQ depending on how long they have been playing the game. Great players are conditioned over time to protect on a two-strike count, and will add a buffer to their mental strike zone and will swing at anything that looks like it's going to come inside that zone. A 14-pitch inning for Gray, way to go!!!

Little League rules say that if one team is up by 10 runs after 4 innings, or up by 15 runs after 3 innings, the game ends. Boerne's first All-Star game concludes in grand fashion, and now the parents can let out their breath...Whew, we won the first one, thank God. The parents are literally shaking we are so nervous for our kids. However, Boerne wins game 1 with 15 runs on 14 hits, and 4 homeruns, and that means we get to come back two days later, on Friday night for game 2! Cooper's 71% strike percentage pitching was key for his 34 pitches, and he'll be ready in case he's needed again in the next few days. Gray pitched very well too, throwing 64% strikes. Neither pitcher allowed a hit, and we walked one batter, striking out 8. Gio Garza threw 54% strike percentage for his 54 pitches and Eli Rodriguez threw 70% for his 23 pitches. Ingram only got to bat 10 players, and their remaining three players (Melton Lippman, Kaiden Legg, and Brantley Doege) didn't get an opportunity at the plate. This game sends Ingram to the loser's bracket.

Fredericksburg lost to Medina Valley 10-0 and then Fredericksburg beat Kerrville 17-4, so Ingram and Fredericksburg face off in the semi-final game. Ingram beats Fredericksburg in a nailbiter 9-8. That earns Ingram the right to play in the final elimination bracket game.

Game 2 Medina Valley @ Boerne

Since we played Wednesday night, as soon as we won the game, we had to pack up the kids, get back to our vehicles, and drive about an hour home to Boerne from the field. The kids were starving, so dinner consisted of Whataburger drive-through to eat on the way home since we were going to get back home around 1030p, and knowing that we had to be back here on Friday night.

One of Kaleb's preferences that we have developed over the last three years or so, is to always arrive at the ballpark two hours in advance of our game. That allows him to get into the batting cage, hit a couple buckets of balls (80-100 balls), throw a football to warm up (it was good enough for Nolan Ryan and Phil Mickelson), and then get into regular throwing with the rest of the kids as they generally arrive about an hour early.

Game 2 kicks off at 8pm two days later, the baseball version of Friday Night Lights, and we are playing Medina Valley, a group of kids we know very well, and that Kaleb has played with multiple times in various travel ball tournaments over the last few years. Medina Valley is a farming community just west of San Antonio and has been named the "Apple Capital of Texas." Like many communities in Texas, this town has grown up around Medina Lake and is known for its small-town charm, local friendliness, and warm personality.

Even though we feel confident in our team our heart is back again in our throat as soon as the first pitch is thrown. Medina gets to bat first and so we've got Caden in to pitch. Caden is built similar to Cooper, he's a stocky kid and he's already 5'6", so when you see this tall, stocky kid that also throws almost 70 mph from 46 feet, you figure out real quick how good you really are. Harris Hitzfielder watches ball one, swings at strikes one and two, fouls one off, watches balls two and three, and then strikes out swinging. Drew McDougal looks at strike one, watches ball one, and then looks at both strike two and three. Walker Kohlleppel watches balls one and two, swings at strike one, watches ball three, fouls one off, and then watches strike three. A nice 17-pitch inning and 3 up, 3 down for Caden to start things off!

Julian leads off the bottom of the 1st for Boerne, facing Walker Kohlleppel on the mound for Medina, and pops the first pitch up to Hunter in right field. Cooper swings at strike one and then grounds out to the Drew at shortstop. Kole is batting third today, he watches balls one and two, swings at strike one, watches ball three, and then singles on a hard grounder that gets by TJ at third to get into left field. Caden, perhaps warmed up because he was pitching today, comes in, fouls off the first pitch and hits a screeching rocket homer over the center field wall!! Yes, and Boerne is on the board!

Remember I said that he was a tall, stocky kid? Well, this Boerne team is full of them, and even though the boys are swinging USA bats, several of the kids are still able to clear these Ingram fences that are about 200' from home plate. He scores 2! Gray comes in, fouls off the first pitch, watches ball one, fouls off another, watches balls two and three, and then rips a line drive to Jase in left field for a single! Doc watches balls one and two, and then pops out to Drew at shortstop to end the inning, Boerne 2-0.

TJ Fulks looks at strike one, watches ball one, and then swings and misses at strikes two and three. Hunter Alston swings at strike one, watches strike two, watches ball one, and then swings and misses at strike three. Justus Keller watches ball one, swings and misses at strikes one and two, and then watches strike three. A 12-pitch inning for Caden, let's go!!

Aiden's up in the #7 spot for Boerne, watches balls one and two, watches strike one, and then hits a grounder to Drew at short for the first out of the bottom of the 2nd. Jett swings at strike one and then grounds out Walker on the mound. Dylan takes a swing at the first pitch of his at bat and sends his first home run over the center field wall! Kaleb looks at strike one, swings at strike 2, watches ball 1, fouls off one, and then watches strike three. Boerne's now up 3-0 at the end of the 2nd inning.

Hollis Bartlett watches ball one, looks at strike one, looks at ball two, fouls one off for strike two, and then watches strike three. Jase Marquez watches strike one, watches balls one and two, watches strike two, and watches strike three. Ricky Rodriguez fouls the first one off, swings at strike two, and watches strike three. Caden has a 3 up, 3 down on 14 pitches and we go to the bottom of the 3rd.

Gage leads off for Boerne, watches balls 1, 2, and 3, and then hits a pop fly to Justus at second, and reaches on an error. Ben watches strike one, fouls off the next one, then watches four balls in a row. Julian returns to the box, watches ball one, ball two is a wild pitch allowing Gage and Ben advance, and then Julian rips a double to the Drew at short that ultimately scores two!! Cooper watches balls one and two, fouls the first strike off, and then doubles to Hollis in center field, scoring Julian! We are rolling! 6-0!

Medina Valley changes pitchers and brings Drew McDougal to the mound. Kole watches strike one, watches balls one and two, swings at strike 2, watches ball 3, and then watches strike three for the 1st out. Caden watches ball one, fouls the next one off, looks at strike two, and then grounds out to Hunter, now playing short, since Drew went to the mound. Cooper advances to 3rd on the throw. Gray rips a double to center and scores Cooper! Doc fouls off his first pitch, and then hits his first home run of the tournament over center field, scoring two more! Aiden watches balls one and two, Aiden fouls off strike one, watches ball three, watches ball two, and draws the walk on a 3-2 count.

Medina Valley changes pitchers again and brings in Jase Marquez. Walker was at 48 pitches (54% strike percentage) and so he might be needed in one of the future games. At 50 pitches or less, he can pitch again with 2 days' rest. Jett watches ball one, swings at strike one, watches the wild pitch ball two that lets Aiden advance to 2nd, looks at strike 2, and then flies out to Hollis in center. Boerne has now taken the lead of 9-0 at the bottom of the 3rd.

Caden's still on the mound, throws ball one, gets Ethan Portela to swing at strike one, and then walks him on 3 straight balls. Westin Lewis, #11 batter comes to the plate, hits a grounder but reaches on an error by Gage at 1st and is able to get to 2nd on the same throw. Jagger Dyer, the #12 batter in Medina's lineup, watches the balls 1-3, looks at strike one, and then draws the 5-pitch walk. Bases loaded, no outs for Boerne. Harris Hitzfelder watches ball one, swings at strike one, watches strike 2, watches balls 2 and 3, and then goes down swinging for strike three.

Drew McDougal swings at strike one, watches strike two, watches ball one, and then goes down swinging for strike three. Walker Kohlleppel watches strikes one and two, watches balls one and two, fouls one off, watches ball 3, fouls another one off, and then watches ball 4. And Boerne "walks" in a run...Arrrghh. Excellent plate discipline by the MV team to swing at the third strike but let the balls go by. TJ Fulks watches strike one, watches ball one, watches strike 2, fouls off one, and then swings and misses at strike 3. Medina bloodies Boerne for the 1st time, and now the score is 9-1.

Dylan watches strike one and then gets to 1st on a ground ball single to Harris at short. Kaleb grounds into a fielder's choice to Justus at second base, and Dylan is out going to 2nd, and Kaleb is safe at 1st. Gage watches four straight balls and takes his base. Ben watches balls one and two, and then grounds out to Walker at third base, with both Kaleb and Gage advancing on the throw. Julian returns to the plate, a wild pitch scores Kaleb from 3rd and Gage gets to 3rd. Julian watches ball 2, and then singles on a ground ball to Harris at short, and Gage scores to end the game at the end of the fourth inning, Boerne 11, Medina Valley 1 (10 runs after four innings is a run rule). The parent's breath a collective sigh of relief. Even though Boerne maintained great control over the game, that little slip in the fourth was enough to put your heart back in your throat and keep you on edge until that last run scored.

Boerne's pitching doesn't allow Medina Valley any hits, one error and three walks, resulting in one run. Caden throws 58% strike percentage with a total pitch count of 77 and an incredible 12 strike-outs. Boerne collects 10 hits, three walks, and only two strikeouts. Walker pitched 54%, Drew pitched 55%, and Jase pitched 44% for a total of 105 pitches. Boerne got 25 at-bats this game, so we were able to just make it into our lineup for a third time. Medina Valley got to the plate 16 times.

This game sent Medina Valley to the loser's bracket, which means they had to play Ingram. Medina Valley then beats Ingram 9-1 in the elimination bracket final game. That means they earn the right to re-match Boerne in the championship game Sunday evening! Medina Valley played fantastic against both Ingram and

Fredericksburg, batting .537 as a team and accumulating 19 runs on 29 hits, 10 walks, only 8 strike-outs, and four kids took a hit-by-pitch.

Game 3 Boerne @ Medina Valley

The goal with each of these District tournaments is to complete them in 5-6 days, which builds in a small buffer for weather delays/rain-outs, so the first two games kicked off on Monday, June 17th and this championship game is scheduled for Sunday, June 23rd at 7:00pm unless a second game is needed, which is scheduled for the following evening on Monday at 8pm.

This is where it gets really interesting from a baseball pitching strategy perspective. Medina Valley is now playing in their 4th game in 6 days, as they played in the opening round (Boerne had a bye), they beat Fredericksburg, but then lost to Boerne in Round 2, which sent them to the loser's bracket, and then they had to win that game to earn the right to re-match Boerne in this Championship game. Medina Valley played us Friday night and lost, had to play the next day Saturday against Ingram, which they won, and now they are playing again on Sunday night.

Each game, each team is going to have to throw probably 65-100 pitches. Based on every we have learned about youth pitcher health, including Eric Cressey's podcasts, Patrick Jones' podcasts, and other sources, kids under 15 should be throwing no more than 100 pitches per week in games, and as we mentioned earlier, LL restricts it to 85 pitches per day. That means that Medina Valley has completely exhausted the arms of at least 3 of their kids, but if their top kid threw in Game 1, then he has recovered enough to pitch in this do-or-die game as he has had 5 days' rest. The team has thrown a total of 276 pitches in the three prior games, with Hunter throwing 94, Walker throwing 48, Drew throwing 45, Jase throwing 29, and TJ, Harris, and Hollis throwing 20 each.

Many Little League teams have one or two ace pitchers, a 12-year-old that throws 70+ mph, can throw strikes consistently (we define consistent as throwing 60% strike percentage or better), and has 1-2 off-speed pitches, a curveball and/or a change-up. That combination makes them really dangerous (like, Maverick and Goose dangerous, so in a good way 😊). Then they have 2-3 more kids that "can pitch" but do not possess all three of those qualities together. They won't throw as hard, they will not be as consistent, and they might not have a good secondary pitch.

Every so often you'll find a kid, like Luis Yepez from Venezuela, Antonio Guerrero from Mexico, or Lin Chin-Tse from Taiwan that throws 78-82 mph, and that puts a lot of pressure on a team, because few kids at 12 years old are prepared to step into the box and actually battle against that pitcher. More importantly than having one great pitcher though, would be to have 4-7 really good pitchers, with strike percentages consistently above 60%. However, as Donald Rumsfeld famously quoted, "you go to war with the army you have, not the army you want or wish to have at a later time."

To give you an insider's viewpoint and provide some additional context, our Spring season Little League team went 8-6 against our opponents. We had 10 players on the team, and one of the rules for the Spring season is that you aren't supposed to "stack" the teams. Our 12 All-Star kids got separated onto four different teams, so there were roughly three "really good" players per team.

For the 14-game season, Kole Newson batted .618, Kaleb Christ batted .595, and Aiden Munoz batted .526. We had one other kid bat .320, one bat .258, four kids bat between .100 and .200, and three kids bat under .100. This is absolutely to be expected. Little

League gets kids at all different skill levels and all the kids are wanting to improve. Kole pitched 23 innings, Aiden pitched 14, and Kaleb pitched 9, for a total of 46 innings pitched, or 68% of all the 72 innings pitched during the spring season. Kaleb's strike percentage was 68%, Kole's strike percentage was 66%, and Aiden's strike percentage was 53%. When you look at these three kids, they walked 22 kids out of 74 total walks, so 30% of the total walks for the team. For strikeouts, these three kids struck out 55 of the 122 strikeouts, or 45% of the total.

Strike percentage is a key metric for youth pitchers, defined as how many strikes you throw divided by the number of total pitches. Nolan Ryan's lifetime strike percentage was 65%. You can argue that in the MLB pitchers are going to throw "competitive balls" a lot to try to induce swings and misses or swings and soft contact. With kids, that is not the right focus. You want kids to throw strikes. If they are accurate enough to throw on the corners, then that's great.

When you talk to high school coaches, they want kids that can throw strikes. Walks are what kills a team. We set a goal of Kaleb throwing 70% strikes per game. Many coaches will change pitchers once a kid walks 3-4 batters to try to keep control of the game and still figure out a way to win. With Kaleb, we have set a higher standard than that, we set a goal to only walk one batter (or preferably less) for the entire game. We don't ever pitch around any kid, because if they beat us by barreling up the baseball and hit a home run, then we'll tip our cap to them, but we are going to make them beat us, we are not going to give them a free base. If you look at our Williamsport team and you see that even Kaleb, our 11-year-old batted .595 and threw 68% strike percentage during the regular season, you start to understand how good, and deep, our pitching and hitting lineup really was.

Let's get back to this championship game. Medina Valley is the home team, so Boerne bats first. Julian faces off against Hunter Alston, fouls off the first three pitches, watches ball one, and then looks at strike 3. Tension in the stands goes up a bit because we don't expect our lead-off hitter to strike out. Gray swings at strike one, and then hits a fly ball to Ricky in right field, who dropped the catch, and so Gray reaches second base on the error. Cooper watches the first two balls, fouls the next one off, and then rips a double to Jase in left field, scoring Gray. The parents collectively exhale a little, as now Boerne takes a 1-0 lead in the top of the 1st inning. Caden watches swings at strike one, watches ball one, and then hits a ground ball to Harris at third base, which results in a double play to end the inning. At least we scored one run, but now our defense needs to step up and get three quick outs so we can go bat again.

King Julian takes the mound, throws the first two pitches for balls, regroups and fires a hard fastball for a strike that Harris Hitzfielder watches go by, fouls off strike two, watches ball three, fouls the next one off, and then Julian gets him swinging and missing at strike 3. Whew...Leadoff batter strike out, always a great way to start an inning. Drew McDougal comes to the plate, watches balls one and two, watches strike one and two, watches ball three, and swings and misses at strike 3. Ok, exhale...first two batters down. Great job Julian, keep it up kiddo! Walker Kohlleppel watches strike one, watches balls one and two, swings at strike two, and then swings at strike three, our catcher drops it, but is able to grab it and still get Walker out at first. Okay great, first inning down, got through the Top 3 in their lineup and we won the inning.

We always tell the kids that their goal is to "win every inning." That way they focus on the immediate things they can try to do correctly and not worry about the bigger picture. Now it's time to extend our lead. Kole leads us off, swings at strike one, fouls off strike two, and then swings and misses at strike three. Crap...now they have done it to us too. This is a dogfight.

Doc comes to the plate, watches ball one, fouls off strike one, and then flies out to the Hollis in center field. Dylan watches the first three pitches for balls, watches strike one, and then singles on a fly ball to Jase in left. Jett comes to the plate, watches ball one, and then singles on a ground ball to Jase in left and Dylan advances to second. Aiden swings at the first pitch and smashes a fly ball to TJ in right for a triple! Dylan and Jett both score!! A heck of a two-out rally! Whew...ok, two more runs home, so now it's 3-0. Gage comes to the plate swings at strikes one and two, fouls off the next one, and goes down swinging at strike three. Ok, let's go play defense.

TJ Fulks comes to the plate to lead off, fouls off the first pitch, watches strike two, watches ball one, and watches strike three. This is such an important point, and one that takes getting kids to a higher level of baseball IQ before you see them consistently make the right decisions in the moment. Baseball is an incredibly dynamic game, meaning the variables and circumstances change very quickly, and only those who have truly mastered what all those variables mean, what impact they can have for their team, and have practiced to an expert-level, have a better-than-average chance of doing the right thing in the moment. For this kid, this game is do-or-die. There is no tomorrow if you don't win this game. If you have two strikes, your objective should be to swing at anything close to a strike, foul it off at least, but do not let the defense get you out simply by throwing a strike and you watching it.

Hunter Alston comes to the plate and looks at ball one, looks at strike one, swings at strike two, swings at strike three but is able to get to first because of a passed ball, then he gets to second on an error by our first baseman, Kole. Justus Keller swings at strike one, watches ball one, swings at strike two, fouls the next one, and then pops up the next pitch for a foul tip out. Hollis Bartlett comes to the plate, and the first pitch is a ball way outside, and so Hunter advances to third. Hollis watches ball two, swings at strike one, fouls off the next one, and then watches two more balls to draw his walk and get on first. 2 outs and runners on the corners, our hearts are beating like drums! Come on boys, let's get that final out and keep our lead! Jase Marquez comes to the plate, watches ball one, looks at strike one, swings at strike two, and goes down swinging for strike three and the third out of the inning. Whew, we can take a breath. We dodged a bullet, and didn't allow them to score.

Top of the 3rd inning and Kaleb is the leadoff batter. He watches ball one and two from Alston, and then hits a hard grounder to Drew at shortstop and is able to reach first. Ben watches ball one, watches strike one, watches ball two, and then hits a line drive to Jase in left, a double and getting Kaleb to third! Julian singles on a hard grounder to Drew at short, scoring Kaleb and advancing Ben to third.

That play shows great baseball IQ. Kaleb is the runner on third, no outs, all we need to do is put the bat on the ball to score the run, and Julian executes his job to perfection with his grounder. The very first pitch is close enough that he is swinging hard and trying to barrel up the baseball. The fact that he reached 1st instead of being thrown out is simply a bonus, but when we talk about capitalizing on the little mistakes, this is an excellent example. Medina Valley should have gotten at least one out on that play, but now we've scored a run and have another base runner. Gray comes in to bat and hits a double to Hollis in center field, scores Ben, and Julian gets to third. Again, great baseball IQ executed in the moment. Cooper as well swings at the first pitch and hits a single to Hollis again, scoring Julian and Gray! Caden comes to the plate, watches ball one, and then rips a home run over the left field wall for a two-run bomb! The top four guys in the lineup executing to precision exactly what you want MLB players to do! This is incredibly fun to watch play out in front of us! Well done boys!! Kole watches ball one, watches strike one, and then flies out to TJ in right field. Doc fouls off the first pitch, swings at strike two, watches the next two pitches for balls, fouls off the next one, watches ball three and gets hit by ball four to get on base.

We go back to baseball IQ. At the plate, it's simple. We want to let balls go by and swing at strikes. These Little League umpires are really good, and they are not calling anything outside the plate. The strike zone for Little League is "armpits to the top of the knees," but if it's off the plate, it's a ball. That lets the really good hitters be selective about what pitches they will swing at, because they have that certainty. We have some umpires in other tournaments where anything between the two white lines (6" off the plate on both sides) is a strike, and sometimes curveballs that end up in the other batter's box get called as strikes too. However, for this District to LLWS tournament, the umpires are awesome and consistent!

Anytime we swing at a ball, we made a mistake and we give a "free strike" to the pitcher. When we know that their pitchers are going to have to throw 65-100 pitches in a game, and they are always going to start off with their best pitcher available, our goal is to let him rack up his pitch count as quickly as possible. If we can force him to throw 30 pitches in the first inning, and another 30 pitches in the second inning, his arm is wearing down coming back in for a third inning, or the coach may even decide that he needs to protect that arm for a future game. Doc just created a 7-pitch at bat. Technically, a quality at-bat (QAB) is 6 pitches or more. Anytime a batter can force a pitcher to throw him that many pitches means that you are probably seeing every pitch he has available, you are wearing him down physically, and you are also frustrating him which makes him more prone to error.

Dylan comes to bat and swings at strike one, watches ball two, watches strike two, and then hits a hard grounder single to Drew at shortstop, which advances Doc to second base. Jett watches strike one and two, watches balls one and two, and then hits a hard grounder to Jase in left field for a double, scoring Doc and advancing Dylan to third! Boerne 10-0! We are starting to breathe a little easier, but we know we've got 3 more innings that we've got to maintain control here, so there is a little breathing room, but we can't get complacent. Aiden watches ball one and two, fouls off the next strike, and then hits a line drive to Drew in right field for a double! He scores Dylan and Jett! Gage swings at the first pitch and sends a hard grounder to the TJ at third, getting a single, and sending Aiden to third. Kaleb watches ball one, and Gage steals second, to put both runners in scoring position. Kaleb swings at the next pitch and fouls it off. He swings at the next pitch and hits a line drive to Jase in left, scoring Aiden!

Boerne 13-0, and we are all praying to get to 15 runs so we can run rule them after the third inning and end this game right there! Ben fouls off the first two strikes, watches balls one, two, and three go by, and then hits a ground ball to the Harris at shortstop for a fielder's choice, so the defense gets Kaleb out going to 3rd. Gage scores and Ben gets to first. 14-0! Come on boys, get at least one more!! Julian returns to the plate with two outs, watches balls one and two, fouls off the next pitch, and then hits a line out to Hollis in center...CRAP!!! Now we have to play at least four innings, and Medina Valley gets at least two more at bats. Their #9,10, and 11 guys are on deck, so that means the top of their lineup will get at least one more bat!!!

Julian's focus shifts a bit. Boerne has a 14-0 lead. The only thing that kills us at this point are to walk kids, so now our goal is to throw 100% strikes, if they can hit it, that's fine, but let's let our defense work. It's unlikely they would get 10+ runs before they rack up three outs, so let's just play the odds. Ricky Rodriguez, their #9 batter comes to the plate. He's swinging aggressively, fouls off strikes one and two, watches the next two pitches for balls, fouls off a third strike, and then grounds out to second. Julian's pitch count is at 46 pitches, and we have a commanding lead, so we are going to let one of our other pitchers close this game out. Doc comes into pitch. He quickly fires strike one at Ethan Portela, who swings and misses. Doc shows him no mercy, firing two more hard strikes, and Portela swings and misses at both. Two down. Westin Lewis watches ball one, watches strike one, swings at strike two, and watches strike three. We end the third with three up, three down! On to the fourth, and hopefully final inning of this game!

Hollis Bartlett comes in to pitch as Hunter Alston had gotten to 86 pitches. Gray watches ball one, and then rips a line drive to Drew, now in center for a double. Cooper at the plate, watches balls one, two, and three, and then hits a hard ground ball to the Jase in left field for a single, advancing Gray to third! Caden fouls the first pitch off, swings and misses at strike two, watches ball one, fouls the next one off, and watches strike three. Kole watches balls one and two, and then hits a line drive single to Drew in center, scoring Gray and getting Cooper to second. Doc comes in and watches balls one and two, Cooper steals third, Kole steals second, and Boerne keeps the pressure on! Doc watches balls three and four, and draws the walk.

Bases loaded and Dylan comes to the box. First pitch line drive single to Jase in left field scores Cooper and everyone advances! Jett swings at strike one and hits a line drive to Drew in center fielder, where they get the ball and throw it into second in time to get Dylan out. Kole scores and Doc advances to third. Aiden flies out to Drew in center fielder to end the top of the fourth 17-0. Here we are, three outs away, in control, but we've got to finish this off to advance to the Section Tournament!

Jagger Dyer, their #12 batter watches ball one, watches strike one, and then lays down a bunt, which Doc pounces on from the mound and gets him out at first. Now back to the top of their lineup. Harris Hitzfelder watches ball one, fouls the next one off, watches ball two, swings at strike two, and watches strike three. One out away!! Drew McDougal, watches balls one and two, swings at strike one, and then watches balls three and four to get on base. Shoot! We had a chance to close the game out right there, but we allowed them to crack open the door. No worries, let's get this next batter! Walker Kohlleppel watches strike one, watches ball, one, two, three, and four. Are you kidding me? We are pulling our hair out, we've got two outs and we just walked two batters in a row! That's okay, let's focus on this next batter. TJ Fulks watches ball one, both runners steal, and so now we've got runners at 3rd and 2nd with two outs. TJ watches strike one, watches ball two, fouls off strike two, and then watches strike three. Boerne has done it!! They've won District and will be advancing to the Section Tournament!

17-0 final score, Boerne allowed no hits, walked three batters and had 11 strike-outs. Boerne had 19 hits, drew 2 walks, and only had 4 strikeouts. When you look at the game in the rearview, or just from the statistics, you'd say, wow, what a boring game. Trust me, with this game being the deciding factor between going to Section or having to play a second elimination game, this game was a rollercoaster of emotion the entire two hours! Medina threw 105 pitches in that game to our 33 total batters, with Harris throwing 62% strike percentage on his 85 pitches and Hollis throwing 55% for his 20 pitches. Julian threw 61% strikes for his 46 pitches and Doc threw 53% for his 30 pitches, and we faced a total of 16 batters.

The fans erupt, the kids get to pose with the District Champion banner and the scoreboard in the background, and it means that Boerne gets to return to Ingram the following weekend for the Section Tournament! That picture appears in the Boerne Star, the local newspaper, the next day on June 29th and the boys have their first taste of fame!

Quick Re-cap: 3 games and 3 wins, Ingram 15-0, and two games against Medina Valley, winning 11-1, and 17-0. We allowed one run in 3 games, while scoring 43 runs. Oh, and by the way, we threw three no-hitter games. Our pitching roster for those games was Cooper, Gray, Caden, Julian, and Doc. We had eight home runs, with Caden getting three of them, and one each for Julian, Gray, Dylan, Doc, and Jett. Since Medina Valley had already lost one time to Boerne, this was their second loss, and so they were eliminated, which left Boerne as the only team to not have accumulated two losses. Otherwise, there would have been an "if" game the next evening on Monday at 8pm.

Game 4 Boerne @ Northern Little League (San Angelo

It's another blisteringly hot evening in Ingram, and with the game starting at 6p, it still feels like we are on the red side of the sun. It won't cool off until 830 or so, when the sun finally gets low in the sky... And by cooling off, we mean dropping down to 98 or so!

Many folks will tell you that District "feels" much harder than the Section event. It's the first few games where the kids are truly tested, and so there is an incredible anxiety to it all. We celebrated each win, but we tempered it in talking with the boys that we have to remain laser-focused, because if we let any game momentum start to go against us, that can be a death blow. So you are "living on the edge" throughout this entire series.

However, we arrive at Section now with these three wins behind us, and a consistent theme of each of our 12 boys executing in their respective moments. However, we have really not been "tested" defensively yet to this point, and on one of the defensive opportunities we had, we committed an error. Now, we know these kids are 12 and so they will absolutely make errors, and we work very hard in practice to minimize those, and so we have some anxiety relating to seeing how the boys will respond against a team when they start to put the bat on the ball.

The Texas West Section 3 tournament has five teams in it as well, Northern LL from San Angelo, McAllister Park LL from San Antonio, Uvalde LL, Eagle Pass LL, and Boerne. This tournament starts on Friday, June 28th and it intended to finish by either Tuesday, July 2nd or Wednesday, July 3rd, if that second elimination game is necessary.

San Angelo is a really neat town in West Texas, in that it's the largest town without an interstate, and its home to about 120,000 people. Back in the 1900's, it was the "Wool Capital of the World," as it was a major stop on cattle drives in the American West. Angelo State University is now affiliated with Texas Tech University in Lubbock, and so there is a significant investment in education in the area. There is a strategic blend of history, modernization, all wrapped up with small-town charm and a "we know all our neighbors" feeling.

Boerne is the away team to start the night, so Austin Epperson in at pitcher for Northern, and Julian leads us off. He grounds out to the shortstop Aiden for the first out of the game. Gray watches ball one, swings at strike one, watches strike two, and hits a line drive single to left. Cooper fouls the first pitch off, watches ball one, swings at strike two, and flies out to the center fielder, with Gray remaining at first. Caden watches balls one and two, and then hits a ground ball to short where they quickly flip it to second base, getting Gray out to end the inning. They just got us in a 12-pitch inning and we fail to score with our leadoff hitters, so now we've got to go play defense. Our blood pressure shoots up again. Let's go boys!

Cooper starts us off on the mound, throws a first pitch ball to Brooks Belcher, who swings at the second pitch and flies out to right field. One up, one down. Let's go, boys! Colt Barker swings at strike one, and hits a grounder back to Cooper who fields it and gets him out at first. Ok, good, two up, two down, just like we drew it up. Leo Speciale watches strike one, fouls the next pitch off, and goes down swinging for strike three! A fantastic 7-pitch first inning for Cooper! All right, let's go to the top of the second and get some hits!

Kole leads us off, watches ball one, fouls the next one off, and then hits a ground ball to third base for a single. Doc watches ball one, and then hits a grounder to short and is out at first. Kole advances to third on the throw. Aiden fouls the first pitch off, watches balls one and two, swings at strike two, watches ball three, and then hits a line drive single to the right fielder, scoring Kole! Ok, we are on the board, 1-0!! Dylan watches balls one, two, and the third is a wild pitch, so Aiden steals second. Dylan watches ball four and draws the walk. Jett looks at strike one, looks at strike two, fouls the next one off, and swings and misses at strike three for our first out. Kaleb watches ball one, Aiden steals third, and Dylan steals second. Kaleb hits a grounder back to the pitcher, who gets the out at first to end the top of the 2nd inning.

Cooper starts Jose Gonzalez off with ball one, and then hits him with his second pitch. Colson Koehn comes into the box, watches ball one, swings at strike one, watches balls two and three, watches strike two, and swings and misses at strike three. Maddox Carr watches strike one, watches strike two, and swings and misses at strike three. Austin Epperson, the pitcher, watches strike one, swings at strike two, and swings and misses at strike three to end the second and not allow any runs. A 14-pitch inning for Cooper, and he is looking really good tonight! That is such an important thing for kids, to be able to quickly shake-off (or flush, whatever word you want to use) a bad outcome like the hit-by-pitch there, re-focus, and come back full of confidence and do your job! Well done Coop!

Gage leads off for Boerne, watches four balls a row and draws the walk. Ben watches ball one sail by, Gage steals second on that wild pitch, Ben watches ball two, and then hits a single to short, and Gage is able to get to third. Julian comes to the box for the second time through our lineup and he watches ball one fly by, letting Ben get to second on the wild pitch. Julian watches balls two thru four and he walks. Gray watches balls one, two, and three, watches strike one, and then draws the walk with ball four, walking in Gage for our second run.

Cooper swings at strike one, watches balls one and two, swings at strike two, and then hits a hard ground ball to the right fielder, scoring both Ben and Julian, while Gray gets to third. Caden watches a wild first pitch, while Cooper gets to second. Caden watches strike one, watches strike two, fouls the next one off, and goes down swinging for strike three. Kole watches ball one, watches strike one, and then hits a hard ground ball to the left fielder, scoring both Gray and Cooper!

It's now 6-0, and Northern changes pitchers to try to change the momentum of the game. Austin has already thrown 62 pitches, and we are not even through the 3rd inning. Colt Barker comes into pitch for Northern. Doc singles on the first pitch by hitting a hard grounder to center field, and moves Kole to second. Aiden watches a first wild pitch, letting Kole and Doc both move up a base. Aiden watches ball two, and then hits a hard ground ball to third, who can't come up with it, so he reaches on an error. Kole scores and Doc remains at second. Dylan watches strike one, watches ball one, swings at strike two, and swings at strike three.

Jett watches ball one, fouls off the next two, and then hits a fly ball to right field for a single. Doc scores and Aiden gets to third. Kaleb swings at strike one, Jett steals second, and then Aiden steals home. Kaleb fouls the next one off, and then rips a fly ball to right field for a double, scoring Jett! Boerne is now up 10-0! Gage watches balls one and two, ball three is a wild pitch and Kaleb advances to third. Gage watches strike one, and then watches ball four to draw the walk. Gage steals second. Ben watches ball one, ball two, watches strike one, fouls off strike two, and then smokes a fly ball to center field for a double, scoring Kaleb and Gage! Julian watches strike one, watches ball one, and grounds out to the shortstop, ending the top of the 3rd inning with Boerne having a commanding lead of 12-0!

Camden Uriste comes into bat for Northern, fouls off the first pitch, swings at strike two, and swings and misses at strike three. Aiden Wiens swings and misses at three straight strikes for out #2. Estaban Gonzalez watches ball one, and then hits a ground ball to Aiden at second, for an out at first base. Cooper continues his mound domination with an 8-pitch inning to end the 3rd!

Gray leads it off with a fly ball to left field for a double! Caden swings at strike one, watches ball one, fouls off the next two, watches ball two, fouls off another strike, and then pops out to the first baseman. Kole hits a rocket home run to left for his first home run of the summer, scoring 2! Doc hits a ground ball and reaches first on an error by the first baseman. Aiden swings at strike one, and then rips a line drive to center field for a double! Dylan watches strike one, swings at strike two, fouls off the next three strikes, and refuses to go down. He hits a hard grounder to shortstop who can't field it cleanly, Doc and Aiden both score, and Dylan is able to get to second base.

Jett hits a ground ball single to center field, scoring Dylan. Kaleb watches ball one, swings at strike one, fouls off the next two, watches ball two, and then watches strike three for the final out in the top of the 4th, but Boerne has blown the game open with a 17-0 lead! All we need are three out to finish this game and advance in the brackets!

Kole comes in to close out the game for Boerne even though Cooper only threw 28 pitches in the game, with 22 of them being strikes, so an incredible 79% strike percentage! Adrian Esparza is the #9 batter for Northern, he watches balls one and two, swings at strike one, and then hits a fly ball to Doc in center for the first out. Jaylen Urteaja watches balls one and two, watches strike one, watches ball three, watches strike two, and swings and misses at strike three. Two down, one to go. Isaiah Ojeda, Northern's #13 batter is their last hope to extend the game. Northern decided to have a roster of 13, instead of 12, so everyone has to bat. He watches strike one, swings at strike two, and swings and misses at strike three to end the game!

Northern got 0 hits in that game, 0 walks, and 8 strike-outs. They threw 117 pitches total. Colt Barker pitched very well at 71% strikes and Austin Epperson pitched 48% strikes. Boerne only threw 41 pitches with a combined 73% strike percentage. Cooper threw 79% (Boom!!!) and Kole threw 62% (well done)!!! Boerne had 14 hits, 4 walks, and 4 strike-outs. This is now Boerne's 4th game where we haven't allowed a single hit. This game sends Northern to the loser's bracket, where they have to play against Uvalde, who McAllister beat 15-0. This was also the 4th game where we run-ruled our opponents.

Recall the earlier conversation? We are trying to shut these games down as quickly as possible. It's a shame to some extent, because we mentally commit two hours for each game, plus the two hours of warm-up beforehand. Ending a game in the 3rd inning, or after about one hour of play, leaves us slightly unfulfilled. We feel like we blew through that game so quickly we didn't even get to enjoy it, and now it ended even faster than we planned. Obviously very positive for our team, but still a strange emptiness as well.

Game 5 Eagle Pass @ Boerne

We pack up and leave the Friday night game around 8pm, get home around 930p, and have to be back at Ingram the very next day, Saturday, for game 2 at 7p against Eagle Pass. Eagle Pass is a Texas border town about 130 miles southwest of San Antonio and has a bridge that connects to Piedras Negras, which is in the Mexican state of Coahuila. Every March there is an International Friendship Festival hosted to celebrate the shared culture and relationship of the two towns. Having railroad tracks built in the late 1800's that connected Mexico with Galveston and San Antonio caused Eagle Pass to flourish. It is the fastest route between San Antonio and Mexico, also called "La Puerta de Mexico," which translates to Mexico's Door. Laredo, TX is a larger town south of Eagle Pass that now is responsible for a lot of the tractor-trailer traffic between the two countries.

D'Andre Daniel is on the mound for EP, and Gray leads Boerne off tonight. He watches balls one, two, and three, and then rips the first strike to center field for a single. Julian watches strike one, fouls off the next pitch, watches ball one, fouls off the next pitch, watches balls two and three, and then hits a line drive to center field as well for a single, advancing Gray to third. Cooper watches ball one, and then hits a hard grounder to center field, scoring both Gray and Julian! Caden watches strike one, fouls off the next two strikes, watches ball one, and then hits a hard grounder to second base, who errs and allows him to get to first and Cooper to third.

Kole watches strike one and strike two. Cooper is picked off trying to steal third and Caden steals second. Kole watches balls one and then a wild pitch, which allows Caden to get to third. Kole strikes out swinging. Aiden fouls off the first pitch, then watches balls one and two, watches strike two, and swings and misses at strike three. Boerne scores two in the first inning.

Doc is on the mound and D'Andre is the leadoff batter. He watches ball one, fouls off strike one, watches ball two, watches strike two, watches ball three, and watches strike three. Michael Salinas watches balls one and two, watches strike one, watches strike two, and goes down swinging for strike three. Gustavo Esqueda watches strike one, watches balls one and two, swings and misses at strike two, watches ball three, and swings and misses at strike three to end the 1st inning. Doc gets three punch-outs on only 17 pitches!

Doc swings at the first pitch and hits a ground ball to the second baseman and is able to beat the throw. Dylan watches ball one, and then hits a ground ball to the shortstop for a single and both runners are safe. Ben watches ball one, watches strike one, fouls the next one off, watches ball two, and watches strike three. Eagle Pass pulls D'Andre off the mound with 37 pitches and brings in Joseph Nino. Jett hits a ground ball and reaches on an error by the third baseman and all runners are safe.

Kaleb watches ball one, fouls the next one off, watches ball two, swings and misses at strike two, and rips a line drive right to the third baseman for a lineout. Gage watches ball one, watches strike one, watches a wild pitch ball two, gets out of the way so Doc can score, and the runners move up one base. Gage watches strike two, and watches strike three for the third out, but Boerne gains another run to go up 3-0.

Joseph leads off and pops out to Jett at shortstop. Richard Moreno swings and misses at strike one, watches strike two, watches balls one and two, and then goes down swinging. Luis

Riojas grounds out to Aiden at second base for an out at first. Doc's second inning ends quickly by only racking up 7 pitches!!

Gray watches strike one and then pop flies out to second. Julian watches balls one, two, and three, fouls off the first strike, and then rips a fly ball deep to right field for a triple! Cooper hits a fly ball to left, good for a sacrifice fly and scores Julian! Caden watches the first three pitches for balls, watches strike one, fouls off strike two, and then draws a walk with ball four. Kole watches ball one and then flies out to the right fielder. They get us with a 16-pitch inning but we scored 1!

Damian Guerrero swings at strike one, fouls off strike two, watches balls one and two, and then goes down swinging for strike three. Jakob Garcia watches balls one and two, swings and misses at strike one, watches strike two, and then watches balls three and four to draw a walk. Omar Rodriguez swings at strike one, watches strike two, and then watches strike three for the second out of the inning. Asael Kancheff watches ball one, watches strike one, watches ball two, and then we catch Jakob stealing second, with Aiden tagging him out.

Aiden leads off the top of the 4th, watches ball one, watches strike one, and watches balls 2, 3, and 4 to draw the walk and get our lead off runner on first. Doc watches ball one, and then turns and gets paled by ball two for a hit by pitch. Dylan watches balls one, two, and three, and then hits a line drive to center field for a single, loading the bases. Ben watches strike one, fouls off strike two, watches ball one, fouls off another one, watches ball two, fouls off a 3rd pitch, and watches ball three and four to walk in a run. Jett watches strike one, watches balls one and two, fouls off the next two, and then hits a ground ball to the shortstop, who gets Dylan out going to 3rd. Doc scores and then other runners are safe. Kaleb watches a wild pitch for ball one that allows Ben to get to third and Jett to get to second, swings and misses at strike one, swings and misses at strike two, watches ball two, fouls off a strike, watches ball three, and hits a fly ball to right field for a sacrifice fly, scoring Ben and advancing Jett to third. Gage fouls off the first pitch, swings and misses at an outside pitch that gets by the catcher, and allows Jett to score, and then watches strike three to end the inning, Boerne up 8-0.

Asael Kancheff returns to the plate since Jakob's stealing was the third out, and he watches strike one, swings and misses at strike two, watches ball one, and watches strike three. Leonardo Saucedo, Jr. fouls off the first pitch for a strike, swings and misses at strike two, and watches strike three. Robert Daniel III fouls off the first pitch, watches balls one, two, and three, watches strike two, and then draws ball four for the walk. Doc is now at 54 pitches, so Boerne brings Gray in to pitch. Jeremiah Pargas swings at strike one, watches strike two, watches balls one and two, and then hits a ground ball to Aiden at second base for an out at first.

Gray watches the first three pitches from Joseph for balls, fouls off the first strike, and then watches ball four to get our leadoff runner on first. Julian fouls off the first pitch, fouls off the second pitch, watches ball one, fouls off a third pitch, watches balls two and three, and then rips a fly ball over the center field wall for another Boerne homerun, scoring 2 more! Cooper watches balls one and two, fouls off the first strike, watches ball three, watches strike two, and then hits a line drive to the right fielder for a single.

EP pulls Joseph with 79 pitches and brings in Richard Moreno to try to corral this Boerne offense. Caden watches ball one, and then hits a line drive single to right field. Kole watches ball one and then hits a line drive single to center field, scoring Cooper and moving Caden to third. Aiden watches ball one and two, Kole steals second, Aiden fouls off strike one, swings and misses at strike two, and then hits a ground ball to third who gets him out at first. Kole advances to third on the throw. Doc watches ball one and then hits a fly ball to center for a single. Dylan watches strike one, watches ball one, swings at strike two, watches balls two and three, and is then hit by pitch.

EP pulls Richard with only 17 pitches, and brings in Robert Daniel III to finish the game. Ben watches ball one, swings at strike one and two, and then rips a line drive to right field for a single, scoring Doc and Dylan advances to third. Jett hits a fly ball to right field for a single, scoring Dylan and getting Ben to second. Kaleb hits a fly ball to the center fielder, who drops it, but they then throw Ben out trying to score at home, and Jett gets to third. Gage pops out to the third baseman to end the inning, but Boerne is now up 15-0 at the middle of the 5th inning. This is the longest baseball game that Boerne has played yet, as all the games in District ended at or before the end of the 4th inning.

D'Andre watches ball one, fouls off strike one, watches ball two, swings at strike two, fouls off the next three in a row, and then watches balls three and four, drawing a walk and getting on base. Michael watches ball one, fouls off strike one, swings at strike two, and then goes down swinging for strike three. Gustavo watches a first pitch ball get past the catcher, and Derrick advances to second. Gustavo fouls off the next pitch, watches ball two, and then pops out to Aiden at second for a second out. Joseph swings at strike one, watches balls one and two, fouls off strike two, watches ball three, fouls off another strike, and then draws the walk. D'Andre steals third, so we've now got runners on the corners with two outs. With two outs, Richard hits a fly ball over center field wall to score three runs for Eagle Pass! Luis, their #6 batter comes to the plate to try to extend the game, watches strike one, watches ball one, fouls off strike two, and swings and misses strike three!

Boerne continues their dominating run with a win over Eagle Pass of 15-3! This is the fifth game now that we have run-ruled our opponents. Eagle Pass threw 140 pitches (54% strikes combined) in that game, and had to face our entire lineup three full times, 36 at-bats. That puts them at a real disadvantage, being down 1.5 pitchers. Joseph Nino at 79 pitches (51%) is done for the next few days. D'Andre Daniel threw 37 (57%) so they are going to want to use him again, Richard Moreno only threw 17 (47%), so he can go again, and Robert Daniel III only threw 7 (86%). They have to come back Sunday and play at 5p, and if they win, play again Monday at 7p, to then get to the championship game on Tuesday. They are looking at having to use at least two of those guys, if they could go complete games, which is unlikely, and then needing both D'Andre and another closer to play on Tuesday, if they can win their way all the way back.

Eagle Pass had 1 hit in that game, drew 4 walks, and had 10 strike-outs. Finally after 4 games, Boerne allows 1 hit in the 5th game. That is an incredible accomplishment for our pitchers! Boerne had 14 hits in that game, drew 4 walks, and had 5 strike-outs. This sends Eagle pass to the loser's bracket. Northern beats Uvalde 15-6, so that earns them the right to play Eagle Pass, and they win that game 5-2.

Game 6 Boerne @ McAllister Park

The way the brackets worked out for the Section Tournament is that we played Friday night, Saturday night, and because we won, we get to play again on Sunday at 7pm, so three nights in a row we are back in Ingram. This is now the semi-finals game against an always competitive McAllister Park (MP) program. McAllister Park encompasses Northern San Antonio, so they have quite a pool of kids to pull from.

McAllister clenched invitations to Williamsport back in 2009, 2012, and 2016. They were state champions in 2013, 2014, 2015, 2017, 2018, 2021, and 2022. This program has a long history of excellence. With the first five games ending by run-rule, this is shaping up to be Boerne's first "real test." With McAllister Park having over 2,000 kids, technically they now have two charters, which means they have two difference clubs, so they have an American club and National club.

This is how we talked about it with the kids as well. We wanted them to be very focused and mentally prepared for an incredibly tough game. We believe we have a very strong team, however, the vast majority of these MP kids were initially selected for All-Stars at 10 years old and have been working diligently the last two years to get to this 12U All-Star season, so they can make another run at Williamsport.

Maverick Kidd starts off on the mound for MP and Gray leads off for Boerne. Gray watches strike one, watches balls one and two, and hits a fly ball that is dropped by the right fielder to reach first on an error. Julian swings at strike one, and then hits a ground ball to the second baseman, who gets Gray out at second. Cooper watches strike one, and then hits a fly ball to right field for a single. Julian advances to second. Caden watches strike one, fouls off strike two, and then hits a grounder to shortstop, who flips it to his second baseman, who turns the double play to end the inning. Oh boy, another first inning where we fail to put points on the board! Okay, let's try to relax and watch our boys go play some defense!

Julian is in to pitch in this all-important game. Ozzy Mallen fouls off strike one, watches ball one, fouls off strikes two and three, watches ball two, hits a ground ball to Jett at shortstop and he is out at first. Jett O'Hara swings at strike one, watches ball one, swings at strike two, watches ball two, and watches strike three. Kash Libson watches strike one, swings at strike two, and swings at strike three. Julian is solidly in command, taking out 3 batters with only 14 pitches.

Kole watches ball one and hits a hard grounder to left field for a double to start off the top of the second! Doc fouls off strike one, fouls off strike two, watches balls one and two, and then hits a fly ball to center field that is caught for out number 1. Aiden rips a fly ball to center field for a triple, scoring Kole! Dylan watches ball one, swings at strike one, watches ball two, and hits a ground ball to shortstop who can't come up with it, and he gets to first on the error, and scores Aiden. Ben swings at strike one, watches a wild pitch go by, allowing Dylan to get to second, watches strike two, watches balls three and then gets hit by the next pitch to take his base.

Jett connects on the first pitch of his at-bat with a ground ball to shortstop for a single and loading the bases. Kaleb watches ball one and hits a fly ball to right field that is good for a sacrifice fly to score Dylan. Gage hits a fly ball to left field that is caught to end the top of the second.

Alex Puentes faces off against Julian and swings at strike one, swings at strike two, watches balls one and two, and then swings and misses at strike three. Maverick Kidd swings at strike one, swings at strike two, watches balls one and two, and swings and misses at strike three. We drop the third strike but get Maverick out at first. Barrett Thomas fouls off strike one, watches ball one, watches strike two, watches ball two, and watches strike three for the final out of the second. Julian records 13 pitches and 3 outs for that inning!

Gray watches strike one and then watches four straight balls to draw the walk. MP wants to save Maverick, so they pull him at 38 pitches and put Ozzy into pitch. Julian watches ball one and hits a ground ball to center field for a single. Cooper watches four straight balls to load the bases. Caden rips the cover off the ball with a home run to deep center field! His grand slam blows the game open 7-0!!!

MP pulls Ozzy after only 7 pitches, and puts in Jett to pitch and try to get control back in this game. Kole watches strike one. Kole hits a ground ball to short and is out at first. Doc watches ball one, fouls off strike one, watches ball two, watches strike two, watches ball three, and hits a fly ball to center field that is caught for out #2. Aiden watches strike one, swings at strike two, watches ball one, fouls off strike three, watches balls two, three, and four, and draws the 7-pitch walk. Dylan swings at strike one, watches balls one and a second wild pitch. Aiden advances to second on the wild pitch. Another wild pitch for ball three and Aiden gets to third. Ball four and Dylan takes his base. Ben comes up big with a line drive to center field for a single, scoring Aiden! Jett watches ball one, and hits a ground ball to short, who gets Ben out going to second for the final out of the top of the third.

Luke Jackson hits a line drive single to Gray in right field for MP. Julian Bonilla is facing Julian Hurst on the mound. Julian Bonilla swings at strike one, fouls off strike two, watches ball one, and then hits a grounder back to Julian Hurst, who turns and gets the lead runner out going to second. Blake Jarzombek hits a ground ball back to Julian, who turns and gets it to Jett at short for the out at second, and then Jett turns the double play getting the ball over to Kole at first. A 6-pitch inning for Julian on the mound, and we are halfway through this semi-final game!

Kaleb watches ball one, fouls off strike one, watches ball two, and then hits a ground ball to second base and is out at first. Gage watches strike one, watches ball one, watches strike two, watches ball two, fouls off strike three, and watches balls three and four to draw a 7-pitch walk. Gray flies out to the right fielder. Gage steals second. MP pulls Jett O'Hara and replaces him with Blake Jarzombek. Julian is back in the box, and he watches ball one, watches a wild pitch ball two that allows Gage to get to third, and then watches balls three and four.

MP wastes no time, pulls Blake, and puts Luke Jackson into pitch. They are pulling out all the stops to try to stop this freight train called Boerne baseball! Cooper fouls off strike one, swings at strike two, Julian steals second, and Cooper hits a line drive to left field for a double and scores Julian to make the score 10-0! Caden comes back to the plate and smashes a home run over the center field wall to score 2 more! Choo, choo, and the Boerne freight train is coming thru!!! Kole watches ball one, watches strike one, and then hits a line drive to left field for a single. Doc maintains Boerne's aggressive nature at the plate, swinging at strike one and flying out to right field.

Travis Bagley, the #10 batter, swings at strike one, and then gets four balls in a row, to put the MP leadoff runner on first in the bottom of the 4th inning. Bryson Starnes watches strike one, fouls off strike two, watches ball one, and swings and misses at strike three. Graham Winckler watches strike one, watches ball one, fouls off strike two, watches ball two, and swings and misses at strike three. Ozzy Mallen, the top of the lineup for MP, is their last hope to keep the game alive! He swings at strike one, watches ball one, watches strike two, and watches strike three to end the game and send Boerne to the Section Championship game!

MP threw 93 pitches that game (52% strike percentage) and Julian only threw 51, with 34 of them being strikes (67% strike percentage). MP got one hit in the game and drew one walk. So, now we've gone 6 games and have only given up 2 hits total!!! Our pitchers and defense are incredible!! Boerne got 10 hits in the game and drew six walks. Perhaps even more impressive was that Boerne didn't have a single strike-out, whereas MP had 8.

This game sends McAllister Park to the loser's bracket, so they have to play Northern in the semi-final elimination game. Northern beats McAllister Park 3-2 in another nailbiter, and so that earns Northern the right to a re-match against Boerne on Tuesday!

We celebrate that victory because we just beat the team that many folks would have assumed was "the team to beat." Now we've got some confidence, and believe that we can take this Section tournament. However, as we are all painfully aware, anything can happen in baseball, so we celebrate with the boys and we prepare them to come back two days later and finish the job. This is the first glimpse that this could be something really special and we are excited to see how this ride turns out!

Game 7 Northern LL @ Boerne

Drama central! Here we go, we have been flawless through 6 games up to this point, and now we are in the Section Championship game trying to earn our way to Abilene and the State Tournament! Northern LL played their way back through the loser's bracket and so from their perspective, it's payback time, and from Boerne's perspective, we have to take care of business one more time!

It's Tuesday night, and two days before July 4, but everything rests on the outcome tonight! If we lose, we do get to play again Wednesday night, but we sure don't want to put our backs up against the wall that way, so we want to get pressure on Northern early and never remove our boots from their neck!

Caden, who dominated in the box last game, is in to pitch this evening. Colt Barker swings at strike one and then hits a ground ball to left field to get their leadoff runner on first. Leo Speciale swings at strike one and then proceeds to rip a fly ball over the center field fence, scoring 2! And just like that, Boerne, who has never trailed in any game up to this point, finds itself down 2 runs after two batters. The Boerne parents almost have a heart attack. Holy crap, what just happened???

Ok, breathe, let's get some outs, and let's trust in our offense that has put a hurt on every team up to this point, and, don't forget, beat this same team 17-0 just five days earlier. Brooks Belcher swings at strike one, swings at strike two, watches ball one, and goes down swinging at strike three. Great job Caden, that's more like the Boerne boys' we know. Adrian Esparza watches strike one, watches balls one, two, and three, swings at strike two, and then hits a line drive out to Aiden! Whew...okay, two batters, two outs. Let's do that one more time. Jose Gonzalez watches ball one, watches strike one, watches strike two, watches ball two, watches ball three, and watches strike three. Ok, guys, a little rattled with that two-run shot they got off, but then we took care of their next three batters and now it's our turn to put some points on the board. A 21-pitch inning for Caden, which in a normal baseball game is pretty good, but looking at the standard Boerne has set in the first several games, slightly below our elevated standard. 😊

Adrian Esparza's in to start the game for Northern. Julian watches ball one and then hits a hard grounder to center field for a single. Gray watches ball one and two, Julian steals second, Gray watches strikes one, watches ball three, and then hits a line drive to center field for a single, scoring Julian! Okay, there is our first run, now we are only down by one, with Gray on, and the rest of our boys ready to swing behind him...Cooper hits a ground ball to third and reaches on an error. Caden watches ball one and then hits a ground ball to center field, scoring Gray and moving Cooper to third. Ok, now we can take a breath, we've tied the game, we've got another runner in scoring position and no outs.

Kole watches ball one, swings at strike one, watches a wild pitch for ball two that allows Caden to advance to second, watches ball three, and then hits a line drive to center field for a single, scoring Cooper and Caden! Ok, they briefly had a 2-0 lead, but as soon as we got to bat, we caught up and have now made it 4-2, and we're not done with the first inning yet.

Northern brings in Camden Uriste to try to change the momentum of this game, pulling Adrian after only 15 pitches. Doc fouls off strike one, watches ball one, watches ball two, and then is hit by pitch. Aiden swings at strike one, and hits a line drive to left field for a single, scoring Kole and moving Doc to second. Dylan fouls off strike one and then hits a fly ball out to right field. Doc tags up and gets to third and Aiden gets to second on the throw. Ben watches ball one go by the catcher, Doc steals home, and Aiden steals third. Ben fouls off strike one, watches ball two, and hits a ground ball to shortstop, who gets him out at first, but, most importantly, he did his job by putting the bat on the ball and scored Aiden. Jett grounds out to the second baseman to end the 1st inning, with Boerne up 7-2. Okay, we can take a breath. It's going to be okay.

Maddox Carr leads it off for Northern, watches ball one, and then swings and misses at the next three strikes for out #1. Austin Epperson watches ball one and then hits a ground ball back to Caden and gets on first. Aiden Wiens watches ball one, watches strike one, watches ball two, watches ball three, and Austin tries to steal second and is thrown out by our catcher Gray. Aiden watches ball four to draw the walk. Colson Koehn fouls offs strike one, swings at strike two, and hits a ground ball to second for an out at first to end the top of the second. A 14-pitch inning for Caden! It just took him an inning to warm up and now he's rolling!

Kaleb watches three balls in a row, watches strike one, and then watches ball four to get Boerne's leadoff runner on first. Northern yanks Cam after 17 pitches and brings in Jose Gonzalez to pitch, trying anything they can to turn this game their way. Gage watches four straight balls to draw the walk. Julian hits a line drive single to right field, scoring Kaleb and moving Gage to third. Gray watches strike one and then watches three balls in a row. Julian is thrown out trying to steal second, but he is able to let Gage steal home. Gray fouls off strike two, and then rips a hard grounder to the first baseman for a single. Cooper watches ball one, fouls off strike one, and then pops out to the third baseman. Caden watches balls one and two, and then hits a hard ground ball to shortstop for a single. Kole watches three balls in a row, watches strike one, and then watches ball four to take his base. Doc hits a hard ground ball to center for a single, scoring Gray and Caden, and allowing Kole to get to second.

Aiden watches ball one, watches strike one, watches a wild pitch for ball two that Kole and Doc both advance on, and then Aiden hits a hard ground ball to the right fielder, scoring both Kole and Doc. Dylan fouls off strike one, swings at strike two, watches a wild pitch for ball one that lets Aiden advance, and swings and misses at strike three that finally ends the second inning. However, Boerne now has a commanding 13-2 lead!! And we can take a collective breath. It's going to be okay, we've got this!

Camden Uriste watches strike one, fouls off strike two, and then watches four balls in a row to get on base. Isaiah Ojeda watches ball one. Cam tries to steal and Gray throws him out going to second. Isaiah watches three more balls and he too, gets walked. Estaban Gonzalez watches strike one, watches strike two, watches a wild pitch for ball one that allows Isaiah to advance, then watches ball two, and swings and misses at strike three. Jaylen Urteaja watches strike one, watches balls one and two, watches strike two, and swings and misses at strike three.

Ben watches strike one, watches ball one, and then smashes a home run shot over the right field wall!! Jett watches ball one, watches strike one, and then hits a fly ball to center field that is caught for out #1. Kaleb watches balls one and two, and then rips a line drive to left field for a single. Gage swings at strike one, watches a wild pitch for ball one that lets Kaleb advance, and then hits a line drive triple to right field! Gage is so fast and it's so much fun to watch him run! He scores Kaleb! Julian watches strike one, watches ball one, and then rips a line drive to right field for a double! Gray watches ball one and then obliterates a ball over the right field wall to score two and end the game!

Boerne has done it!! We win 18-2 over Northern, and Boerne has earned a trip to Abilene for the State Championship! We run rule them after the 3rd inning as well, so this is our 7th run-rule game!

Northern got 3 hits in that game, 3 walks, and 5 strike-outs. Boerne had 15 hits, 3 walks, and only one strike-out. Northern threw 80 pitches with three different pitchers (cumulative 50% strike percentage) while Caden only needed 55 pitches, with 30 of them being strikes (55% strike percentage). We've now only given up 5 hits in 7 games, an incredible testament to the depth of our pitching lineup and our defense!

We have beaten the teams through both District and Section, and now it's time to pack up and get on the road to Abilene for the State Tournament. We expect that we are going to see some really intensive competition there, so we prepare the boys for things to simply continue to get much harder from this point forward! The Boerne Star puts us in the newspaper again, and now we are starting to draw some attention and from around the country.

We created our GameChanger app with an abbreviation so that our family/friends could find it but we didn't want any of the other teams around the country to be able to "follow" our team that closely. We are still in "stealth mode" because we have done well to this point, but at the end of the day, if you don't win State, you never get to go to Regional, and if you don't win Regional, you don't get to go to Williamsport. We were hoping that no one would know that this Boerne Freight Train was coming!

As you can see from these first seven games, every single one of our boys executed crucial plays in the moment to help our team secure these wins. This particular format, and we can't stress it enough, requires 12 really good, complete, baseball players.

Game 8 Boerne @ West Brownsville LL

Winning that game against Northern meant that we got ourselves an invite to go to Abilene, TX in the middle of July for the State Championship Tournament. If you have ever been in Houston in mid-summer, when the temperature is 100 degrees and the humidity is 100%, yes, you know, it's miserable. If you drive west to San Antonio, it's 110 degrees but the humidity is around 70%. That means that you don't sweat if you are in the shade. If you drive to Abilene, which is north and west of San Antonio about 200 miles, or a 3.5-hour drive then you start to figure out what living on the sun is like. It's hotter and drier than San Antonio, oh and by the way, it's hotter and dustier too. Did I mention it's hotter?

Abilene is home to about 125,000 people and three universities, Hardin-Simmons, McMurry, and Abilene Christian University. There are a bunch of motels in Abilene that we were not interested in, and so we stayed right downtown at the Doubletree, which technically was called the Downtown Convention Center hotel...Yeah, right. Well, it's a farming community, so I'd be willing to bet there are several Agriculture conferences during the year. The Wylie baseball fields are on the south side of town, on the east side of Kirby Lake. Our Little League President Chris Carey is from Abilene, so he was quite excited to "return home."

We drove up early Friday morning because we wanted to get there early, have lunch, have time to loosen up after the long drive, check into the hotel, go get an early dinner, and then be at the Wylie stadium around 5p to start getting ready for our 7p game. We found Joe Allen's Pit BBQ, and ended up eating there 6 times in the four days we were there. A wonderful local BBQ restaurant that feels very homey, had a great food and great service, so that's why we kept going back. They served plain BBQ turkey, which is one of Kaleb's favorite protein-dense meals, and one of the meals we eat frequently before/after baseball tournaments and other sporting events. Let's get to the game, and of course, now all the parents are nervous and on edge!

There are four teams in this state tournament, Midland Northern, University (Fort Worth), West Brownsville, and Boerne. Midland beat University in a close game just before ours, 10-8.

We thought it was a long drive for us at 3.5 hours, but Brownsville is another 5 hours south of San Antonio, so for those families this was an 8-9 hour drive. Brownsville is a Texas border town, right next to Matamoros, Mexico, and is on the Gulf of Mexico, so it's right next to South Padre Island, a popular South Texas beach. 20 years ago, high school and college spring breakers would come party on South Padre Island, and then drive across into Matamoros where the legal drinking age is 18, but that's another story.

Sebastian Hernandez is on the mound for Brownsville, and Julian leads off for Boerne. He swings at strike one, fouls off strike two, and hits a line drive single to the center fielder. Yes!! Our leadoff batter got on base! Gray fouls off the first pitch, and hits a ground ball to the shortstop. They are able to get Julian out going to second on the fielder's choice, but Gray gets to first in time to avoid the double play. Cooper hits the first pitch as a hard ground ball to right field for a single, and Gray advances to third. Caden watches strike one, swings and misses at strike two but the catcher can't hold onto it and lets it get behind him, so Gray scores for our first run, and Cooper advances to second! Caden swings and misses strike three for our second out. Kole takes a big swing at the first pitch and hits a rocket line drive home run over the right field wall, and Boerne announces that we are in the house! A two-run bomb in the first inning!

Aiden fouls off the first pitch, and hits a ground ball to third that they successfully handle and get the third out. Top of the first and we jump out to a 3-run lead! Ok, we can take a little breath. The long drive didn't negatively affect the boys' hitting ability, and so let's go play defense!

Cooper is on the mound for Boerne. Logan Frady comes to the box, watches balls one, two, and three, watches strike one, swings at strike two, and watches ball four to get their leadoff runner on base. Crap...hopefully the drive didn't affect our pitching arms. Ok, let's settle down and get to work.

Alec Parra watches ball one, watches strike one, watches strike two, and watches strike three. Ok, good, now we are back on track a little. Max Barron watches a wild pitch for ball one that allows Logan to advance to second. Max watches ball two, swings at strike one, and then hits a line drive to center that is caught by Doc. Ok, great, two down. Sebastian Hernandez, their starting pitcher, fouls off the first two pitches and then hits a line drive to center that is also caught by Doc! First inning done and we've taken the lead 3-0! A 17-pitch inning for Cooper!

However, if these Brownsville boys keep hitting line drives like this, eventually a few of them are going to put the on base! Let's go hit!!

Doc swings at strike one, and then hits a grounder back to the pitcher, who gets him out at first. Dylan swings at strike one, and then hits a ground ball to the shortstop, who gets him for the second out. Ben swings at strike one, then hits a ground ball that short can't come up with and reaches on an error. Jett fouls off strike one, and then hits a ground ball to third, who gets the ball to second and gets Ben out. An 8-pitch inning for Hernandez and this is a battle!

Isaac Guerra watches balls one and two, swings at strike one, watches strike two, and then swings and misses at strike three. Calix (Ace) Rosales watches strike one, watches ball one, fouls off strike two, and then swings and misses for strike three. Dante Guerra fouls off strike one, watches ball one, watches strike two, watches balls two and three, and then hits a ground ball to Kole at third base for the last out at first. A 15-pitch inning for Cooper, let's go!!

Kaleb watches ball one, two, and three, watches strike one, swings at strike two, fouls off strike three, and then watches strike three. Gage watches strike one, watches ball one, watches strike two, fouls off strike three, and then swings and misses at strike three. Julian watches ball one, two, and three, watches strike one, watches strike two, and then watches ball four to draw the walk. Gray watches strike one and then pops out to shortstop for the third out. A 20-pitch inning for Brownsville and we blanked!

RJ Alvear, their #8 guy in the lineup watches ball one, watches strike one, swings at strike two, and watches strike three. Sebastian Cortez fouls off strike one, watches ball one, swings at strike two, and watches strike three. Joey Camacho fouls off strike one, watches strike two, and swings and misses at strike three. A great 3 up, 3 down, 11-pitch inning for Cooper!

Cooper watches ball one, two, three, watches strike one, and then watches ball four to draw the walk. Caden watches ball one, swings at strike one, and then hits a hard ground ball to right field for a single, and then advances when they throw it to 3rd trying to get Cooper out. Kole watches strike one, fouls off strike two, and swings and misses at strike three.

Sebastian Hernandez is now at 52 pitches, so they so pull him and bring in Calix (Ace) Rosales. Aiden watches four straight balls to draw the walk and now the bases are loaded. Doc watches ball one, and then Doc does what he has done all season, rips a line drive over the center field wall for a grand slam!! Boerne takes a 7-0 lead! Dylan watches ball one, ball two, and then hits a ground ball to third who grabs it and gets him out at first. Ben watches four straight balls and gets on base. Jett swings at strike one, watches balls one and a second wild pitch, allowing Ben to advance to second, swings at strike two, and swings at strike three for the third out. Doc's grand slam has blown this game open for Boerne in the top of the 4th! Now we need to get through at least two, maybe three more at-bats for Brownsville for the win!

Anthony Gonzalez watches strike one, watches strike two, watches ball one, and then hits a ground ball to Julian at first for out #1. Cooper is now at 47 pitches (66% strike percentage), and so we switch Doc in to pitch. Angel Mejia, their #12 batter, watches balls one and two, swings at strike one, and then hits a ground ball to Kole at third, who gets him out. Brownsville did have 13 on their roster, but one of the kids was hurt, so they only played 12. Logan returns to the box, fouls off strike one, and the watches four balls in a row. Alec watches ball one and then hits a ground ball to Jett at first, who flips it to Aiden at second to get Frady out for the final out of the inning.

Brownsville brings in Anthony Gonzalez to close. Kaleb watches ball one and then pops out to short. Gage watches ball one, and then the next pitch hits him, so he takes his base. Julian watches a wild pitch for ball one that allows Gage to advance, and then hits a line drive to left field for a double, scoring Gage! Gray watches three balls in a row, watches strike one, and then watches ball four to draw the walk. Cooper hits a ground ball to second, scoring Julian, and they get Gray out going to second. Caden hits a fly ball to right field, who drops it, and Caden is able to get to second, with Cooper getting to third.

Kole watches ball one, fouls off strike one, watches strike two, fouls off strike three, watches ball two, fouls off another strike and the pops out to the catcher on a foul tip. Boerne is now up 9-0 in the middle of the 5th! Ok, we are in control of this game, but we can't let our guard down.

Max Barron watches ball one, swings at strike one, fouls off the next two, and then swings and misses at strike three. Sebastian Hernandez watches ball one, watches strike one, and then hits a ground ball to right field for a single. Isaac Guerra fouls off strike one, watches ball one, swings at strike two, fouls off strike three, watches balls two and three, fouls off another strike, and then lines out to Julian at first. Ace Rosales watches strike one, watches ball one, fouls off the next two pitches, and then hits a ground ball to Aiden at second for an out at first. A 21-pitch inning for Doc and Brownsville is doing all they can to make us work for it!

Aiden hits a line drive to center field that is caught for out #1. Doc watches ball one, two, and then hits a line drive to left field for a single. Dylan swings at strike one, watches balls one, two, and three, and then hits a ground ball to second, who flips it to their shortstop to get Doc out going to second. Ben fouls off strike one and then rips a line drive to left field for a double! Dylan scores, Ben advances to third on the throw, and then Ben scores on an error by the catcher! Jett watches ball one, and then hits a line drive to left field for a single.

Kaleb watches ball one, watches strike one, and hits a ground ball to short, who gets him out at first. However, Boerne has a 11-0 lead going into the bottom of the 6th inning! This is the longest game that Boerne has had yet, and the first time we've had to go to a 6th inning. 3 outs away boys, let's go!

Doc is at 32 pitches, so we bring Kole in to close out the game. Dante Guerra watches balls one two, and three, watches strike one, and watches ball four to draw the walk. RJ Alvear watches strike one, swings at strike two, watches ball one, and swings and misses at strike three for the 1st out. Sebastian Cortez watches ball one, swings at strike one, swings at strike two, and then hits a single to center fielder Gray, who is able to field it and get it to Aiden to get Dante out going to second. Joey Camacho hits a line drive to right for a single, so now we have runners at 1st and 2nd with two outs. Anthony Gonzalez hits a ground ball to shortstop and that loads the bases.

Oh my gosh, bases loaded and we only need one out!! Come on boys you can do it! Angel watches strike one, watches ball one, and then hits a ground ball back to Kole who gets him out! Whew...

Boerne wins the game 11-0, but that 0 doesn't show how close they came to scoring several times! That game is also the first one that we went to the bottom of the 6th inning! Now that we've had to go all six innings, we are back to wishing we could have just run-ruled them by the third inning! See how crazy this becomes, and how our thoughts and emotions are all over the place?

Brownsville got 3 hits in that game, drew 3 walks, and struck-out 8 times. Boerne had 9 hits, 5 walks, and 6 strike-outs. Brownsville threw 105 pitches with a 59% strike percentage. Sebastian Hernandez threw an impressive 73% and Anthony Gonzalez threw 54%. Boerne conversely threw 97 pitches with a 63% strike percentage. Cooper threw 66%, Doc threw 59%, and Kole threw 61%.

Hopefully you are starting to see a pattern emerge here. The Boerne boys are really good hitters, which means they have plate discipline. If they get deep in a count, 2-0, 3-0, they'll watch another pitch or two to try to draw the walk. However, they are also swinging at strikes and trying to hit the ball hard.

That is a learned skill, that takes years to develop (and is still developing) in these 12-year-olds. You don't get that by hitting balls once or twice a week. You get that through consistent 4-5-6 times per week hitting balls, practicing soft toss, and live batting practice. With baseball, it is almost always the same. You'll see a kid that becomes a pretty good defensive player first, then he'll develop his ability to pitch/throw strikes, and lastly, they will develop their batting skills so they become a good batter (meaning they bat over .400 consistently).

This is one of the reasons it's so important for Little League kids to get year-round practice, because you won't develop this as well if you are only doing it for 4 months per year. Jimmy Gonzales, a retired local MLB scout that owns Jimmy Gonzales Baseball Academy, says "hit every day. Even if it's just off a tee into a net in your backyard, hit every day."

We expected to see some better competition here at State, and some of the Brownsville kids showed us their batting ability! We've played several Rio Grande Valley teams before in other tournaments, and they hit the ball hard and they hit the ball a long way! We know these kids can hit, we've got to pitch well and when they do connect, we need to be solid on defense!

We send Brownsville to the loser's bracket, and they play against University (Fort Worth) on Saturday, and University wins 13-3 in four innings. So, with the double elimination, that means Brownsville goes home. University has to play their way back through the loser's bracket, so that means they will meet the loser of the Midland North v. Boerne game on Saturday. One more of those teams will be eliminated, and the winner will advance to the State Championship game.

Game 9 Midland @ Boerne

Midland has been a famous town in West Texas for a long time, given its rich history being located in the Permian Oil basin, the second-largest oil shale in the world. If you watch Billy Bob Thornton in the series Landman, then much of that is filmed in Midland. Midland, and its sister town, Odessa about 40 minutes away, are home to thriving communities, have significant investments from a number of large international corporations, and The University of Texas-Permian Basin with a local college campus. Midland residents have the second-highest personal income in the United States.

Midland beat University 10-8 in their first game. So we now face another unbeaten team! Our blood pressure shoots up again, ok boys, let's go!

Sam Thomas is on the mound for Midland. Julian leads off, watches strike one, and hits a ground ball to third base for the first out. Gray watches four balls in a row and takes his base. Cooper swings at strike one, watches balls one and two, and then hits a line drive to left field that is caught for out #2. Caden fouls off the first pitch and then hits a ground ball to short for the final out at first. A 13-pitch inning for Midland and again a start where we don't score! Perhaps our standards (or at least hopes) are a bit too high?

Caden is on the mound for Boerne. Sam Thomas watches strike one, watches strike two, and hits a ground ball to Jett at shortstop for a quick throw to Kole at first and out #1. Ian Bejil swings at strike one and then hits a fly ball to Gage in left field for an out. Raul Pando fouls off strike one, swings at strike two, fouls off the next three pitches, and then watches strike three. An 11-pitch inning for Caden!

Kole watches strike one and then is hit by the next pitch. Doc watches ball one, fouls off strike one, watches ball two, fouls off strike two, and then hits a ground ball to the second baseman, who flips the ball to shortstop to get Kole out. Aiden fouls off strike one, swings at strike two, and then rips a line drive to center for a double! Doc advances to third. Ben watches strike one, watches strike two, watches ball one, fouls off strike three, and swings and misses at the next pitch for our second out. Dylan gets in the box and watches four balls in a row that loads the bases. Jett watches balls one and two, watches strike one, and then watches two more balls to walk in a run.

Kaleb rips a line drive to center field for a single, scoring both Aiden and Dylan! Gage watches four balls in a row to load the bases again. Julian gets ready to hit and then he watches four balls in a row to walk in another run. Gray watches ball one, watches strike one, and then watches three more balls to walk in a third run and makes it 5-0 Boerne. Midland swaps out Sam Thomas for Case Neatherlin to see if they can re-gain control of this game. Sam Thomas threw 51 pitches with a 39% strike percentage. Now the pressure is squarely on Case, as he walks into a bases loaded situation and his team down by 5 runs. Cooper watches ball one, swings at strike one, swings at strike two, and swings and misses at strike three to retire the side. Case breathed a huge sigh of relief, as that is the most difficult place for any pitcher to have to come into, but he did great!

Ethan Cisneros, their #4 batter comes to the plate, watches strike one, watches balls one and two, and then hits a line drive to Cooper in right field for a single. Evan Walker watches strike one, watches ball one, watches strike two, and then hits a line out to Aiden at second. Javier Gonzalez watches the first two pitches for balls, watches strike one, watches ball three that gets by the catcher and allows Ethan Cisneros to get to second base, watches strike two, and then watches strike three. Ivan Valenzuela watches strike one, fouls off strike two, watches ball one, and then smokes a line drive to Ben in left for a double, scoring Ethan Cisneros. Midland is trying to chip away at the lead, as they just got one back. Tebow Tipton watches strike one, watches balls one and two, swings at strike two, watches ball three, and then hits a line drive to Doc in center field for a single.

Caden's at 35 pitches (71% strike percentage) and so we bring Julian in to try to shut down Midland's offense. This was a particularly intense moment. First of all, like all true champions, Julian wanted to pitch the Championship game the next day, and didn't want to have to come into relieve in this game and then not be able to throw in the championship. However, the pitcher doesn't decide who pitches, the coaches do. Bert and Justin believed that Midland was the better hitting team and so we wanted to make sure we didn't lose control of this game. The format of these tournaments means that it can be very difficult to come back from a loss, and so we really focused on winning this game.

After that call, Justin didn't sleep for two nights and was concerned that all of us parents thought he was crazy for making that call. At the end of the day, we trusted in his decision and supported him do what he thought was best in the moment.

Case Neatherlin watches Julian's heater for strike one, watches ball one, swings at strike two, and then watches strike three for the third out and to send it to the 3rd inning.

Caden watches balls one and two, fouls off strike one, and then rips a line drive to left field for a double! Kole watches ball one, fouls off strike one, watches ball two, fouls off strike two, and then hits a screaming fly ball over the center field wall for a two-run homer!! Doc watches balls one and two, swings at strike one, and then hits a ground ball to left field for a single. Aiden swings at the first pitch and sends a hard grounder to third base, who can't come up with it so he reaches on the error.

Ben watches ball one, swings at strike one, watches ball two, and then hits a fly ball to right field that is caught, but it's a great sacrifice fly, as it allows Doc to tag up and get to third base and then Aiden moves to second when Midland throws to third trying to hold the runners in place. Dylan swings at strike one, swings at strike two, and then hits a ground ball to first, which is good enough for Doc to score and for Aiden to get to third. Jett watches a wild pitch for ball one, but then Aiden is out trying to steal home on the passed ball.

Mason Burger watches ball one, swings at strike one, watches strike two, and watches strike three. Jake Stockstill watches ball one, strike one, strike two, ball two, ball three, and strike three. Camden Patterson watches strike one, swings at strike two, and then swings and misses strike three to end the inning. Julian's command performance on the mound continues as that half inning only took 13 pitches.

Jett hits the first pitch and lines out to third base for out #1. Kaleb hits a grounder to the third baseman, who gets him out at first. Gage fouls off strike one, and then hits a hard ground ball to left field for a single. Julian watches ball one, fouls off strike one, and then hits a fly ball to right field for a single that allows super-fast Gage to reach third. Gray watches strike one, watches ball one, and then smokes a line drive to left field for a double, scoring both Gage and Julian! Cooper watches two balls in a row, and then hits a ground ball to second base, who is able to get him out at first.

Boerne takes a 10-1 lead going into the middle of the 4th inning! Ok, we can breathe a little, we just have to keep throwing strikes and not let anything crazy happen.

Sam Thomas watches ball one and then hits a fly ball to Cooper in right field for a single. Ian Bejil swings at strike one, fouls off strike two, and watches strike three. Raul Pando swings at strike one, watches ball one, fouls off strike two, fouls off strike three, and then swings and misses for out #2. Ethan Cisneros watches ball one and Sam steals second. Ethan swings at strike one, but it gets past the catcher so Sam is able to get to third and is able to score on the same pitch. Ethan watches ball two and then hits a ground ball back to Julian who isn't able to come up with it, so Ethan is safe on first. Evan Walker watches ball one, strike one, ball two, strike two, and strike three. Julian needs only 19 pitches for that inning and Midland scores 1 more run, so it's now 10-2.

Caden watches ball one, and then hits a ground ball to short, who gets him out at first. Kole fouls off strike one, and then hits a ground ball to third base for out #2. Doc watches two balls and then hits another grounder to short, who comes up with it, for out #3. Kudos to Case as he only needed 7 pitches in that inning and didn't allow any runs. He's battling like crazy on the mound!

Javier Gonzalez watches ball one and strike one, swings at strike two, and swings at strike three. One out. Ivan Valenzuela fouls off strike one, watches balls one and two, swings at strike two, watches ball three, fouls off strike three, fouls off another one, and then swings and misses. Well done Ivan, an 8-pitch at-bat. Great battle, kid! Tebow Tipton watches ball one, watches strike one, fouls off the next two, and then watches strike three. Julian needed 17 pitches for that inning. Ok, breathe, we have one more inning and we have a really good lead. Let's finish this one boys!

Aiden watches four balls in a row and gets our leadoff runner on base. Ben watches balls one and two, fouls off strike one, and then pops out to third base. Dylan watches balls one and two, watches a wild pitch go by for ball three that allows Aiden to advance, and then hits a single to third base, with Aiden advancing to third on the throw. Jett watches a wild pitch for ball one and Dylan moves to second. Jett watches ball two, fouls off strike one, watches another wild pitch for ball three that allows Aiden to score and Dylan to move to third, watches strike two, fouls off strike three, and then watches ball four to draw the walk.

Kaleb watches ball one and then takes one for the team at he turns his shoulder and is hit by the pitcher to load the bases. Midland, in a last-ditch attempt to change momentum, pulls Case and puts in Raul Pando. Case had thrown 66 pitches already, and so they have already racked up 116 pitches in this game, and it's not over yet. Gage swings at the first pitch and hits a ground ball to short that results in a single, scoring Dylan and moving everyone up one! Julian watches strike one, fouls off strike two, watches ball one, fouls off another strike, watches ball two, and then swings and misses for strike three. Gray watches strike one, watches a wild pitch go by for ball one that allows Jett to score and the runners move up. Gray hits a ground ball to shortstop for an out at first to end the inning.

Case Neatherlin comes to the box, watches balls one and two, swings at strike one, swings at strike two, and watches strike three. Mason Burger swings at strike one, watches strike two, watches ball one, and then watches strike three. Jake Stockstill, their #11 batter is the only thing standing between Boerne and the championship game. He watches strike one, watches ball one, watches ball two, fouls off strike two, and swings and misses for strike three! Julian continues his pitching domination needing only 14 pitches that inning and Boerne advances to the State Championship with a win over Midland of 13-2!

Midland got 4 hits that game, 0 walks (that is HUGE!!!!!), and 15 strike-outs. We celebrate games where we don't walk anyone! Milkshakes for everyone!! They threw 127 pitches to Boerne (49% cumulative strike percentage), resulting in 10 hits, 8 walks, and only 3 strike-outs. Winning this game meant that we sent Midland to the loser's bracket, so they had to battle University for the right to play us again in the Championship.

Remember, Midland beat University in the opening game, so this is University's chance at redemption. University does beat Midland 12-3 on Sunday, which is Midland's second loss so they go home. You could argue that after their 127-pitch game against us and them beating University the first time, they simply ran out of pitching, but they only scored 3 runs in that game vs University's 12, so their offense seemed to perform very similarly to the way it performed against us.

This is an important point and I don't want us to simply blaze past it for the sake of getting to the Championship game. It's very important to measure how your child and/or your team performs at their "average." Anyone individually or collectively can have a great game here or there. However, in baseball, and in any athletic activity, you have to compare your "average" play across a bunch of games so you can get a sense of how good you really are. That forces you to do the hard work of bringing the kids' average consistency up to whatever level you want to achieve.

Coach Nick Saban talks about there only being 5 "choices" in his philosophy on "The Process." It's a framework for achieving elite performance through consistent, disciplined, execution of small tasks. The five levels that athletes can operate at are: Bad, Average, Good, Excellent, and Elite. Getting to Elite status requires going beyond natural talent with special focus, intensity, commitment, choosing to focus on daily actions over outcomes, and fostering a culture of internal standards, self-discipline, and mental toughness.

When you measure your kid's performance and the team's "average" performance against these 5 levels, it requires the parents to swallow the pill that the child has not simply prepared enough yet and needs more practice. Many of the Boerne kids ask their parents, "hey can we go hit?"

The parents would say yes, and so many evenings we would arrive at D-Bat Boerne (a local batting cage) and rent a cage for an hour or grab our membership card and go over to the machines to let the kids take batting practice. When any of us would show up on a random Tuesday, Wednesday, or Friday night, on evenings when we didn't have regular baseball practice, it was quite common to see 2-3 of the other kids and parents there, also putting in extra work.

That is the level of commitment it takes to get to Elite level, and it takes that sustained effort over a period of years to see that "average" performance move up those different steps. For our kids, free time meant there was time to go do more fielding/hitting/bullpen, which they enjoyed doing. Once you have developed the habits of hitting every day, after a couple years, the kids will come to you and ask to go hit. But don't expect them at age 7-11, if they are just learning, to always be the one to want to "initiate practice." Ok, off the soapbox, let's get to the next game!

That game against Midland was the second game where we played six complete innings. We did win both of the game by large margins, but you can see that our opponents are starting to stretch us deeper in games and we are having to go further into our bullpen. We explained to the boys about how this continues to get more difficult the deeper we get and so we simply have to focus on the play in front of us, execute in the moment, and let the results come as they will. We have to be "process-oriented" and if we execute our process, we'll continue to do well in these games.

This win gives us an entire day off, Sunday, before we play again on Monday evening. We go jump in the pool that evening to let the boys cool off. We sleep in the next morning because this entire experience takes an incredible emotional and physical toll on your body, and so you look for opportunities to give your body 9-10 hours of rest. We also know that, given our kids are right in the middle of their growth spurts, they need the 10-11 hours of sleep every night to just to help their bodies recover from the growing they are doing, not to mention all the stress we are putting on them from an athletic perspective.

We go to a local batting cage there in Abilene, inside so that way we can appreciate the air conditioning, get some hitting in, and then go eat and relax some more before we get ready to go play again on Monday night.

Game 10 University LL (Fort Worth) @ Boerne

Boerne has won 9 games in a row and, you could argue, quite decisive victories, outscoring our opponents 129-8. These have been the 9 most stressful games that all of our families have been a part of, and our kids have each played in hundreds of baseball games by this point, when you count both Little League and Select baseball games. And the stress just continues to build, because as we all know, anything can happen in baseball, and we are just hoping and praying that today is not the day that we stumble and fall.

We've got to say thank you to Chris Carey, President of the Boerne Little League, as he and his family were at every game cheering us on and doing more. This is one of those quick, behind-the-scenes moments. So, we've talked about it being hotter than heck in Abilene, and the boys have now played two games, so both jerseys and their pants are dripping wet with sweat, are smelly and nasty, as is common with 12-year-old boys. Chris, being the saint that he is, asks for everyone to deliver their uniforms on Sunday morning to him in the hotel lobby and he will go get them all washed before Monday night's game. So, we've got freshly washed uniforms ready for the next two games, hopefully only one is necessary.

So here we are, Day 4 in Abilene, and hopefully our opportunity to extend our summer playing baseball. University lost to Midland in the opening round, beat Brownsville 13-3, beat Midland 12-3, and now they are ready to come at us guns blazing to take another shot at the Boerne boys! They've had to manage their pitching too as this will be game 4 for them and it's only game three, with a couple extra rest days, for us.

Two Fort Worth teams have been to Williamsport in the past, Northeast Optimist in 1960 and Westside in 2002. Westside battled Valley Sports from Kentucky in the semi-final game. This incredible game went six no-hit, scoreless innings being pitched by both teams!!! The game went to 7, then 8, then 9 innings! Both pitchers had to be pulled because back then the Little League rule was you can only pitch 9 innings. Alvey, the kid from Valley Sports threw 129 pitches and Kelly from Westside threw 118.

Today, we look at those pitching numbers and we say, "that's crazy!" Recall the famous 1974 game when Nolan Ryan threw 235 pitches against the California Angels and then threw multiple 160+ pitch games in 1989 at age 42. We don't even come close to those types of pitch limits these days. The 10th inning comes and goes, and still, no score. The game finally ends 2-1, with Valley Sports emerging victorious in the bottom of the 11th inning! The game went 3 hours and 10 minutes, just short of the all-time longest game in 1998. During these 11 innings, 49 players were struck out! Valley Sports went on to win the World Championship that year. We say all that so that you can understand the history and context with these teams.

Everyone in Fort Worth Little League has been told that story 100 times. So, for years, there are little kids dreaming of being able to take Fort Worth back to Williamsport and win the whole thing for their town! There was some controversy surrounding the Fort Worth Section tournament. Fossil Creek Little League beat University Little League 14-2 with Alex Padilla pitching, however, they didn't continue and so University moved on the State tournament.

Boerne bats first, and so Julian gets into the box. He faces off against Alex Padilla, who leads off pitching for University. Julian watches ball one and then takes the hit on ball two to get our leadoff batter on base! Great start boys! Gray takes the hit on the first pitch! Cooper watches balls one and two, watches strike one, watches a wild pitch for ball three that allows our two runners to advance, and then watches ball four, to load the bases with no outs! Kole fouls off strike one, fouls off strike two, watches a wild pitch for ball one that gets by the catcher and allows Julian to score, but then they are able to throw Gray out at 3rd base. Kole watches ball two, and then swings and misses at strike three.

Caden watches balls one and two, and then hits a line drive to center field for a single, scoring Cooper! Doc watches ball one and then hits a line drive single to left field. Aiden watches ball one, swings at strike one, and then sends a ground ball to shortstop where they are able to get Doc out on the force out to end the inning. Boerne scores 2 runs in the Top of the 1st, and now we have to go play defense! A 21-pitch inning for Alex!

Caden is on the mound for Boerne and he's throwing heat. Jack White is the leadoff hitter, strike one looking, strike two swinging, and strike three swinging. Easton Alexander fouls off strike one, swings at strike two, fouls off strike three, and then swings and misses at strike three. Alex Padilla watches ball one, watches ball two, watches strike one, fouls off strike two, and then swings and misses at strike three. Caden has a masterful first inning performance, with 12 pitches to retire the first three batters.

Jett swings at strike one, swings at strike two, and hits a line drive single to left field! Ben watches ball one and is then is hit by the next pitch. Kaleb watches a wild pitch for ball one that allows the runners to advance, and then watches three more balls in a row.

For the second time, Boerne has bases loaded and no outs! Dylan watches ball one, swings at strike one, fouls off strike two, watches ball two, and swings and misses at strike three. Gage fouls off strike one, watches a wild pitch go by the catcher for ball one, that allows Jett to score and Ben & Kaleb to advance, swings at strike two, and then watches balls two, three, and four. Bases are loaded for a 3rd time!

Julian watches ball one, swings at strike one, watches ball two, fouls off strike two, and watches strike three. Gray watches balls one and two, and then hits a ground ball to first for the third out. CRAP!!! How many times did we load the bases, and we only get one of them home???? At least we forced Alex to throw 28 pitches that inning!

Wyatt Robbins' is in the box and he watches ball one, fouls off strike one, and then hits a grounder to Jett at shortstop for a quick throw to Kole and out at first base. Willie Walker fouls off strike one, and then watches four balls in a row to take his base. Colby Cung watches strike one, fouls off strike two, and then hits a ground ball to Jett at shortstop who is able to tag second base and throw to Kole for a double play and ends the inning. Other than the walk to Willie, it's a quick 11-pitch inning for Caden and he continues his fantastic performance on the mound!

Cooper watches ball one, fouls off strike one, watches strike two, and then watches balls two, three, and four to get our leadoff batter on first! Kole rips the first pitch for a line drive to center field for a double and advancing Cooper to third! Caden watches ball one, ball two, swings at strike one, and then watches balls three and four to load the bases for a fourth time in three innings! Things are looking very good for Boerne, but we need to do a better job of scoring those runs when we get the boys in position!

Doc watches ball one, watches strike one, and then watches balls two, three, and four to walk in a run. Aiden watches ball one, ball two, watches strike one, fouls off strike two, fouls off strike three, fouls off another strike, and then watches strike three. Jett watches ball one and then rips a fly ball to center field that is caught, and the runners do not advance.

Ben watches strike one, watches ball one, and then is hit by the next pitch, which walks in another run. That is the second time that Ben has been hit by Alex in this game. Kaleb fouls off strike one, watches ball one, fouls off strike two, watches ball two, watches ball three, and swings and misses for strike three to end the top of the 3rd inning. Boerne now has a 5-0 lead going into the bottom of the third. We forced Alex to throw 34 pitches in that inning, so he's now at 83 for the day.

Julian Duran for University watches strike one, and then lays down a bunt and is able to get to second after an errant throw by Caden to first. Thatcher Peterson watches strike one, swings at strike two, watches ball one, fouls off strike two, watches ball two, fouls off strike three, watches ball three, and then swings and misses for strike three. Bradford watches four balls in a row to draw the walk. Ethan watches strike one, watches ball one, and then lays down another bunt, but Caden is able to get him out at first. William Cothran rips a fly ball to right field for a double and is able to score both Julian D and Bradford. Thomas swings at strike one, watches ball one, fouls off strike two, watches ball two, and then swings and misses at strike three to end the inning. Caden needed 24 pitches for that inning but Boerne stays in control 5-2. University is chipping away at the lead! Let's go hit!!

Dylan fouls off strike one, watches ball one, and then hits a line drive to left field for a single. Alex is now at 86 pitches, so they bring Colby Cung in to relieve. Gage fouls off strike one, and then rips a line drive to right field for a double, getting Dylan to 3rd. Julian watches ball one, watches strike one, and then hits a line drive to center field for a single, scoring Dylan! Gray fouls off strike one, watches strike two, and then swings and misses at strike three. Cooper pops the first pitch up and it's caught by the first baseman.

Kole hits a rocket fly ball to left field that just keeps going and going, a 3-run bomb!!! Caden watches balls one and two, and then hits a ground ball to shortstop, but is able to get on first when he can't come up with it. Doc watches ball one, swings at strike one, watches strike two, and then swings and misses for strike three to end the inning, and Boerne is now up 9-2!

Jack White fouls off strike one, watches balls one and two, watches strike two, fouls off strike three, and then hits a fly ball to center that Doc is able to catch. Easton Alexander watches balls one and two, and then swings at strikes one, two, and three. Alex Padilla watches ball one, swings at strike one, fouls off strike two, and then swings and misses for strike three. Caden only needed 15 pitches to finish that inning, and is at 62 pitches for the day.

Aiden watches balls one and two, and then is hit by pitch to take his base. Jett watches strike one, and then rips a line drive to right field that is caught, keeping Aiden at first. Ben fouls off strike one, watches balls one and two, fouls off the next three pitches, and then watches balls three and four to draw an 8-pitch walk! Kaleb watches ball one and then hits a ground ball to shortstop, where they are able to get Ben out advancing to second, but not turn the double play. Dylan watches strike one, swings at strike two, and then watches strike three to end the inning. An 18-pitch inning for Colby and he's doing everything he can to keep his team in it!

Wyatt Robbins watches ball one, fouls off strike one, and then hits a fly ball to Gray in right field for a single. Willie Walker fouls off strike one and then hits a ground ball to Jett at shortstop who is able to turn the double play to Kole at first base. Colby Cung swings at strike one and then hits a ground ball to Aiden at second base for an out at first. A 7-pitch inning for Caden!!

Gage watches ball one, swings at strike one, and then smokes a fly ball to left field for a triple! Julian watches ball one and then hits a hard ground ball to left field for a single and scores Gage! Gray swings at strike one, fouls off strike two, watches ball one, watches a wild pitch go by the catcher for ball two that allows Julian to advance to third from first, watches ball three, and then rips a line drive to center field for a double, scoring Julian! Cooper watches four balls in a row and takes his base. Kole watches ball one, swings at strike one, and then hits a ground ball to shortstop and they are able to get Cooper on the force at second base. Caden fouls off strike one, watches a wild pitch for ball one that allows Kole to get to second, and then watches ball two, fouls off strike two, and then watches two more balls to load the bases for a 5th time in this game!

Doc hits a ground ball to left field for a single and scores Gray! Aiden watches ball one, watches strike one, and then hits a ground ball to second base, who is able to get Doc out at second, and Kole scores! Jett rips a line drive to center field for a double, scoring Caden and moving Aiden to third base! Ben fouls off strike one, watches ball one, and then hits a fly ball to right field for a single, scoring Aiden and Jett! Kaleb watches ball one, and then rips a line drive to center field for a single! Dylan watches ball one, swings at strike one, watches ball two, watches a wild pitch go by for ball three that allows Ben and Kaleb to advance, and then watches ball four to take his base. Gage watches ball one, fouls off strike one, watches strike two, watches ball two, fouls off strike three, watches ball three, and then watches strike three to end the inning. We go to the bottom of the 6th, and we have a 16-2 lead, so all we need are three outs!

Julian Duran, their #7 hitter, watches ball one and then hits a ground ball back to Caden on the mound for out #1! Thatcher Peterson fouls off the first two pitches, watches ball one, fouls off strike three, and then watches strike three. Bradford, their #9 batter, is all that is left between Boerne and advancing to Waco. He watches strike one, swings at strike two, and then swings and misses at strike three.

They have done it! The Boerne boys are advancing to the Little League Regional Championship in Waco! Boerne got 15 hits in that game, 10 walks, and had 9 strike-outs. University got three hits, 2 walks, and had 8 strike-outs. Caden had sole possession of the mound and only needed 78 pitches to get through their 20 batters, and threw a fantastic 68% strike percentage! University threw 167 pitches and averaged 49% strike percentage. The boys get their picture taken and are crowned the "Texas West State Champions."

We checked out of the hotel that morning, knowing that if we lost and needed a game two, we could check back in later that evening. Thankfully that wasn't necessary, so we drive home that night and get home after midnight that Monday night, but at least thankfully we are back in our own beds in Boerne, and we know that we've got two weeks off before we have to play our first game in Waco on Thursday, August 1st.

The local newspaper, the Boerne Star reports on July 20th about our victory in Abilene, and for the first time, we start more significant fund-raising efforts. Now it gets very real! We are State Champions and we are one Regional Tournament away from the dream that is Williamsport!

We have to give a huge thank-you to Jeremy Affeldt, local business owner of Free Roam Brewery and a former MLB player who was drafted by Kansas City in 1997, and is a 3-time World Series Champion in 2010, 2012, and 2014 with the San Francisco Giants. He was very vocal and helped to organize various events with his downtown brewery being a very convenient meeting location, and we will be eternally grateful for everything he did for our team and our town. He held "watch parties" at his brewery, and so during all the regional and Williamsport games there was a large crowd in there cheering the boys' on! Or maybe they were just there for the suds? He'll argue, and we'll let him win, that they were there for both! 😊

There is plenty of drama that surrounds these tournaments. This Fossil Creek v. University story is just one example. You hear stories about various Little League teams and/or programs that bend and/or intentionally subvert various rules in order to get their teams to go further in these events. Rio Vista Little League was apparently disqualified for having one to two players they shouldn't have. The really famous case was Danny Almonte from the Dominican Republic in 2001, and there were reports of him having two birth certificates, one showing he was 12 and another showing he was 14. His team was disqualified after reaching the semifinals. The Jackie Robinson West Little League in Chicago was stripped of their 2014 accomplishments, including winning the US Championship tournament at Williamsport after it was found that they had ineligible players on their roster. Waterbury, CT had a protest filed against them as well for allegedly having some ineligible players as well.

Game 11 Texas West @ Arkansas

Waco...Welcome to the Little League Regional Tournament. For seven days every August, Little League players and families descend and take over the town. This baseball tournament provides a little over a $1.3 million economic boost to the town during this week. Even though we just played two weeks ago, it feels like it's been forever. The coaches wanted to get the boys to Waco a little early, so we drove up Tuesday, July 30th in the morning, even though our first game was not until Thursday at 10am.

Waco is famous for being the home of Texas Farm Bureau Insurance, Magnolia Market (from the Chip and Joanna Gaines Fixer Upper TV Show), Baylor University, Texas Ranger Hall of Fame Museum, Dr Pepper Museum, and the Texas Sports Hall of Fame. Now that we are 3 hours east of Abilene, the temperature fluctuated between 95-103 degrees, and the humidity is about 70%. Abilene is 45-50% average humidity, and so Waco is 20% more humid than where we were two weeks ago. In meteorological terms, the humidity comfort levels range from humid to muggy to oppressive to miserable. We didn't see any of the dry or comfortable days, lol.

The Regionals tournament is different because the Little League actually takes over past the state tournament. Waco is home to the Little League Southwestern Region Headquarters, and so all games are played at the Marvin Norcross Stadium, which is right next to the Baylor University Equestrian Center and the Baylor University Golf Practice Facility. This stadium holds about 2,000 people, and one of the nice things about Little League events is that they are free to the public. Many folks from around Texas and surrounding states make the journey every August to Waco to come watch these teams, in addition to the parents and extended family that come because their kids are playing that year. Many of the life-long fans of Little League try to come watch as many of these games as they can. Billy Martin showed up in Waco, and then he also came to Williamsport to watch the tournament. He was the Houston pitcher who threw the first no-hitter in tournament history in 1950! He was recognized as a "Diamond Moment" in the 75-year history of the LLWS!

There are seven teams in this tournament, Arkansas (Junior Deputy Baseball LL from Little Rock), Louisiana (Greater New Orleans LL), Mississippi (Clinton Baseball Association LL), New Mexico (Roadrunner White LL from Albuquerque), Oklahoma (Tulsa National LL), Texas East (Lamar LL from Houston), and Boerne, which is now Texas West. Mississippi sent their Hub City LL from Hattiesburg to the LLWS in 1977. Oklahoma had teams make it to Williamsport in 1964 and 1988. We'll talk about Arkansas, New Mexico, and Louisiana as we play them.

All the boys and coaches were provided rooms courtesy of Little League in the La Quinta hotel downtown. Many of the parents booked in the Aloft Hotel that shares the parking lot with the La Quinta, that way we can walk back and forth. That also means you have all 7 teams staying together in one hotel, 84 kids plus 21 coaches, so the La Quinta was a madhouse every day. La Quinta cooked breakfast for the boys, and then Little League provided gift cards to the coaches that were to be used for the lunches and dinners for the boys. We also have to give a Texas "thank you" to Rudy's BBQ, a Texas BBQ chain that graciously supplied breakfast tacos to the boys on multiple mornings. Kaleb's favorite breakfast food is bacon & egg tacos, so he says that his great play was a direct result of Rudy's breakfast tacos.

The boys also got a further taste of what stardom is like. Axe bats provided each of the boys with a complimentary bat. The more interesting thing though, for the boys, was that each of these games are televised live on ESPN+. The competition continues to improve to, so, while Boerne has gone undefeated in its first 10 games to get to this point, each of the other programs have also won 8-12 games to get to this point. This takes on a whole new level of stress and anxiety for the families, as now, every pitch, every swing, and every error, is seen by thousands, if not millions of folks around the world, and the boys are now only one step away from realizing the dream which is to get to the Little League World Series in Williamsport.

Arkansas has been to Williamsport three times; National Little Rock in both 1952 and 1953, and Burns Park in North Little Rock in 1979. Arkansas comes to Williamsport with big dreams to take their state back to the grand stage! This is what makes Little League World Series incredibly popular, but also an emotional rollercoaster, because you've got these twelve kids now representing an entire state, and doing their absolute best in every play for the millions of people back home!

The team gets a good breakfast in them, arrives at the batting cages around 8a for batting practice, and then they head to the field for a second hour of warmup and getting ready. Arkansas starts off with Beau Holbert on the mound, Julian watches strike one. He fouls off strike two, and then Holbert hangs a curveball up in the zone, that Julian is able to smoke to left center in the gap for a stand-up double. Gray watches strike one, swings at strike two, and then hits a chopper ground ball to third base that bounces over his glove and gets into right field for a single and Julian advances to third. Holbert throws Cooper that same high curveball, and Cooper hits a ground ball in the gap between short and third base for a single to left, scoring Julian! Seven pitches into the game and we take a 1 run lead! See, we are supposed to score in the first inning every time! Kole watches balls one and two, fouls off strike one, and then Holbert throws that same high curve ball, is able to get it in on Kole's hands, but he is able to get enough of it to hit a ground ball up the middle to center field for a single, they throw home to try to get Gray, but the ball comes in high and Gray slides under it for the second run!

Holbert starts Caden off with that same high curve ball, he hits a grounder to the third baseman, who fields it and immediately runs to third, but Cooper beats him to the bag! Bases loaded, no outs! Let's go Boerne! Doc swings at strike one, and then hits a knuckle ball to right field on a line drive that the right fielder is just able to stick out his glove and catch it down on his left side as he is running toward the fence. It catches the boys off balance, as they had already started to the next base, so they have to quickly reverse course and get back to their bags. The right fielder throws it into the shortstop at second, who quickly flips it to first base and gets Caden out before he can get back for the first double play of the game. Holbert throws a nice curveball that starts to drop down out of the zone to Aiden, who hits a fly ball to center field to end the inning. A 15-pitch inning for Beau!

Cooper is on the mound for Boerne and Brady McCrillis watches strike one, and then hits a ground ball to Jett at shortstop who is able to get him out at first. Kyler Brown watches strike one, swings at strike two, and then hits a line drive to right field that Doc, coming over from center, is able to snag and quickly get it in to hold him to a single. Gabriel Scaife swings at strike one, fouls off strike two, watches ball one, watches ball two, and then is hit by a changeup that gets away from Cooper. Abel Gill fouls off strike one, and then Cooper is able to induce a soft contact ground ball with his curve, but the ground ball just gets by Kole at third, and so Arkansas loads the bases with one out. Jonas Berry fouls off strikes one and two, watches ball one, fouls off strike three, watches ball two, and then swings and misses for strike three. Garrett Brosius fouls off strike one, watches ball one, watches ball two, watches ball three, watches strike two, fouls off strike three, fouls off three more pitches, and then finally watches ball four to walk in a run. A 10-pitch at bat for Garrett and he is able to bring a run home to make it 2-1.

Hyatt Bankhead watches strike one, watches strike two, watches ball one, and then half swings really early on a changeup to outside corner for strike three to end the inning. Whew...Way to get us out of that inning Cooper with minimal damage! A 32-pitch inning for Cooper and that shows you how much tougher these games get as you get further along! Cooper knew it too as he made the "sheath the sword" move as the boys return to the dugouts!

Gage watches ball one, swings at strike one, swings at strike two, and then gets that same high curveball and is able to hit a line drive up the middle to center for a single! Ben hits a towering fly ball to the left fielder for out #1. Jett watches ball one, swings at strike one, swings at strike two, fouls off strike three, and then Holbert is able to throw that curveball inside a little, that Jett thinks might hit him so he turns his shoulder, but it drops over the corner for strike three. Dylan watches ball one and then rips a line drive to left field for a single!

Kaleb watches strike one and then, with his new Axe bat, smokes a line drive to shallow center for a single, the center fielder throws home to try to hold Gage at third but the throw is wide right, so Gage scores, and both Dylan and Kaleb advance. Julian gets intentionally walked, and now the bases are loaded for Boerne! Little League rules say that 4 balls do get added to the pitch count for an intentional walk. Gray watches ball one, fouls off strike one, and then smokes a line drive to deep left field, scoring both Dylan and Kaleb! Cooper watches ball one and then hits a ground ball up the middle to center field for a single, loading the bases once again with two out! Kole watches ball one, swings at strike one, fouls off the next eight pitches, and then protect swings at a pitch to the top of the zone, pops it up, and the catcher is able to go make the catch for out #3. Boerne extends their lead to 5-1! A 34-pitch inning for Beau! This is a battle!

William Groce to the plate, watches ball one, watches strike one, watches ball two, fouls off strike two, watches ball three, fouls off strike three, and then Cooper gets him on a good curveball and he hits a ground ball to third and Kole is able to get him out at first. Jack watches ball one and then hits a shallow fly ball to center field that drops in for a base hit.

Sam hits a ground ball to Aiden at second base, who makes a good spin move to his left to flip the ball to Jett to get the lead runner out. Beau watches balls one and two, watches strike one, swings at strike two, and then hits a fly ball to deep left field over Dylan's head that gets to the wall, but then Dylan throws it all the way to Kole at 3rd just as Sam rounded third base, and Boerne gets him hung up in a pickle, and after one throw back and forth, Julian tags him out as he is going for home. A 15-pitch inning for Cooper!

Arkansas pulls Beau at 49 pitches and brings in Garrett to relieve. Caden watches three balls in a row, and then Garrett throws him a high curveball that drops into the zone and Caden hits a line drive up the middle to center field for a single. Doc watches three balls in a row, watches strike one, and then is able to extend his bat out to the outside corner to catch a curveball and send it to deep center field as a fly ball, but the center fielder is able to make the catch near the wall over his shoulder, and so Caden was already halfway to 3rd base, so he turns around, but they get him out at first, doubling it up. Aiden fouls off strike one, and then hits a ground ball out on the end of the bat back to the pitcher for an out at first. An 11-pitch inning for Garrett!

Dustin fouls off strike one and then lays down a bunt to 3rd base, and Kole isn't able to get to it in time, so he is safe at first. Brady McCrillis hits a ground ball to Jett at shortstop and he is able to turn the double play. Kyler Brown watches balls one and two, and then waits on a curveball right to the middle of the zone, sending a home run over the left field wall, to make it 5-2! Justin, Boerne's GM, decides to pull Cooper at 52 pitches, who threw an impressive 69% strike percentage, and bring Kole in to pitch. Gabriel Scaife swings at strike one, watches ball one, fouls off strike two, and then chases a high fastball at the top of the zone and misses for strike three! A 10-pitch inning for Boerne, let's go!!! They are going to keep trying to chip away at our lead!

Gage watches ball one, fouls off strike one, swings at strike two, and then hits a high pitch way up the air for a fly ball to right and an out. Ben watches ball one, watches strike one, swings at strike two, and swings and misses at a curveball to the outside corner for strike three. Jett watches ball one and then is able to wait on a high curveball, barrel it up, and hits a fly ball to the left fielder for out #3. That 10-pitch inning put some pep into Arkansas' step and they are coming back swinging and try to tie this game up!

Abel Gill watches strike one, watches ball one, swings at strike two, and then hits a ground ball a few feet in front of the plate, but Kole is not able to pick it up and get it to first, so their leadoff runner is aboard. Jonas watches ball one, watches strike one, and then hits a line drive to left field to get two runners on. Garrett watches ball one, fouls off strike one, swings at strike two, watches a wild pitch for ball two while the runners advance, and then hits a ground ball back to Kole at first, who checks the runner at third, throws it to Julian at first for the out, and then Julian throws it home to Doc who is able to tag Abel out as he tries to score!

Hyatt Bankhead fouls off strike one and then lines out to Gray in center field to end the 4th inning. We narrowly avoided them scoring several there, but with quick defensive instincts we were able to take advantage of their aggressive base running and hold them to no runs even after they got their two leadoff hitters on base! A 14-pitch inning for Kole, let's go!!

Dylan watches ball one, and then waits on a high curveball and hits a line drive to center that is caught for the first out. Kaleb watches strike one and then flies out to center field as well. Julian watches balls one and two, watches strike one, watches ball three, and then waits on curveball and is able to hit a hard ground ball to left field for a single! Gray waits on a curveball that drops in low and so he barrels up a fly ball to center field that is caught for out #3. A 10-pitch inning for Garrett and this thing is back and forth! Our hearts are in our throat!

William watches ball one, swings at strike one, watches balls two and three, fouls off strike two, and then watches ball four high and outside to draw the walk. Jack hits a ground ball to Jett who is able to get it to Aiden for the lead out, but Jack is able to beat the throw to first and avoid the double play. Sam fouls off the first two pitches, and then hits a ground ball to Aiden, who flips it to

Jett, who catches it bare-handed, tags 2nd and then throws to Julian at first for the double play to end the 5th inning! A 10-pitch inning for Kole!

Cooper swings at an outside curveball diving in low, catches it on the end of the bat and sends a ground ball to third base, who is able to get him out at first. Kole watches three balls in a row, swings at strike one, and then watches a curveball way outside for ball four and takes his base. Caden gets the barrel down to a curveball dropping out of the zone, and hits a fly ball to shallow center that is caught for the second out. Doc watches ball one, fouls off strike one, and then watches three balls in a row to draw the walk, and get runners on 1st and 2nd with two outs.

Aiden watches balls one and two, and swings at a curveball and is able to hit a hard grounder to third base, who can't come up with it, so the ball dribbles into left field. Kole comes around and scores, and Aiden advances to second on the throw. Gage waits on a hanging curveball up in the zone and is able to hit a line drive to center field, scoring Doc! Ben hits a deep fly ball to center field that is caught to end the top of the 6th. Boerne scores two to take a 7-2 lead! A 17-pitch inning for Garrett! 3 outs away from our first win at Regionals! Let's go!

Beau, their #11 hitter, fouls off the first two pitches, and then hits a hard ground ball in the gap to left field for a single. Dustin watches balls one and two, fouls off strike one, watches ball three, fouls off strike two, and watches ball four to get runners on first and second. Boerne brings Julian in to try to quickly end this game, even though Kole has thrown an impressive 62% strike percentage in his 37 pitches on the mound. Brady watches balls one and two, the third pitch is a hard curveball that goes wide left and so the runners advance. Now we've got a 3-0 count, no outs, and runners at 2nd and 3rd.

Nail biting and the Boerne families are on the edge of their seats, come on boys, don't let this one get away from us! Brady watches strike one, fouls off strike two, and then swings and misses at Julian's nasty curveball for strike three. Kyler watches strike one, watches strike two, and then swings and misses at Julian's curveball for strike three and out #2. Come on boys, just one more!!! Gabriel, Arkansas' last hope to keep the game alive, comes to the plate. He swings at strike one, watches ball one, swings at strike two, fouls off strike three, and then watches strike three, a really good hard curveball on the inner third of the plate that jelly-legs him, and that ends the ballgame! PHEW!!!!

A 7-2 victory over Arkansas, and they held Boerne to only 11 hits, 7 runs, 3 walks, and 2 strikeouts. Boerne's pitching was able to hold them to 7 hits, 3 walks, and 6 strike-outs. Boerne continues its pitching accuracy with a 71% strike percentage on 103 pitches. Arkansas pitched well too at 65% for their 96 pitches.

Texas West and Arkansas broke the record for double plays in a Southwest Region Tournament game with five. That is the first game we have scored fewer than 11 runs, and the closest game we have had yet. That puts us on edge, knowing that the rest of this Regional tournament is going to be a really tough test, but at least we get to celebrate today! We left the stadium, went to go find a good lunch, refuel and rehydrate, went to go relax the rest of Thursday afternoon, and get to bed early that evening so that way we would be ready for New Mexico first thing in the morning.

Game 12 Texas West @ New Mexico

Winning on Thursday against Arkansas meant that we got to play again the next day, Friday at 10a again against New Mexico. Arkansas got sent to the loser bracket and they would face Texas East on Saturday, who won Thursday against Mississippi, but then lost on Friday to Louisiana, and so that was an elimination game for both of those teams. New Mexico got the bye, with there being 7 teams, so their first game was against us. New Mexico has appeared in the Little League World Series one time in 1956, where the Lions Hondo team won the whole thing! This New Mexico team arrives with the hopes to take their state back to Williamsport as well!

It's another beautiful day in Texas, not a cloud in the sky, and it's going to be a hot one! Reid Alcaraz is on the mound for New Mexico and Julian steps into the box. He watches strike one, watches ball one, fouls off the next three in a row, watches ball two, and then hits a curveball chopper ground ball to third base and they field it cleanly and get him out at first. At first the ump called Julian safe, claiming that the first baseman's foot came off the bag, but upon replay, they called him out. This is another fun benefit of the regional tournament, in that we have live replay, just like MLB games. The level of professionalism in the way these games are run is really incredible.

Gray watches ball one, watches ball two, watches strike one, watches ball three, and then Gray gets caught with that same curveball, hits a ground ball to shortstop and they get him out at first. Cooper fouls off strike one, watches strike two, and then protects on a high curveball up in the zone, and hits a ground ball to second base for the final out. Shoot!! 3 up and 3 down. In our first 11 games, there have only been three games where we have failed to put points on the board in the first inning. Ok, a lot of baseball left, let's go play defense and then get back to the plate. A 15-pitch inning for Reid and he shut down the Boerne offense!

Caden takes the mound for Boerne and throws strike one to Gabriel Martinez, who watches it whiz by. He fouls off strike two, watches ball one, and then waits on a high curveball and sends a line drive to shallow center that Doc is able to get to and catch for out #1. Colby Gaulden watches balls one and two, watches strike one, watches strike two, watches ball three, and swings and misses at a good fastball on the outer third of the plate for strike three. Tyriano Cordova watches strike one, watches balls one and two, watches strike two, fouls off strike three, and then gets fooled on a high curveball that drops into the zone for strike three. A 16-pitch inning for Caden and he's looking good, so we try to relax just a little.

Kole watches strike one, watches balls one and two, swings at strike two, and then connects on a high curveball and skies it to foul territory in right field and they are able to come over and make the catch. Caden swings at strike one, fouls off strike two, and then just misses a fastball up the zone for strike three. Doc fouls off strike one and then is able to put the curveball on the ground where it bounces off the shortstop's glove and he is able to get to first. Aiden watches ball one, fouls off strike one, and then barrels up that same high curveball that Kole got and hits a line drive to left, and the left fielder is able to get under it for the 3rd out.

Oh boy...Even in the 3 games where we failed to score in the 1st inning, we ALWAYS scored in the second inning, and now we have just blanked twice... A 13-pitch inning for Reid! All the Boerne families are chewing their nonexistent nails further into the nailbeds. It's okay, Caden's got good control of this game on the mound, and we keep swinging, we'll break-through their defense at some point.

Lucas Baca watches ball one, watches strike one, watches ball two, swings at strike two, and then watches that same high curveball to the outer half of the plate for strike three and out #1. Brycen Rogillio watches ball one, watches strike one, watches ball two, and then is able to catch up to Caden's fastball and send a hard ground ball between Kole, playing first base, and the first base bag for a single. Harry Bunton watches ball one hits a ground ball to Aiden, who flips it to Jett and they turn the double play to end the inning! That is the fourth double play for Boerne here at Regionals, and an incredible 11-pitch inning for Caden!

Gage gets the sign to bunt so he can use his blazing speed to try to beat the throw, but the bunt is just a little too much back toward the pitcher, so he is able to make the grab and throw to first to get him out before he makes it down the line. Ben watches strike one, swings at strike two, watches ball one, watches ball two, fouls off strike three, watches ball three, and then hits a curveball as a high fly ball to shallow center and the centerfielder, Beckett Locker, on a dead run is able to make the catch. Jett swings at strike one, swings at strike two, fouls off strike three, watches balls one, two, and three, and then rips a high curveball to the right-center gap but Beckett is able to get over and snag that one too at a full sprint.

Ok, we are officially in uncharted territory here, with 3 innings and no runs. It's fine though, it's not a question of "if" we will score, it's simply a question of "when." We hope. A 15-pitch inning for Reid! He's locating his curveball really well and forcing our batters to try to barrel it up. Can we recruit that kid?

Omar Flores watches ball one, watches strike one, and then just gets under a fastball to pop it up behind third base and Jett's able to come over, calls off Ben who is also right there in shallow left, and make the catch. Beckett Locker watches strike one, watches ball one, watches ball two, fouls off strike two, watches ball three and four to draw the walk. One of the things that parents love to see is the really good sportsmanship of the players in these Little League tournaments. Kole fist bumps Beckett when he gets to first base, as if to say, both of us are simply really happy to be here playing baseball and just want to congratulate you on doing your part to help your team. Tucker Kollar watches strike one and then hits a rocket to left-center gap that bounces over the fence for a ground rule double!

Boerne pulls Caden at 35 pitches (57% strike percentage) and brings in Doc to relieve. Reid comes to the plate and watches ball one, watches strike one, watches strike two, watches ball two, watches ball three, and then hits a ground ball to Aiden at second, who quickly fields it and throws home to Julian, who is catching, in order to tag Beckett as he's coming home. Julian brushes his leg as he dances by, and is initially called safe at home, but upon official review, they call him out. WHEW!!!

We avoided that by the skin of our teeth...Jake Stevens watches ball one, fouls off strike one, watches ball two, swings at strike two, and then Doc gets him with an elevated fastball to the outside corner for a swing and miss strike three! A 22-pitch inning for Boerne and this game is tense!

Dylan watches balls one and two, watches strike one, fouls off strike two, and then watches balls three and four to take his base. That last pitch was a low curveball that just dropped out of the zone, and Dylan did a great job of taking that pitch. Ok, here we go, leadoff runner aboard, let's make some things happen!

New Mexico pulls Reid at 50 pitches and brings in Gabriel to relieve. Gabriel is a big lefty pitcher that throws hard. Kaleb swings at strike one, watches ball one, fouls off strike two, watches balls two and three, fouls off strike three, fouls off two more pitches, and finally misses on a fastball to the outer half of the plate. A tough 9-pitch out for Kaleb, trying to do anything he could to move Dylan to second and get him in scoring position. Julian watches strike one, watches ball one, swings at strike two, and then watches balls two, three, and four. That last pitch was a low curveball outside, and Julian didn't chase, so now we've got 2 runners on with 1 out!

Ok, boys, this is our time, let's go! Gray gets into the box and the first fastball comes in high and in, and he turns his left shoulder and takes the hit to load the bases for Boerne! This cannot be over-stated. Too many kids dive out of the way of getting hit, but that is simply something that coaches and parents need to "condition" into the kids. It can be the difference between winning and losing, and the pain doesn't last that long anyway. If you are going to play this game for a long time, you might as well get used to getting hit with the baseball. Any high school coach that watches a player dive out of the way will be benched immediately, if not thrown off the team, so you might as well establish good habits at ages 10-14 years old. Cooper watches balls one and two, and then just gets under a fastball to hit a high fly ball to right field, that is good enough to for a sacrifice fly and Dylan is able to tag up and score, and both Julian and Gray advance when the right fielder threw it home! Finally! Boerne on the board, 1-0, and two more runs in scoring position! Kole fouls off strike one, watches strike two, and then just misses that fastball to the outside corner for strike three. Finally, a 28-pitch inning for New Mexico and our first run!

Jordan Frick, their #12 batter, comes to the plate, watches ball one, watches strike one, watches strike two, and then tries to protect on a high fastball, but hits a chopper ground ball to Jett at short, who is able to run up, make the scoop, and get it to first for out #1. Gabriel swings at the first pitch fastball to the outer half and is able to hit a line drive over Jett's head into the gap in left center and get all the way to the wall for a stand-up double! Colby watches strike one, swings at strike two, fouls off strike three, watches ball one, and then swings and misses at Doc's high fastball for strike three.

Tyriano rips the first pitch fastball on a line drive to right field, Ben scoops it up and throws it home, but it's just offline enough that Gabe is able to come in and score, and now it's tied up at 1-1! Needless to say, we are on the edge of our seats and now looking for someone else's nails that we can chew on...Lucas fouls off strike one and then hits a line out to Jett at short to thankfully end the 4th inning. Ok, take a breath, we aren't losing, it's just back to a tie game, and now it's time to go hit! A 13-pitch inning for Doc but they scored 1!!!

Caden watches balls one and two, fouls off strike one and two, and then watches a slider start off the plate and come back in on him for strike three. Doc fouls off the first two strikes and then goes after a high fastball but misses for strike three. Aiden watches balls one and two, watches strike one, fouls off strike two, and then watches balls three and four to draw the walk. New Mexico pulls Gabe at 35 pitches and brings in Tyriano to relieve. Gage fouls off strike one, watches ball one, and then rips a line drive single down the line in left for a single! Ben watches ball one, watches strike one, and then watches balls 2-4, with the last one being a high curveball that just stays up, and Boerne loads the bases with two outs!

Jett watches ball one, watches strike one, fouls off strike two, watches ball two, and then hits a hard ground ball that just gets past the second baseman, who dives but couldn't get there, and it gets through the gap to right field, scoring both Aiden and Gage! Gage comes sliding in, just beating the throw home to the plate, and his slide makes the catcher miss the ball, so both Ben and Jett advance one base. Dylan fouls off three pitches in a row and then hits a deep fly ball to left to end the inning, but we take the lead 3-1! YES!!! A 31-pitch inning for New Mexico, and now we are starting to crack open the door!

Brycen fouls off strike one, and then watches four balls in a row, and their leadoff runner gets aboard. Harry watches ball one, fouls off strike one, watches strike two, fouls off strike two, and then gets under a high fastball to pop it out to Aiden at second. Boerne pulls Doc at 35 pitches (60% strike percentage), and brings Julian in to close the game out. Omar watches strike one and then hits a chopper back up the middle just left of the mound that Julian can't quite field cleanly, and now we have 2 runners on with one out. Beckett watches ball one, swings and misses at a nice curveball that just drops off the table, but the ball gets behind Caden and the runners advance! Now we have the tying run in scoring position with only one out! Brycen swings at strike two, and then Julian gives him that curveball again, and he swings and misses for strike three! A huge out for Boerne and now Tucker comes to bat. He watches strike one, swings at strike two, and then is able to get his bat on Julian's curveball to the outside corner to hit a tailing fly ball into foul territory in right field, and Doc is able to come over and make a sliding catch to end the inning!! The momentum turns to Boerne, let's go hit! A 29-pitch inning for Boerne but we didn't let them score! PHEW!!!!!!!

Kaleb watches strike one and then just gets on top of a fastball outside to hit a ground ball to second base for an out at first. Julian fouls off strike one and then just takes the cover off the ball with a no doubt home run solo shot into the trees right over the ESPN camera booth in center field! New Mexico immediately brings in Harry to try to change the momentum. Gray watches strike one, watches ball one, swings at strike two, and then just obliterates a high fastball and pulls it down the left field line to the wall for a stand-up double! Cooper rips a hard single to right, and the fielder can't come up with it, so Gray rounds third and gets home easily, for Boerne to take a 5-1 lead!!

Kole fouls off strike one, watches ball one, watches a changeup come way up out of the hand of Harry and go over Kole's head into the backstop, and Cooper will get to second base on the wild pitch. Kole fouls off the next two pitches and then just gets on top of a curveball to hit a ground ball to shortstop who is able to get him out at first. Cooper makes it to third. Caden watches strike one and then watches four balls in a row to get on. Doc swings at strike one, watches ball one, Kole (courtesy runner for our catcher Caden) steals second, so now we have two runners in scoring position, and then Doc watches ball two, and then just gets under a fastball to pop it up behind him but the catcher is able to get back and make the catch to end the inning. Ok, we took a while, but now we've got a 5-1 lead and only need 3 outs!!! Let's go boys, let's finish this!!! A 24-pitch inning for New Mexico, and now we are starting to stretch it out!

Reid, their #10 hitter, comes to the plate, Julian gets a fastball in on his hands and Reid pops out to Kole at first for out #1. Jake watches strike one, strike two, and then Julian throws him the heater middle-in for strike #3 and Jake watches it for strike three. Now their #12 hitter is all that is left between extending the game and a win for Boerne! Jordan watches strike one, swings at strike two, and then Julian jelly-legs him with a high curveball that just drops back into the zone for strike three! Holy crap, the tightest game so far, but we were able to emerge victorious! A 7-pitch inning to close it out for Julian! Wow!!!

New Mexico had 5 hits, two walks, and had 8 strike-outs. They held us to 6 hits, gave up 5 walks, and 5 strike-outs, so those three walks and our slightly better strike percentage (66% vs. theirs of 61%) were difference makers. We were also fortunate to have some timely hitting, but our bats didn't show up today like the normally have. We need to go have a word with that Axe sales rep! 😊

Prior to today, our lowest was 9 hits against Brownsville. How many times have we already seen in the 12 games we've played thus far that you need 12 good hitters, because several of these games will come down to what your #9-12 batters can do for you at the plate! It's almost inconceivable to believe that it is only noon on Friday, most of the real world is working, and we've been at a baseball field for the last 4 hours, but seems like much longer. That game was so tense!

Winning on Friday meant that we earned a day off and we would not play again until the semi-final game on Sunday, August 4th at 3p. We took the boys for a good lunch and then some went swimming to offset the 100+ degree heat. We'd get together for a practice on Saturday, definitely do plenty of hitting, but keep things pretty low-key so everyone can be at 100% for the game

Sunday. After what we have just experienced in these first two games, we're going to need to bring our A-game!

Our two "go-to" restaurants in Waco end up being Terry Black's BBQ and Texas Roadhouse. Since we won Friday night and wouldn't play again until Sunday, we had all day Saturday off. We took Kaleb to the pool for a while and then took him back to the hotel and dropped him off after dinner.

The boys figured out that our Aloft hotel had a pool table in the lobby, so whenever they were simply hanging out at the hotel, many times we'd find them in our lobby as opposed to theirs.

Saturday evening Betty and I were able to make our way to Melody Ranch, a local country dance hall, and spend a bit of "adult time" together while Kaleb was getting his much-needed rest for Sunday's game. Melody has live music every Saturday night. Betty and I typically get to these country dance halls around 8p, dance to the first set or two of the band, and then head back home, or in this case, to our hotel. That gives us 2-3 hours of dancing, but then we still get a good night's sleep before all this baseball drama continues the next day!

Louisiana beats Texas East later on Friday 3-0, so that puts Louisiana in the semi-final game against us for Sunday. Do you see a "theme" in these scores? Many of the scores at District, Section, and even state had teams scoring 10-20 runs, and here we are at Regionals and there was only one blow out game, and the rest of the games have been decided by 1-4 runs.

New Mexico's loss sends them to the loser's bracket so they had to play Saturday at 2p (really, 2p on Saturday afternoon when it's 1,000 degrees outside?) against Oklahoma, who lost to Louisiana in the first round, but was able to beat Mississippi 10-0 in the first loser's bracket game. Mississippi played Texas East on Thursday in the first round, and Texas East beat them 4-0, so Mississippi didn't score a run in the Regional tournament. They will take that information back home and re-tool for next year. New Mexico would beat Oklahoma in a nail-biter 1-0 game, and then ultimately lose to Texas East in another nail-biter game 3-2 on Sunday before our first game against Louisiana.

Game 13 Texas West @ Louisiana

Louisiana did something unique this year. The Greater New Orleans (GNO) Little League partnered with the Jefferson Parish Parks & Recreation Department (JPRD) to extend the opportunity to play Little League to the kids in Jefferson Parish. This partnership allowed nearly 1,000 kids with more accessible and more affordable opportunities to play baseball. They charged just $25 per family, which got kids their jersey, hat, and all the registration fees.

This is such a great example of the importance of Little League and local community partnerships around the world, where else could you play baseball for an entire season for just $25? GNO-JPRD has a population of around 800,000, so they have quite a pool to select the best players, versus our 22,000 in Boerne. Louisiana has sent 9 teams to Williamsport in the past, with Eastbank (River Ridge) LL winning the World Series Championship in 2019 against Caribbean! They lost their first game against West, and then won the next 6 games in a row to come back from the loser's bracket to win it all!

For this Regional Tournament, they beat Oklahoma 4-1 and Texas East 3-0, and so here we are in the winner's side of the bracket, in for the proverbial fight of our lives! A proven Louisiana program vs the "upstart" team from Boerne. Let's go!! We love our underdog stories!

Christopher (CJ) Newsone Jr is in to pitch for Louisiana, the lanky right hander. Julian watches strike one, watches ball one, watches strike two, and then grounds out to shortstop. Gray watches strike one, watches ball one, watches strike two, fouls off strike three, watches balls two and three, and then rips a hard grounder to right field for a single! Cooper fouls off strike one and then gets on top of a curveball for a chopper ground ball up the middle that is grabbed by the shortstop and turned for a double play! That was the 20th double play of the Regional Tournament and yet again we fail to score in our first at-bat! A 13-pitch inning for CJ and we are looking for some nails we can chew on!

Caden is on the mound for Boerne and Zayne Barrett watches ball one, watches strike one, watches ball two, and then pops out to Aiden at second for out #1. Dominic Barranco watches ball one, watches strike one, and then turns his shoulder on a high fastball inside that hits him, and he gets to first. CJ grounds into a fielder's choice to Aiden and Boerne gets Dominic out going to second base. Two outs, runner on first.

Cy Kirklin watches ball one, watches strike one, watches ball two, fouls off strike two, and then hits a ground ball to left field for a single and now we've got two runners on. Chase LeBlanc watches strike one and then rips a line drive to Cooper in left field for the third out. Ok, inning #1 down and no runs by either team. A 15-pitch inning for Caden, let's go!!

Kole Newson fouls off strike one and the hits a sky-high fly ball to left-center, the left fielder dives for it and he can't make the play, so it's a double for Kole! Caden watches strike one and then hits a hard ground ball up the middle to center field for a single, and Kole gets held at third. Doc fouls off strike one, watches balls one and two, swings at strike two, watches a breaking ball bounce in the dirt on the outside that gets away from the catcher and Kole comes into score! Boerne takes a 1-0 lead! Ok, well, if we don't score in the first inning, let's make sure we do so in the second, just to keep all the parents' blood pressure under control.

Doc fouls off strike three and then takes an inside pitch for ball four to draw the walk. Gage watches strike one and then hits a ground ball to shortstop, who flips it to second, but Gage streaks down to first and avoids the double play. Aiden watches balls one and two, watches strike one, fouls off strike two, and then hits a hard ground ball in the gap to right field for a single and scores Caden! Boerne takes a 2-0 lead! Dylan watches four balls in a row to draw the walk and load the bases! Jett watches balls one and two, watches strike one, fouls off strike two, watches ball three, fouls off strike three, and watches the curveball fly up and out of his hand for an easy take on ball four to walk in a run! Patience and great hitting discipline at the plate on full display!!! Boerne takes a 3-0 lead!

Louisiana pulls CJ at 56 pitches and brings Benjamin Florane into relieve. 56 pitches in less than two innings, see what we mean by pitch count? Kaleb fouls off strikes one and two and then rips a line drive to right field for a single and scores Aiden, and he continues to be excited about that Axe bat! Boerne takes a 4-0 lead! Ben watches ball one, watches strike one, fouls off the next three pitches, watches balls two and three, and then watches and outside curveball come back over the corner from the lefty pitcher for strike three. Julian watches ball one, fouls off strike one, and then pops out in foul territory near the dugout and the first baseman is able to get under it and make the catch. Ok, Boerne takes a good lead and now we've got to play defense! An incredible 43-pitch inning for Louisiana that we just created! Well done boys, keep it up!

Landon Valladares fouls off strike one, watches balls one and two, fouls off strike two, and then swings and misses Caden's heater for strike three! Benjamin Florane hits a ground ball to Aiden at second for a routine out at first. Lane Pastor watches strike one, watches balls one and two, and then lines out to Gray in center field for out #3! An incredible 10-pitch inning for Caden!

Gray watches ball one and then flies out to right field. Cooper watches ball one, fouls off strike one, watches ball two, then hits a ground ball to shortstop who doesn't come get it fast enough and he beats the throw to first! Kole Newson watches three balls in a row and then hits a ground ball to third base and they get Cooper out at second. Caden watches strike one, fouls off strike two, watches ball one, and then rips a line drive to deep center field and CJ makes a leaping grab to reach up and over the fence to rob him of a home run right underneath the ESPN cameraman's scissor lift just behind the fence! Did that just happen?? That one is definitely one for the highlight reel...ESPN play of the week! A 14-pitch inning for Louisiana and this is intense!!!

Kole Cao watches ball one and then hits a line drive single to the right center gap. Kamren Lew lays down a good sacrifice bunt to advance Kole Cao to second and he gets thrown out at first by Caden bare-handing the ball and getting it over to Julian. Sayid Jabbar watches balls one and two, fouls off strike one, watches ball three, watches strike two, and then watches a high curveball just miss for ball four to put two runners on. Brandt Deeke watches strike one, watches strike two, fouls off the next two pitches, watches balls one and two, and then swings and misses at a really good curveball that dropped down over the plate for strike three.

Zayne Barrett watches ball one, swings at strike one, watches balls two and three, watches strike two, and then watches an inside pitch for ball four to load the bases. Dominic Barranco hits a ground ball to Aiden who flips it to Julian at first for the final out and thankfully, not allowing any of those runs to score! Halfway done with this game and it's a rollercoaster!!! A 23-pitch inning for Boerne, but we were able to keep them from scoring with two runners on!

Doc watches balls one and two, watches strike one, fouls off the next two strikes, and then flies out to right field. Gage hits a ground ball to shortstop but the throw is wide and low and so Gage reaches on the error. Aiden fouls off strike one, watches ball one, and then hits a line drive to center field that is caught for out #2. Dylan fouls off strike one, watches ball one, fouls off strike two, watches balls two and three, and then hits a shallow fly ball to left field that drops for a hit! Jett flies out to right field to end the inning. A 16-pitch inning for Louisiana and they are throwing strikes and forcing us to barrel up the ball!

CJ smokes a hard-line drive to deep center field wall and gets to second base! Cy Kirklin fouls off strike one, watches strike two, fouls off strike three, and then watches a hard fastball to the outside corner for a strike three call! Chase watches ball one and then rips a curveball on a hard-line drive over Jett's head at short and into the left-center gap that gets all the way to the fence! CJ scores to get Louisiana on the board 4-1!

Landon Valladares rips a line drive that is caught by Kole Newson in left field and Chase has to remain at second. Benjamin Florane watches strike one, watches ball one, Chase tries to do a delayed steal from second but Doc sees it and quickly throws to third to tag him out and end the inning. PHEW...our blood pressure just shot through the roof!! This game is too close! Finally, a 10-pitch inning but they get one back!!

Kaleb grounds out to shortstop. Ben watches ball one and then grounds out to shortstop as well. Julian fouls off the first two strikes and then grounds out to shortstop as well, who does a reverse pivot to throw him out at first. SHOOT!! A 6-pitch inning for Louisiana! Are you kidding me? We are on our feet and pacing....

Ben Florane is back at the plate because Chase got the out while trying to steal for out #3. He swings at strike one and then hits a ground ball back up the middle to center field that is good for a single! Lane watches strike one, swings at strike two, watches ball one, and then half-heartedly swings at a nice curveball by Caden for strike three. Kole Cao gets hit in the helmet by ball one and takes his base, so now we have two runners on and only one out. Kamren Lew watches strike one, watches strike two, fouls off strike three, and then watches Caden's really good high looping curveball drop into the zone for strike three looking and a huge second out! Caden's fifth strike-out today!

Sayid Jabbar watches a first pitch high curveball bounce up and over the glove of Doc, and now the runners advance! Sayid watches balls two, three, and four to load the bases again! Oh crap...Boerne pulls Caden at 75 pitches and brings in Julian to shut this game down. Brandt Deeke watches strike one, swings at strike two, watches balls one, two, and three, and then throws his awesome drop-off-the-table curveball that Brandt swings over for a huge strike three and 3rd out to end the 5th inning! PHEW!!!! A 21-pitch inning for Boerne! We wipe the Texas sweat from our brows and we go into the 6th! Come on boys, one more inning!!!

Gray flies out to left field. Cooper grounds out to shortstop. Kole Newson watches ball one, fouls off strike one, and then lines out to shortstop as well for the 3rd out. Good grief, we can't get anything past that kid!! A 5-pitch inning for Louisiana! Ok boys,

3 more outs!! That's all we need, but we've got to get through the top of their lineup to do it!

Zayne watches ball one, swings at strike one, watches ball two, swings at strike two, and then watches Julian's nasty curveball drop in for strike three. 2 more!!! Dominic watches strike one, watches ball one, swings at strike two, fouls off strike two, and then grounds out to Jett at shortstop who comes over on the run and it able to snag it and get it to Kole Newson at first. CJ watches ball one, watches strike one, and then hits a chopper grounder up the middle to center field for a single, and this game is not over yet!! He is a little slow getting back to first, so Aiden makes a quick throw to first, but Kole's not ready for it, the ball gets by him, and so CJ gets to second base! Cy hits a fly ball over third base, and Jett on the run comes over behind him and makes the catch in shallow left field to end the game!! A 14-pitch inning to end it!!

That game was dramatic!!! Louisiana had 6 hits, 3 walks, and 7 strike-outs to get the 1 run. Boerne had 6 hits, 3 walks, and only 1 strike-out to get our 4 runs! Caden's 59% strike percentage and Julian's 63% strike percentage, combined with their velocities 65-74 mph, were crucial to keep Louisiana's bats quiet. For Louisiana, CJ threw 61% and Ben threw 64%, so they did well too, but the depth of Boerne's hitters really showed here. Thanks for your pep talk and making sure your bats performed, Mr. Axe bat rep! 😊 Total pitch count for both teams was Louisiana at 98 v. Boerne at 94!

Wow!!! How many times have we seen the guys in the bottom of the lineup come through at crucial times? This means Louisiana gets sent to the loser's bracket and they have to play again in 21 hours against Texas East.

Game 14 Louisiana @ Texas West

Here we go!!! Region Championship game on Tuesday, August 6th at 6p, and we have to re-match Louisiana!!! Louisiana narrowly beat Texas East yesterday 6-5 at 2p in the afternoon, so here they are having to play another game 26 hours later. Meanwhile, Boerne has been off since Sunday around 5p, so we've had 48 hours between games to get ready to play tonight! I would say that we went for massages, went for spa treatments, lounged at the pool, but the only truth in those statements is the pool time we did take advantage of to escape the Waco heat and humidity! Louisiana had to manage their pitcher lineup too, because this is their 5th game in 6 days.

Julian's on the mound for Boerne because we are bringing the big artillery out! He only threw 19 pitches against Louisiana on Sunday, so he's going to go as far as he can today. CJ swings at strike one, watches strike two, and then grounds out to Kole Cao at first base for out #1. Zayne B watches strike one, watches ball one, swings at strike two, watches ball two, and swings and misses at Julian's fantastic curveball for strike three. Chase swings at strike one, watches strike two, and then gets jelly-legged by Julian's curveball dropping right into the zone for strike three. An 11-pitch inning for Julian, 3 up and 3 down! Let's go hit!

Chase LeBlanc is pitching for Louisiana. Julian watches strike one and then watches four balls in a row to draw the walk. Gray watches ball one, fouls off strike one, swings at strike two, watches ball two, and then swings and misses at Chase's good curveball for strike three. Cooper watches ball one and then hits a hanging curveball on the outside to deep right for a fly ball out. Caden swings at strike one, watches balls one, two, and three, watches strike two, and then watches a knuckleball on the outside corner for strike three. Shoot, so we were able to get one runner on but not do anything with him! An 18-pitch inning for Chase! This is going to be a dogfight!

Cy K watches ball one, watches strike one, watches strike two, watches ball two, and then is able to turn on a curveball to squeeze a ground ball between 3rd and shortstop to get on first. Landon V swings at strike one, swings at strike two, and then is able to get on that same outside curveball, hit it hard down the third base line all the way to the wall, and Cy rounds third and is able to get home to take the lead, 1-0! Landon advances to 2nd base on the throw. Dominic fouls off strike one, watches ball one, watches strike two, fouls off strike three, and then hits a chopper between the pitcher and 3rd base, which Julian springs on and flips to first, but he's not in time, and the ball gets away from Kole, so Landon scores on the error, and now it's 2-0 Louisiana.

Two days are not enough for nails to re-grow, so we just start chewing on our fingers... Ben F watches ball one, watches strike one, swings at strike two, and then watches a nice changeup come in for strike three and thankfully, out #1. Lane P swings at strike one, watches strike two, and then watches that outside curveball drop in beautifully for strike three! Kole C watches a high pitch for ball one that bounces off the top of Caden's glove and gets behind him but rebounds quickly off the backstop, so he grabs it and throws to second, but neither Aiden nor Jett can make the catch, so Dominic gets to second, and then gets to third before Doc can grab the ball and get it in. Kole watches strike one, swings at strike two, watches ball two, watches a curveball in the dirt for ball three that gets past Caden and so Dominic comes in to score! It's now 3-0 Louisiana! Kole swings and misses at Julian's curveball for strike three and thankfully we finish that inning, but the damage is done, they've gotten three runs. A 26-pitch inning for Julian! We're fine though, we can trust our bats, let's go hit!

Kole Newson swings at strike one, swings at strike two, and then smokes a hanging curveball to deep center that one hops the fence for a ground rule double! What a great way to answer! Let's go!! Doc watches strike one, watches strike two, fouls off strike three, and then hits a ground ball to shortstop, who is able to get it and throw it to third base to tag Kole and get the lead runner out. Gage watches balls one and two, swings at strike one, swings at strike two, and then swings and misses at curveball that just drops off the table for strike three and out #2.

Dylan watches strike one, watches ball one, fouls off the next two, watches ball two, watches ball three spike in the dirt and get past the catcher to get Doc to second base, and then swings and misses right over top of Chase's really good curveball for strike three. Shoot!! A 19-pitch inning for Chase! Now we've failed to score in the first two innings! Come on boys, you can do it, let's go play defense and then we'll chip away at that 3-0 lead!

Kamren hits a ground ball to Jett at shortstop and he's able to make the play at first and get out #1. Sayid J watches strike one and then grounds out to Aiden at second for out #2. Brandt watches strike one, watches strike two, then starts to walk back to the dugout on a curveball that he thinks is strike three, but the umpire calls ball #1. He then watches ball two and then swings and misses at a fastball at the outside corner for strike three. An 8-pitch inning for Julian, so that is exactly what we needed! Now it's time to go wake our bats up!

Aiden hits a fly ball to center field for out #1. Jett fouls off strike one, swings at strike two, and then hits a line out to center field.

Kaleb watches four balls in a row to get on base. Ben swings at strike one, swings at strike two, fouls off strike three, and then watches another curveball that comes in low and just grabs the strike zone for strike three. A 12-pitch inning for Chase and he's doing a great job keeping Boerne's bats quiet!

CJ watches strike one, watches balls one and two, fouls off strike two, and then watches a high curveball drop right back into the zone for strike three. Zayne B fouls off strike one, watches ball one, swings at strike two, and then watches that same high curveball drop right into the zone for strike three and Julian's 8th strikeout of the day! Chase watches ball one, watches strike one, watches ball two, swings at strike two, and then hits a ground ball to Cooper at third who is able to grab it and throw it to first to get the last out of the inning. A 14-pitch inning for Julian! Ok boys, we've played with these kids long enough, let's get those bats going!

Julian watches strike one and then hits a low middle fastball deep into the left-center gap for a one hopper over the fence for a ground rule double! Gray watches ball one and then turns his shoulder into ball 2 to take the hit and now we have two runners on! Cooper hits a ground ball into the gap to left field to load the bases! Finally! Let's go Boerne, have a big inning here!!! Caden watches ball one, fouls off two strikes in a row, watches ball two, and then hits a curveball inside on the ground to left field to drive in a run! Bases are still loaded with no outs! Kole hits a hard ground ball up the middle to center field and he scores a run! Doc goes down to hit the knuckleball and nukes it over the left field wall for a grand slam!!! He gets mobbed at home by the team and Boerne takes a 6-3 lead!!

Louisiana changes pitchers and brings in their lefty Kole Cao to pitch. Chase was at 63 pitches and a 62% strike percentage. Gage watches balls one and two, and then grounds out to their shortstop. Dylan watches balls one and two, swings at strike one, watches ball three, watches strike two, and then just missed a fastball at the top of the zone for a swing and miss strike three. Aiden watches balls one and two, and then flies out to deep right field that they barely catch on the run and at full extension to end the fourth inning, but now, Louisiana is chasing! A 24-pitch inning for Louisiana and we have finally broken through!

Cy fouls off strike one and then hits a hard ground ball into the left field corner and is able to beat the throw to second base for a double. Louisiana is not going to go quietly into the night! Landon swings at strike one, watches three balls in a row, swings at strike two, and then watches a curveball just miss on the outside corner for ball four to get their two leadoff runners on base, and we are back to a nailbiter!!!

Dominic B watches strike one and then grounds the ball back to Julian who quicky spins, Cooper hadn't gotten to third yet so he throws it to Aiden at second to get the out, but by the time Aiden gets the ball to Kole at first, the runner had already gotten there. So now we have runners on the corners and one out. Ben F fouls off strike one, watches strike two, fouls off strike three, watches ball one, and then lines out to Jett at short, so none of the runners can move, and now we have two outs!! Lane P watches ball one, swings at strike one, watches strike two, and half-heartedly swings at a nasty outside curveball for strike three to end the inning and thankfully not allow any more Louisiana runs! An incredible 19-pitch inning for Julian!

Jett watches ball one, watches strike one, watches strike two, and then rips a line drive to the 3rd baseman, who watches it bounce off his glove, and Jett gets to first on the error. Kaleb fouls off strike one, swings at a nasty slider for strike two that gets by the catcher so Jett gets to second, fouls off the next two pitches, and then swings and misses at a high outside slider for strike three. Ben watches ball one, swings at strike one, watches ball two, swings at strike two, and then swings and misses at that slider middle out for strike three. Julian watches strike one, watches ball one, fouls off strike two, watches ball two, and then swings and misses at that outside slider for strike three. Louisiana answers with their own 19-pitch inning!!

Kole watches strike one and two, then hits a ground ball to third, Cooper grabs it but the throw to first is a little off and gets by Kole N, so Cao is able to get to second. Kamren watches three balls in a row, watches strike one, fouls off strike two, and then Julian's nasty curveball drops off the table to get strike three. Julian got to 85 pitches (71%) and so Doc comes into relieve. Sayid watches strike one, watches ball one, swings at strike two, and then throws a heater fastball over the outside corner for strike three looking.

Brandt D watches a wild pitch go over Caden's head for ball one that allows Kole Cao to advance to 3rd, and then swings at strike one, and then hits a ground ball to Kole Newson at 3rd base, that takes a hard bounce but he is in front of it, it hits the heel of his glove and slides into his stomach, and he grabs it and throws to Julian at first to get the last out and that does it!!!

After 5 ½ innings and a come-from-behind to take the lead, Boerne has done it! A 16-pitch inning to end the game! The boys are going to Williamsport!!! The crowd in Waco erupts! The boys rush the mound, they throw their gloves high in the air, they shake Louisiana's hands, and then they hoist the championship banner in victory!!!!

Boerne threw 95 pitches in that game with a combined 71% strike percentage. Louisiana threw 94 pitches in that game with a combined 62% strike percentage. We only walked one of their batters and they walked two of ours. We had 7 hits to their 4 hits. You see how tight and close these games have become? Talk about on the edge of your seat the entire game!!

We finish the game around 8pm and shortly thereafter, the fans empty out of the stadium, and so the families are the only ones left. The field is eerily quiet as dusk settles in and the Little League officials call the Boerne family together in the stands for a meeting.

We sit down and they tell us, congratulations on a great tournament. Guess what, your boys will be on a 6am flight on Friday morning from San Antonio airport to Newark, where they will board a bus and be shuttled to Williamsport, PA. There are on-campus dorms in Williamsport; Little League takes care of everything, but there are a few things you are going to need to pack for them and then you are basically turning your kids over to us for the next three weeks. You don't need to worry, we run this like a well-oiled machine, and they will be in good hands.

They also said that they recommend us getting on our phones while we are sitting there and figure out where we want to stay, because there are only a few hotels in Williamsport and they book up fast. What???

So as we are sitting there trying to absorb the fact that we just won the Regional Championship and listen to what is going to happen at Williamsport, while we are also having to frantically search on our phones to get hotel reservations. First world problems, yes, we are aware, but after two months of hot summer baseball, we are realizing the dream has come true, and that it's not over yet, we are now signed up for three and a half more weeks of baseball craziness to a place that none of us have been before. Stunned by the speed with which this is all happening, we pack up, grab some dinner in a drive-through, and drive home to Boerne, getting home again around midnight, knowing that we've only got two days' to get them ready and then they'll take off.

This is a significant strain on the families, as we have been in four different cities for basically almost 5 days each already in the last 7 weeks, and now we are facing another three-week stretch in Williamsport. Thankfully Ingram was within driving distance, but both Abilene and Waco required week-long stays. Several of our team members were juggling work commitments with their spouses, and some of our folks that were able to work remotely, were doing work as possible from the hotels at the odd times they were able to grab some screen time and taking calls from the parking lot. Yes, I know these are first-world struggles, and it's a wonderful thing to face this type of challenge, and we wouldn't change it for the world.

It also speaks to the generosity of the Boerne and Kendall County community, because without their support, this would not have been possible. Each family was already on the hook for about $4,000 in expenses from just from Abilene and Waco, and for the upcoming 3-week stay in Williamsport, you are looking at close to $10,000 per family when you factor in flights, hotel, rental cars, and food. For 12 families, that works out to roughly a $180,000 investment to get all the way there. Little League pays for the flights to get the kids to/from their respective cities, boards the kids in Williamsport, and takes care of feeding the boys for the entire time, but the families' expenses are all on the families. For the international families, those flights are even more expensive, so thank you, thank you, thank you to anyone that has ever donated to any team for this Little League dream, because you want both the kids and the families to thoroughly enjoy this experience, and not be inhibited by financial restrictions if at all possible.

We are also reminded of how grateful we are to have it so good in the USA. We were told a story about one of the Little League teams from a Latin America country (we won't say the name because we don't want to embarrass them), and they were interviewing one set of parents of one of the kids, who had two other kids beside their baseball player, and they were talking about making the decision on which two kids were going to get to eat that day, and which one was not. That was just utterly heart-breaking, but we know, especially in the many impoverished nations around the world, that is a daily fact of life, and so our prayers, hearts, and donations go out to those families.

Friday morning arrives at 2a, yes you read that right, 2 o'clock in the morning, and we meet in the nearby HEB Fair Oaks parking lot. Have I mentioned yet all the late nights and the early mornings? Hopefully you don't like to sleep very much because there is plenty to keep you awake during all this baseball. We have police cruisers and several shuttle vehicles to take the boys in a police escort to the airport. Little League, true to their word, emailed the coaches later that Tuesday evening a list of exactly what the boys would need, and so we've been able to pack appropriately. It's a surreal experience though, turning your 11-

and 12-year-olds over to your three coaches and knowing that they will be halfway across the country for the next several days before we all get up there to see them again. The boys get to the airport and the local San Antonio TV news crews are there to interview them about the upcoming trip and get some video. They make a stop at the airport Starbucks, and Kaleb gets introduced to a double-smoked cheddar bacon egg sandwich and a pink drink, and he now asks for those on every road trip. Peer pressure at 12 years old, good grief! That was his first caffeine drink. He's never drank a coke in his life. He lives on milk, protein shakes, water, lemonade, Gatorade, and now, the occasional (like once every other month) pink drink.

Kaleb takes the team mascot, a stuffed fish appropriately named the Boerne Bass, and shares that with the reporters. They have explained to us that the boys will be very busy, because they will be getting uniforms, equipment, being interviewed, moving into their dorms, meeting the 19 other teams that have made it to the tournament, and doing some practice as the coaches put together a schedule.

I recall my dad driving with me to college nearly 30 years ago, then me taking him back to the airport to put him on a plane back home, and this experience brings up very similar memories, except now I'm the parent in this situation. I'm scared to death to turn over my 11-year-old, but I've got full confidence that he is independent enough that he will be fine, and I've got a lot of faith in our coaches, because they are all incredible men and fathers, and I know that they will take the best care of our boys during this entire trip.

Turn to page 85, The Lead-In to Williamsport, to continue the story from here...

www.ingramcontent.com/pod-product-compliance
Lightning Source LLC
LaVergne TN
LVHW020706110826
845149LV00012B/2126